CH

THE NEGRO IN THE AMERICAN REVOLUTION

THE DEATH OF
MAJOR WILLIAM MONTGOMERY
WHILE LEADING THE BRITISH
ATTACK ON THE FORT AT
THIS POINT.

SEPT 6TH
1781

Jordan Freeman at the Battle of Groton Heights, Connecticut, September 6, 1781, about to launch the spear which killed British Major William Montgomery. Freeman himself was killed a few minutes later. Tablet, in Old Fort Griswold, New London, Conn. Courtesy of the Library of Congress. Washington, D.C.

THE NEGRO IN THE
AMERICAN REVOLUTION

With a New Foreword by Thad W. Tate
and a New Introduction by Gary B. Nash

BENJAMIN QUARLES

Published for the Institute of Early American History and Culture,
Williamsburg, Virginia, by
The University of North Carolina Press
Chapel Hill and London

The Institute of Early American History and Culture
is sponsored jointly by The College of William and Mary
and the Colonial Williamsburg Foundation.

Library of Congress Cataloging-in-Publication Data

Quarles, Benjamin.
The Negro in the American Revolution / by Benjamin Quarles;
with a new foreword by Thad W. Tate and a new introduction by Gary B. Nash.
p. cm.
Originally published: 1961.
Includes bibliographical references and index.
ISBN 0-8078-4603-1 (pbk.: alk. paper)
1. United States—History—Revolution, 1775–1783—Afro-Americans.
2. Afro-Americans—History—18th century. I. Institute of
Early American History and Culture (Williamsburg, Va.) II. Title.
E269.N3Q3   1996
973.3′ 150396073—dc20   96-21111
                                                CIP

The paper in this book meets the guidelines for permanence
and durability of the Committee on Production Guidelines for Book Longevity
of the Council on Library Resources.

00 99 98 97 96   5 4 3 2 1

TO RUTH

CONTENTS

FOREWORD

At a time when African American history has become such a complex and active field of study, it is perhaps difficult to appreciate fully the pioneering quality of Benjamin Quarles's *The Negro in the American Revolution* when it first appeared in 1961. Quarles's extensive bibliography in this book indicates that no substantial study of American blacks before the nineteenth century had appeared for a quarter of a century, apart from Luther Porter Jackson, *Virginia Soldiers and Sailors in the Revolutionary War* (1944), and Lorenzo Greene, *The Negro in Colonial New England, 1620-1776* (1942). To these should also be added Frank J. Klingberg, *An Appraisal of the Negro in Colonial South Carolina* (1941), a work that emphasized the activities of the English benevolent organization, the Society for the Propagation of the Gospel. The scholarship of the small group of historians with an interest in African American history who had immediately preceded Quarles focused almost exclusively on the nineteenth century and later—on the antislavery movement, the Civil War, and the circumstances of blacks after emancipation.

In their study *Black History and the Historical Profession, 1915-1980* (1986), August Meier and Elliott Rudwick identified Quarles—along with John Hope Franklin—with an important shift in the approach that a new group of scholars began to take in the writing of black history by the 1940s and 1950s. Meier and Rudwick found in their work a greater concern with "collective experience of the race" than with celebration of "individual black achievement," and likewise, "a greater emphasis on integrating black history with the study of the broader American past" (p. 119). Certainly Quarles's study of blacks in the Revolution was written in that vein. In his preface he explicitly noted that he had "tried to present a group portrait rather than a study of individuals," although important individual blacks were by no means absent from his account. But he sought to deal broadly with every aspect

of the black experience in the Revolution: support for and active service on both sides of the struggle, aspirations for freedom by blacks
themselves, and the influence on at least some white patriots of the
contradiction between the perpetuation of black slavery and the waging
of a war in the name of human liberty.

Benjamin Quarles, born in Boston, Massachusetts, in 1904, entered Shaw University at the age of twenty-three, graduating in 1931.
His interest in black history kindled by an undergraduate teacher, he
went on to graduate study at the University of Wisconsin, at Madison,
receiving in 1940 the first doctorate in history awarded by that institution to a black. From 1939 to 1953 Quarles taught at Dillard University. He then joined the faculty of Morgan State University, where he
remained until retirement. He now lives in Baltimore.

Although his graduate mentors had initially advised against pursu-
ing research in black history, Quarles stood firm, and under the direction of William B. Hesseltine, he completed a dissertation on
Frederick Douglass, which he revised and published in 1948. When he
completed a second major work, *The Negro in the Civil War* (1953), and
devoted his earliest published articles to nineteenth-century themes,
Quarles seemed, like many of his immediate predecessors and contem-
poraries, committed to African American history of the nineteenth
century.

It is not entirely clear what turned his research interests for a time
in the 1950s away from the nineteenth century, to which he would return in virtually all of his subsequently published work. Perhaps his
earlier interest in the war experience of blacks in the Civil War had
suggested a look back to the Revolutionary War. In 1958 his article
"Lord Dunmore as Liberator," which was later adapted as a chapter in
this book, appeared in the *William and Mary Quarterly*. A year later another article, "The Colonial Militia and Negro Manpower," was published by the *Mississippi Valley Historical Review*. Acceptance of his article on Dunmore must have played some part in his submission of his
book manuscript to the Institute of Early American History and Culture. Quarles recalls choosing the Institute because he believed that it
constituted the most authoritative voice in the field of early American
history. The Institute's decision to publish *The Negro in the American
Revolution* pleased him very much, for he expected that it would ensure
a wide readership for the book.

In several of its major scholarly reviews Quarles's book received generally favorable notice, although not without a few reservations. One could find in them at least a hint that the idea of a book-length treatment of the subject had taken a group of white reviewers somewhat by surprise. To be sure, they admired the thoroughness of the research, even in the face of some skepticism about available sources; and they regarded the discussion of military participation in the Revolution by blacks as the strongest and most significant feature of the study. Reviewers were less prepared, however, given the prevailing interpretation of the Revolution, to accept a second major thrust of Quarles's treatment—his emphasis on the ways in which the struggle for American independence gave a strong stimulus to black aspirations for freedom. They found the point inadequately developed, even a "shadowy and esoteric corner of the history of the Revolution." And although there was praise for the book's treatment of a neglected subject, one reviewer concluded that the role of blacks in the Revolution was sufficiently minor that the subject was of more importance for black history than for the history of the Revolution.

Quarles's book, however, quickly found an important place in the historiography of the Revolution and tapped as well the rapidly developing interest in African American history. In 1966, when the University of North Carolina Press launched a new series of paperbacks, the book was one of the initial eight titles chosen for inclusion. Successive printings of both hardcover and paperback editions followed. As the bicentennial of the Revolution approached, the book remained virtually the only available full-length study of blacks during the Revolution. Its continuing popularity, in fact, led the Press and the Institute in 1976 to raise with the author the question of a possible revised edition. After giving it careful thought, Quarles concluded that he was too heavily committed to other projects to undertake the task. And so the original version of the work has remained in print for thirty-five years. In the process *The Negro in the American Revolution* has gained a place as one of the half-dozen best-sellers among 145 books published by the Institute over the past half century. And more recent historical writing, such as Sylvia Frey's *Water from the Rock: Black Resistance in a Revolutionary Age* (1991), has supported and elaborated Quarles's more controversial conclusion that the Revolutionary era markedly strengthened blacks' desire for their own freedom.

The Negro in the American Revolution has, then, earned the status of a landmark. It is a work that defines an important turning point in the study of the black experience in the Revolution, and it testifies as well to the enduring quality of the scholarship of Benjamin Quarles. By understanding how the Declaration of Independence also spoke to the black struggle for freedom, his study was seminal in seeing the Revolution's meaning for other groups previously marginalized by historians. The issuance of this new paperback edition by the Institute of Early American History and Culture and the University of North Carolina Press seems an appropriate and welcome recognition of Quarles's achievement.

Thad W. Tate
February 1996

INTRODUCTION

In the mid-1950s, when Benjamin Quarles began working on his study of the role of some 500,000 enslaved Africans and a small number of free blacks in the American Revolution, he was laboring in a peculiar historiographical vacuum on this important topic. This peculiarity can be explained only by the unique development of black history itself and the connection between that development and the plight of African Americans in the United States.

At midcentury, the thin collection of secondary literature on the black Americans' revolution was composed of several antiquarian books by pioneering nineteenth-century black historians, a slender pamphlet that had been written in 1940, and a few short passages in several general histories of African Americans. This slim record was all that prevented complete historical amnesia on the one-fifth of the American revolutionary population that was black. Almost all of this work was inspired—and limited—by the yearning for a serviceable history that would lead toward a genuine biracial democracy.

When William C. Nell wrote *The Colored Patriots of the American Revolution* (1855), he enlisted his pen in the abolitionist cause. Leading a campaign to integrate the public schools of Boston in the 1840s, associating closely with William Lloyd Garrison's abolitionist crusade, and publishing Frederick Douglass's *The North Star*, Nell meant to stimulate racial pride while countering white Negrophobia that had spread rapidly in the early nineteenth century. Hence, rather than trying to understand how those of African descent in the colonies— mostly enslaved—reacted to the revolutionary tumult, Nell focused almost entirely on black contributions among those of a small fraction of all African Americans to the colonists' struggle for independence. Appearing with brief recommendations from Harriet Beecher Stowe, who hoped *The Colored Patriots* would "redeem the character of the [Negro] race," and Wendell Phillips, who hoped Nell's efforts might "stem the tide of prejudice against the colored race," the book reached the public in 1855, just as news of "bleeding Kansas" was reported in the penny newspapers. This was the first historical work of a black historian to be published in the United States.

Working from skimpy published records, oral testimonies, and funeral eulogies of black men who achieved fame after the Revolution, Nell indiscriminately wove together stories of black revolutionary involvement with accounts of prerevolutionary slave revolts such as those in New York City in 1712 and South Carolina in 1738 and descriptions of exemplary black citizens in the first half of the nineteenth century. Never hiding the cards he was trying to play, Nell ended the book with a long section on "The Condition and Prospects of Colored Americans"—most of it featuring black accomplishment and virtue in the antebellum North. Nell knew all too well that white prejudice and hostility had blocked the way forward for all but a small number of African Americans, but he hoped that inspiring stories would raise black hopes and command some degree of white respect.

Intent on showing that the blood of blacks fell as copiously as the blood of whites, Nell waxed eloquent about figures such as James Forten, the fourteen-year-old Philadelphia son of a free black. Forten enlisted on Stephen Decatur's privateer as a powderboy in 1780 and soon "found himself amid the roar of cannon, the smoke of blood, the dying, and the dead" in a naval duel between Decatur's *Royal Louis* and the British ship *Lawrence*. When his ship was captured after another battle at sea, the young Forten wore the colors of patriotism nobly, refusing the offer of the British captain to transport him to England to stay with his son who had befriended the black American lad. "NO, NO!" exclaimed Forten, according to Nell, who based his account on oral recollections, "I am here a prisoner for the liberties of my country: I never, NEVER, shall prove a traitor to her interests."[1]

If Nell's attempt to show that black Americans partook of the "Spirit of '76" was massively unbalanced, ignoring entirely the huge number of blacks who fought with the British, his approach can be understood by appreciating the depth of white racial hatred in the antebellum North that all abolitionists had to reckon with. One wonders whether Nell knew from southern blacks who had migrated north to Boston that Virginia, South Carolina, and Georgia slaves had fled to the British in huge numbers in 1779–80. But if available to him, what could the historian-activist have done with this evidence? We can imagine how he would have concluded that to publicize the general belief among slaves that life, liberty, and the pursuit of happiness were best pursued with the British would have only crippled the abolitionists' cause.

For another century, all African American historians of the black revolutionary experience followed in Nell's footsteps, confident that Clio's power resided in her ability to engender black self-esteem and mitigate white hostility. William Wells Brown's *The Negro in the American Rebellion: His Heroism and His Fidelity*, published in 1867, stayed firmly in Nell's mold, as indicated by the subtitle.[2] It is not known whether Brown had read David Ramsey's *History of the Revolution of South Carolina*, published in 1858, where Ramsey claimed that two-thirds of South Carolina's slaves had fled to the redcoats when the British campaign threw the low country into prolonged crisis. But how would Brown have imagined he could yoke Clio to the advancement of black Americans if he treated the large black defection to the British? Rather, he stuck with Nell's approach, glossing the material he found in Nell's *The Colored Patriots of the American Revolution*.

George Washington Williams, who published the first deeply researched history of African Americans, was equally patriotic in two hefty books he published in the 1880s. A veteran of the Civil War and a volunteer in Mexico's overthrow of Maximillian, Williams became a notable minister, journalist, and—most passionately—a historian. In his *History of the Negro Race in America from 1619 to 1880: Negroes as Slaves, as Soldiers, and as Citizens* (1882) and in *A History of Negro Troops in the War of Rebellion, 1861-1865* (1887) he shared Nell and Brown's nearly exclusive focus on the small number of black Americans who fought to break the chains of slavery on the side of the Americans while ignoring the massive number who fought for freedom on the side of the British. Author of the first comprehensive history of "the Negro race in America," Williams, like Nell and Brown, was fired to the notion that historical studies of black patriotism could muffle white racism, convince whites that African Americans deserved equality and justice, and fortify black pride through recalling exemplary lives. In general, Williams's research was much deeper than Nell and Brown's, but he went little beyond previous anecdotal evidence on blacks in the American revolutionary forces. He probably knew of Jefferson's account of 30,000 Virginia slaves fleeing to the British, of David Ramsey's account of black flight in South Carolina, and published accounts of huge black defections in Georgia. But like his predecessors, Williams understandably sidestepped this aspect of the black revolutionary experience. Encountering white hostility himself, he probably regarded discretion as the better part of valor. Black Americans released from bondage could hardly be perceived as loyal Americans by whites if they knew that a large majority of revolutionary blacks had fought for a British victory in the American Revolution. Thus, Williams contributed to the prevailing myth by describing how "in every attempt upon the life of the nation . . . the Colored people had always displayed a matchless patriotism and an incomparable heroism in the cause of Americans."[3]

The founding generation of professional black historians, led by W. E. B. Du Bois, Carter G. Woodson, and Rayford W. Logan, were dedicated to social science methodology in the early twentieth century, but they too were hog-tied by the same problem that their predecessors faced. The end of legal slavery had not stifled discrimination or prevented the reduction of southern blacks to peonage after the Civil War; it only magnified the need to alter the white image of black Americans. In fact, the first small corps of African Americans to receive their doctorates launched their careers in the early twentieth century at just the time when pseudoscientific racism was cresting.

If the new purportedly dispassionate social science methodology professed by the emerging black intelligentsia could not transcend their predecessors' focus on black heroism in America's causes,[4] this was equally true in general surveys of black American history that began to appear in the Progressive Era. Booker T. Washington and Benjamin Brawley, writing for the general public and black high school students, both played up the blood sacrifices of African Americans on behalf of the Americans' "glorious cause."[5] Washington, leader of the accommodationist wing of early-twentieth-century black leaders, allowed that southern slaves ended up in the British army, but that happened not because they defected from their masters but because they were "carried off by the British troops." To counter any notion that African Americans were faithless, even though they were enslaved, Washington quoted Charles Pinckney of South Carolina, who in the House of Representatives in 1820 alleged what was manifestly untrue, that "it is a most remarkable fact that, notwithstanding, in the course of the Revolution, the Southern states were continually overrun by the British, and that every Negro in them had an opportunity of leaving their owners, few did; proving thereby not only a most remarkable attachment to their owners, but the mildness of the treatment, from whence their affection sprang."[6]

Brawley's use of the terms "Builders and Heroes" to describe African Americans characterized his *Short History of the American Negro* (1913). By definition, this description foreclosed explorations of those who fought against the Americans in their struggle for independence. In his much longer *Social History of the American Negro* (1921), Brawley noted that after Dunmore's proclamation in November 1775, "in great numbers the slaves in Virginia flocked to the British standard" and that South Carolina and Georgia lost one-fifth or more of their slaves to the British. But Brawley's account ended with a trumpet flourish about how African Americans "worked for a better country" and "died in faith, not having received the promises, but having seen them afar off."[7]

Carter G. Woodson might have been the historian to shatter the prevailing myth about the patriotism of black Americans in the nation's founding. The second African American to receive a doctorate in history (after W. E. B. Du Bois), Woodson "was virtually single-handedly responsible for establishing Afro-American history as a historical specialty."[8] Woodson created the Association for the Study of Negro Life and History in 1915, launched the *Journal of Negro History* in the following year, and published steadily in his attempt to professionalize the study of black history. Yet Woodson was caught in the same trap that limited his predecessors—the need to counter debilitating white racism and the concurrent imperative to enhance black self-esteem.

Woodson's treatment of the black revolutionary experience was more realistic than that of his predecessors, devoting for the first time some attention to how slaves in every part of the country fled to the military camps of Cornwallis, Clinton, and Howe. In *The Negro in Our History*, first published in 1922 and then reissued periodically through the 1960s, Woodson recounted the "appreciable share in defending the liberty of the country" that was due to free black patriots in the North. But for the first time he dared to include a paragraph on "Negroes with the British," where he mentioned 25,000 slaves in South Carolina who fled to the British and perhaps three-quarters of the Georgian slaves who did likewise.[9] Nonetheless, readers of *The Negro in Our History* would draw the conclusion that for the most part black Americans, enslaved and free, were valorous, patriotic Americans.

If the doctorate-holding black historians of the early twentieth century were able to step only gingerly in confronting the widespread pro-British black sentiment during the Revolution—that in fact the

Revolution involved a massive slave rebellion—their blinkered perspective can be understood by appreciating how thoroughly it was shared by hyphenated Americans. The historians of German-Americans, Italian-Americans, Irish-Americans, and other ethnic elements similarly nurtured group pride and legitimacy by advertising the record of the heroic contributions to nation building and patriotic bloodshed they had made. In this way, like African Americans, they believed they could secure acceptance into the nation's mainstream.[10]

The position of African American historians is also better understood by remembering the dismal record of white historians on the black American Revolution. One searches futilely in the scores of textbooks published before the 1930s for more than an occasional sentence about the revolutionary involvement of thousands of black Americans. From the multivolume histories of the United States by George Bancroft, John Fiske, and Edward Channing to high school textbooks by Charles and Mary Beard, David Muzzey, James Truslow Adams, and many others, the record is so thin on black history in general that it would almost appear that the British and Americans fought for seven years as if a half-million African Americans were magically whisked off the continent. Given this gaping lacunae in the historical record, it is understandable that black historians would draw attention to stories of heroic black patriots such as Crispus Attucks, whose blood fell first at the Boston Massacre, and Peter Salem, who shot through the chest Major Pitcairn of the British Marines as Pitcairn reached the patriot's redoubt in the Battle of Bunker Hill.

Not until 1940 would the peculiar combination of white indifference and strategic black myopia be shattered. Herbert Aptheker's pamphlet *The Negro in the American Revolution*, one of the first fruits of a prolific Marxist historian, set the stage for turning upside down the historical understanding of the black revolutionary involvement. Where earlier historians of black history had riveted attention on the contributions of African Americans to "the glorious cause," understated the impediments to black enlistment in the state militias and Continental army, and ignored the British lure of freedom for enslaved Africans, Aptheker approached the problem very differently. Perhaps steeled by the bitter wars between labor and capital and devoted to the American Communist Party's recruitment of black Americans, he began from the pragmatic position that the Revolution offered the most disadvantaged fifth of colonial society a set of options heretofore unavailable in their quest for freedom—a freedom not measured in ideological stances or political interests but defined by escape from slavery.

Aptheker did not slight the service of black Americans to the revolutionary army and navy; in rehearsing this, he estimated (apparently for the first time) that, given the white hostility against black enlistment for most of the war, only about 5,000 blacks embraced the patriot cause. However, against that number, he figured some 100,000 blacks who escaped their masters and mistresses to join the British forces or—in small numbers—fled to the interior, where they lived as maroons or faded into Indian communities. The dirty little secret about massive black defection from slavery, among a coerced labor force that white historians had pictured as docile and contented, was now out of the bag.

As noted already, such a revelation that many thousands of enslaved Africans made personal declarations of independence by fleeing to the British would hardly have served the purposes of William Nell, George Washington Williams, or early-twentieth-century black historians in their efforts to gain acceptance of American blacks among the generally hostile white population that surrounded them. Writing in 1940, Aptheker labored under no such imperative. Already his pamphlet *Negro Slave Revolts, 1526-1860* (1939) had broken through the white historiographical wisdom that stressed slave passivity.[11] Now he brought forward his account of how "the Negro people played what at first glance appears to have been a dual role [in the Revolution] from 1775 to 1783"—service in the American forces "when they were permitted to do so" and wholesale flight to the British in search of freedom. Aptheker astutely understood what would become a major theme of Benjamin Quarles's *The Negro in the American Revolution*—that the "varied and superficially contradictory activities" of black Americans during the war had "one common origin, one set purpose—the achievement of liberty." Here, as in every epoch of African American history, "the desire for freedom is the central theme, the motivating force," reasoned Aptheker.[12]

Aptheker's stunning formulation, though sketched only briefly in a forty-seven-page pamphlet, provided a new conceptual spine for historians studying the black American Revolution. But this reconceptualization took form only slowly. John Hope Franklin, who, with Quarles, would be heralded for many decades as the leader of the second generation of professional black historians who appeared on the scene in the 1940s, did not capitalize on Aptheker's striking reformulation. In his *From Slavery to Freedom*, published in 1947 and thereafter republished in many editions for half a century, Franklin clung mostly to the old paradigm, though he was more interested in the collective black experience than individual black heroism and more intent on integrating black history with mainstream American history than inculcating black pride. In a chapter on the American Revolution, entitled "That All Men May Be Free," Franklin discussed the military side of the war under the subheading "Negroes Fighting for American Independence." One paragraph within this section discussed slaves flocking to the British, though Franklin tempered this statement with the addendum that slaves fled "in large numbers even if they had no intention of reaching the British lines." This statement aside, the weight of the narrative fell on the 5,000 patriot blacks rather than the antipatriots who were fifteen to twenty times as numerous.[13]

As this historiographical survey suggests, the broader, more clear-sighted, and less heroic treatment of black revolutionaries, anticipated by Aptheker, did not reach fruition until 1961, when it became a cardinal element in Quarles's bold book. In the first paragraph of his preface, Quarles explains that "the Negro's role in the Revolution can best be understood by realizing that his major loyalty was not to a place nor to a people, but to a principle. Insofar as he had freedom of choice, he was likely to join the side that made him the quickest and best offer in terms of those 'unalienable rights' of which Mr. Jefferson had spoken."

In two hundred pages, Quarles demonstrated this central notion with a wealth of detail that made his *Negro in the American Revolution* the first full-scale, document-based history of the black revolutionary experience. In almost equal space, Quarles treated the limited number who fought for freedom and equality on the American side and the far greater number who saw their future in taking up the British offers of unconditional freedom for those (including white indentured servants) who would join them.

Quarles's wealth of detail, gathered from a much wider range of printed sources than surveyed by previous historians, showed how eagerly free blacks, mostly in the North, joined the revolutionary forces when they were allowed to and how slaves who might gain their freedom by serving in place of their patriot masters willingly took the risk that they would survive combat and disease to take up life as freemen. In this part of the book, Quarles greatly broadened the scope of Luther Porter Jackson's brief study, published in 1944, of Virginia soldiers and sailors who fought for American independence. Quarles held with Aptheker's estimate that about 5,000 blacks served with the American forces.

In assessing the motives and roles of black patriots, Quarles veered away from the emphasis that Nell, Williams, and other black historians placed on heroic individual behavior. His main task was to present a "group portrait" of those who fought with the white Americans, reflecting the sociological sensibilities that had infected the historical profession after World War II and the much ripened state of black scholarship by the mid-twentieth century, where attention to the mass of black historical actors had begun to replace the emphasis on a few, heroic figures. Nell and Williams told the stories of the first to fall in the Boston Massacre, the "colored patriot" who led 700 captured British soldiers from Bennington, Vermont, to Boston; the black soldier who carried the day at Bunker Hill. Quarles, on the other hand, presented archetypes of revolutionary blacks—those who ran away from masters to enlist; those who served in place of their masters for freedom; those who were already free and willingly enlisted; and those who served for freedom only to be reenslaved.

Quarles's meticulous research also reaped considerable benefits in demonstrating how natural rights principles, which empowered the first abolitionist crusade that gained momentum in the 1770s, collapsed when the question of enlisting black colonists reached the fore. Quarles definitively established "the fear of putting guns into the hands of a class of persons most of whom were not free" for the first three years of the war and how the reversal of this policy, practiced at the state and continental levels, was driven mostly by the manpower shortage rather than any widespread desire to extend inalienable rights to those who were black.

The most lasting contribution of Quarles's book is three chapters on the huge number of enslaved Africans who escaped bondage by reaching the British lines. The American public is still largely unaware of this turn of events, judging by the silence in almost all textbooks from which young Americans learn their history and by the disinterest in this story by the media. Quarles's scholarship on the black flight to the British has inspired other scholars to deepen greatly our knowledge of this flight, and his judgments about this phenomenon remain mostly unchallenged today. He deftly probed the British reluctance to incite slaves to insurrection, particularly because thousands of American loyalists in the South owned slaves themselves and partly because

British humanitarianism was feeble. He also adroitly analyzed how practical concerns—the need for black manpower and the need to weaken the American strength—determined the British decisions, in 1775 and again in 1779, to proclaim freedom for slaves who fled their masters. "To the most unobservant field hand it must have been plain," wrote Quarles, "that England had not the remotest idea of making the war a general crusade against slavery, especially since so many of her loyalist supporters would have protested bitterly." Recent historians are less realistic in calling African Americans who fled to the British "Black Loyalists" or "Loyal Blacks." Escaping slaves were hardly loyal to the king or Parliament but were seeking their freedom on the best terms they could find.[14]

Nor did Quarles imagine that life with the British army and navy was a freedom festival. He reported authoritatively on how the unsentimental British on the one hand would use black auxiliaries on land and at sea whenever possible but at the same time give or sell fleeing or seized slaves to loyalists to make up for their losses. White British officers, Quarles explains, suffered no pangs of conscience while treating the slaves of the enemy as booty while operating under Dunmore and Clinton's proclamations that offered freedom to slaves reaching the British lines.

What may be added to the sobriety and clear-sightedness of Quarles's analysis is scholarly detachment, cautiousness, and circumspection in his handling of historical data. He would not include the oft-told incident of the enslaved Pompey guiding "Mad Anthony" Wayne's assault party at Stony Point, where the Americans gained a victory on the Hudson River. Nor does he regard as reliable the contention that Peter Salem, a former slave, killed Captain John Pitcairn at Bunker Hill, even though John Trumbull's famous painting memorializes this piece of black heroism on behalf of the Americans. This story always figured prominently in previous books by black historians. Imposing strict tests that few historians uphold today, Quarles would not include among black revolutionary figures men with a single name; nor did he include among African Americans individuals with typically black names such as William Cuff, Cuff Scott, or Prince Hall.

Quarles also treated black consciousness tenderly. Faced with highly fugitive materials and the paucity of written materials by black Americans, Quarles had to deal with the history of a frustratingly ephemeral people. Understanding that the thought of the unlettered has to be comprehended primarily by the actions of the anonymous, he took the position that "as far as possible [one must] avoid conjecture as to his unrecorded thought."

Whereas Quarles was bold in taking up Aptheker's treatment of those who fled to and fought with the British, he was decidedly cautious in estimating their number. Quarles had Aptheker's bait of 100,000 to work with, but he went only so far as to say that "tens of thousands" fled to the British and that the British evacuated about 20,000 blacks during or at the end of the war. Subsequent historians have simply referred to Aptheker's estimate or, resifting the evidence, have concluded that Aptheker's estimate is sound.[15]

Quarles made no attempt to estimate what percentage of able-bodied slaves between the ages of fifteen and forty this number might have included. Recent studies of runaway slaves show that in the decades before the Revolution at least two-thirds of fleeing slaves were males in the prime years. It is probable that this pattern prevailed during the war, although a few more women with children, as well as older slaves probably fled when the British moved within a day or two's journey of their residence. It can be surmised that if 80,000 to 100,000 slaves fled their masters during the war, about 55,000 to 65,000 of them were males between 15 and 40—roughly half of the prime agricultural and artisanal black male workers in the South. Indeed, as Quarles concluded, "Whoever invoked the image of liberty, be he American or British, could count on a ready response from the blacks."

Quarles's restraint—in treating documentary evidence cautiously and in bending over backward to move beyond individual heroism in order to paint a collective picture of patriot and loyal blacks—is also demonstrated by his reluctance to situate his study within the fiery conceptual arguments that emerged among historians of the black experience in the 1950s. Kenneth Stampp's *The Peculiar Institution* (1956), which shattered U. B. Phillip's reigning portrayal of a humanitarian slaveocracy, and Stanley Elkins's *Slavery: A Problem in American Institutional and Intellectual Life* (1959), with its provocative thesis that the typical slave had been traumatized and rendered docile by the severity of slavery, were the talk of the history profession when Quarles's book appeared. But Quarles nimbly sidestepped this issue, mentioning neither historian and leaving for his readers to deduce that the African Americans he portrayed, whichever side they fought on, were anything but infantilized and docile Sambos. Though understated, the backbone of his book is formed by black activism on both sides of the revolutionary struggle—a subtext about black agency that is a hallmark of

Quarles's other work in which African Americans appear as important shapers of American history.

That Quarles ended *The Negro in the American Revolution* with the conclusion that the "irreversible commitment of the new nation to the principles of liberty and equality" would eventually embrace black Americans was also consistent with Quarles's moderation and optimism about the future of African Americans. This Whiggish view of the inexorable march toward progress, written in the midst of the Civil Rights movement of the 1960s, was tempered two decades later when Quarles presented a reflective essay—a kind of coda on *The Negro in the American Revolution*—on the black revolutionary experience. In "The Revolutionary War as a Black Declaration of Independence," Quarles recognized the influence of the black nationalist line of thought that had been developed by black historians in the 1970s. This influence is evident in the different voice he assumed in the 1980s, particularly in his less optimistic view of how the lofty principles of the Revolution would be extended to black Americans and in his more vigorous enunciation of the black liberation consciousness that erupted during the revolutionary years. "The hope of black Americans for a new day of equality was not realized; it was a dream deferred," he wrote in 1983.[16]

Quarles's *The Negro in the American Revolution* will be read for many years, as befits any groundbreaking study. Recent scholarship has deepened and broadened our understanding of the African Americans' revolution and the dynamics of race relations that developed in the new nation, but this book is still the place to begin for all students and general readers interested in one of the most pivotal—and still unnoticed—aspects of the American Revolution.

Gary B. Nash
May 1996

NOTES

1. William C. Nell, *The Colored Patriots of the American Revolution with Sketches of Several Distinguished Colored Persons: To Which is Added a Brief Survey of the Condition and Prospects of Colored Americans* (Boston, 1855), pp. 167–70. Nell organized his material by state, which compounded the problem of addressing issues analytically.

2. William Wells Brown, *The Negro in the American Rebellion: His Heroism and Fidelity* (Boston, 1867). Brown also had available George H. Moore's *Notes on the Employment of Negroes in the American Army of the Revolution* (New York, 1862).

3. George Washington Williams, *History of the Negro Race in America* (1882; reprint, New York, 1968), pp. v–vi. For Earl Thorpe's view that Williams was Anglophobic, see *Negro Historians in the United States* (Baton Rouge, 1958), p. 34. Williams's book was followed by Joseph T. Wilson's *The Black Phalanx: A History of the Negro Soldiers of the United States in the Wars of 1775-1812, 1861-1865* (Hartford, 1888), but this book added little to the revolutionary story of black Americans.

4. Thorpe, *Negro Historians*, p. 4. Only Du Bois broke with the optimistic idea that educating whites would cleanse the country of racial prejudice. Thorpe, following Du Bois, argues that history was not an effective "weapon in the fight for racial equality" because white domination and prejudice was not really rooted in "under-emphasis of achievements of non-Europeans" (pp. 6–7).

5. Neither Washington nor Brawley was professionally trained in history, but their books became standard reading for those interested in African American history.

6. Booker T. Washington, *The Story of the Negro, vol. 1* (1909; reprint, New York, 1969), pp. 319–20.

7. Benjamin Brawley, *Social History* (New York, 1921), pp. 52–53, 55–56.

8. August Meier and Elliott Rudwick, *Black History and the Historical Profession, 1915–1980* (Urbana, Ill., 1986), p. 1.

9. Carter G. Woodson, *The Negro in Our History*, with Charles H. Wesley, 10th ed. (Washington, D.C., 1962), pp. 120–24.

10. Meier and Rudwick, *Black History*, p. 10.

11. This pamphlet would become the basis of his doctoral dissertation, published in 1943 as *American Negro Slave Revolts*.

12. Herbert Aptheker, *Negro Slave Revolts, 1526–1860* (New York, 1939), pp. 5–6.

13. John Hope Franklin, *From Slavery to Freedom* (New York, 1947), p. 133. This account remained unchanged in seven subsequent editions.

14. For example, Ellen Wilson, *The Loyal Blacks* (New York, 1976).

15. For the estimate of Richard Morris that 80,000–100,000 blacks were evacuated by the British, although many may have belonged to departing loyalists slaveowners, see *The American Revolution Reconsidered* (New York, 1967), p. 76. For Quarles's later estimated that the South alone lost as many as 65,000 slaves, although some of these where removed by white loyalists, see his "The Negro Response: Evacuation with the British," in *Black History: A Reappraisal*, ed. Melvin Drimmer (New York, 1968), p. 133. Sylvia R. Frey, in her *Water from the Rock: Black Resistance in a Revolutionary Age* (Princeton, N.J., 1991), after rigorous research, concludes that the 80,000–100,000 estimate is sound.

16. "The Revolutionary War as a Black Declaration of Independence," in *Slavery and Freedom in the Age of the American Revolution*, ed. Ira Berlin and Ronald Hoffman (Charlottesville, Va., 1983).

SUGGESTIONS FOR FURTHER READING

Berlin, Ira, and Ronald Hoffman, eds. *Slavery and Freedom in the Age of the American Revolution.* Charlottesville, Va., 1983.

Crow, Jeffrey J. *The Black Experience in Revolutionary North Carolina.* Raleigh, 1977.

Davis, David Brion. *The Problem of Slavery in the Age of Revolution, 1770–1823.* Ithaca, N.Y., 1975.

Frey, Sylvia R. *Water from the Rock: Black Resistance in a Revolutionary Age.* Princeton, N.J., 1991.

Kaplan, Sidney. *The Black Presence in the Era of the American Revolution, 1770–1800.* Washington, D.C., 1973.

MacLeod, Duncan J. *Slavery, Race, and the American Revolution.* Cambridge, 1974.

Nash, Gary B. *Forging Freedom: The Formation of Philadelphia's Black Community, 1720–1840.* Cambridge, Mass., 1988.

St. George Walker, James W. "Blacks as American Loyalists: The Slaves' War for Independence." *Historical Reflections* 2 (1975): 51–67.

White, Shane. *Somewhat More Independent: The End of Slavery in New York City, 1770–1810.* Athens, Ga., 1991.

Wood, Peter H. "'Liberty is Sweet': African-American Freedom Struggles in the Years before White Independence." In *Beyond the American Revolution: Explorations in the History of American Radicalism,* edited by Alfred F. Young. De Kalb, Ill., 1993.

———. "'Taking Care of Business' in Revolutionary South Carolina: Republicanism and the Slave Society." In *The Southern Experience in the American Revolution,* edited by Jeffrey J. Crow and Larry E. Tise. Chapel Hill, N.C., 1978.

PREFACE

In the Revolutionary War the American Negro was a participant and a symbol. He was active on the battlefronts and behind the lines; in his expectations and in the gains he registered during the war, he personified the goal of that freedom in whose name the struggle was waged. The Negro's role in the Revolution can best be understood by realizing that his major loyalty was not to a place nor to a people, but to a principle. Insofar as he had freedom of choice, he was likely to join the side that made him the quickest and best offer in terms of those "unalienable rights" of which Mr. Jefferson had spoken. Whoever invoked the image of liberty, be he American or British, could count on a ready response from the blacks.

On the American side the Negro saw only limited military service until the war dragged on into its third year. This negative attitude toward enlisting the colored man sprang from a reluctance to deprive a master of his apprenticed servant or chattel slave, and from the fear of putting guns in the hands of a class of persons most of whom were not free. In the main, the Negro was thought of as a servile laborer rather than as a potential warrior. But when manpower needs became acute, whether in the volunteer forces, the militia, or the Continental troops, hesitancies and fears were put into the background and the Negro was mustered in.

This procedure typified an attitude toward Negro enlistment that would prevail in America's future wars. From colonial times until the twentieth century, the Negro would be bypassed in the early stages of conflict. But as the struggle grew arduous, civilian authorities and military commanders would turn to the one great remaining manpower pool, and the Negro would emerge from his status as a rejected inferior to become a comrade in arms.

Some twenty months after the war broke out between England and her former colonies—by the close of 1776—grim necessity forced the states to reconsider the decision to exclude Negroes from their armies. Bound by the necessity of conciliating Southern views, Congress still refused to sanction Negro enlistments, but the states went ahead. Early in 1777 Massachusetts included Negroes in the list of draft eligibles, and the legislature of Rhode Island, at its February 1778 session, voted to raise two battalions of slaves. The substitute system encouraged the enlistment of Negroes; a man summoned to service was permitted to get someone to take his place, and to procure a Negro was easier and less expensive than to procure anyone else. In Virginia and in Maryland the change in attitude toward Negro soldiers was a consequence initially of the difficulty of mobilizing white man-power, and later of the southward shift of the main theatre of war.

Unlike their sister states, South Carolina and Georgia stead-fastly refused to legalize slave enlistments. South Carolina's heavy Negro population made her fearful of such a step, and Georgia shared these misgivings. When these states remained adamant even after the fall of Savannah late in 1778, Congress recommended that they raise 3,000 Negro troops, but these two states declined to reverse their stand, and maintained it to the end.

The Negro welcomed the resort to arms. Although not very strong on theory, he fulfilled the pragmatic requirements of a revolutionary. He had little to lose in goods or lands, and he lacked a sentimental or blood tie with England. At any rate, black Americans quickly caught the spirit of '76. In the words of Frederick Douglass, the most prominent colored American of the nineteenth century, the Revolutionary War announced to Negroes "the advent of a nation based upon human brotherhood and the self-evident truths of liberty and equality." There were portents of a new era. Individual slaves petitioned for their manumission; groups of slaves memorialized state legislatures to abolish slavery. For the first time, a gallery of distinguished Negroes made their appearance, among them Phillis Wheatley, precocious poet; Prince Hall, founder of Negro Masonry; and Benjamin Banneker, mathematician and astronomer.

Negro soldiers served in the minutemen companies of Massa-chusetts in the early weeks of the war, in the state militia of the Northern states, and in the state and Continental forces. They saw action in the Continental army at Monmouth, the last major battle in the North. At Yorktown, where on July 9, 1781, the Continental army passed in review, Baron von Closen, an aide-de-camp to General Rochambeau, made note that "three-quarters of the Rhode Island regiment consists of negroes, and that regiment is the most neatly dressed, the best under arms, and the most precise in its maneuvers."

Negroes served on sea as well as land. In the Chesapeake waters of Virginia and Maryland the use of Negro pilots (often impressed slaves) was not uncommon, and the Massachusetts legislature ordered that captured slaves be made to serve on state vessels. Negroes were numbered among the more than twenty thousand seamen aboard the armada of American privateers.

It is not possible to give accurate figures as to the number of blacks in the American armies. Not more than a third of the Negroes who bore arms were racially labeled; moreover, colored combatants were interspersed with whites in what today might be called unsegregated units. It has been estimated, however, that 5,000 Negro soldiers served in the patriot forces, a respectable figure particularly since so many were not free to act.

Although manpower shortage was the paramount factor, the changed American sentiment toward drawing Negroes into the war effort and thus conceding them a higher status was in part a reflection of the humanitarian impulse which inspired the Revolution and was engendered by it. Anti-slavery sentiment mounted rapidly, and action was taken on both Continental and state levels. Above the Potomac, public opinion turned strongly against slavery; by March 1780 Pennsylvania was ready to lead the way by passing an act for its gradual abolition.

War's end brought further gain to the Negro. To the slave soldier, who had borne the responsibilities of citizenship before he could enjoy its rights, it brought freedom and in some instances a land bounty. In New Jersey, slaves belonging to Tories were freed by act of the legislature. Waged in the name of liberty, the war caused many Americans to give a hard look at their own domestic practices. Abolitionist societies multiplied, often under Quaker sponsorship; Northern states, following Pennsylvania's lead, took action to abolish or circumscribe the slave trade and slavery. In the South the wartime decline of the staple crops— tobacco, indigo, and rice—decreased both the value of the slave and the reluctance to give him his freedom.

Thousands of Negroes gained their freedom by joining His Majesty's forces. Faced, like their opponents, by a manpower shortage, the British were receptive to the use of blacks, and in

1779 Commander-in-Chief Sir Henry Clinton issued a proclamation offering freedom to Negroes who would join the royal standard. The British move was countered by the Americans, who exercised closer vigilance over their slaves, removed the able-bodied to interior places far from the scene of war, and threatened with dire punishment all who sought to join the enemy. To Negroes attempting to flee to the British the alternatives "liberty or death" took on an almost literal meaning. Nevertheless, by land and by sea they made their way to the British forces. In the South the British employed hundreds of runaways as shock troops; others served as guides and spies. It was as military laborers, however, that they found their widest use. Negro carpenters, hostlers, blacksmiths, axemen, and miners markedly increased the striking power of His Majesty's armed forces. The British discovered, as had the Americans, that a Negro laborer could perform a service that otherwise would have to be done by a white soldier. When the war ended, hundreds of Negroes were evacuated from Savannah, Charleston, and New York with the departing British forces.

The establishment of American independence did not bring all that many Negroes had hoped for. The idealism of the Declaration of Independence gave way to the conservatism of the Constitutional era. But if the Negro felt that the cause of liberty had lost momentum, his mood was somewhat brightened by the conviction that the Revolutionary era in which he lived had marked out an irreversible path toward freedom, that henceforth there could be no turning back even if there was a slowing down.

The present study proposes to investigate the role of the Negro in the American Revolution and thereby fill a gap in historical knowledge. Some attempt will be made to explore the extent to which changes occurred in the status of Negroes. It is hoped that this work will also throw some light on race relations, or more broadly, human relations, by describing the development of attitudes and practices, civilian and military, toward an American minority in a period of crisis.

Battle narrative has not been presented in any detail. Unlike the Civil War, the War of Independence had no all-Negro units; hence the military history of the Negro soldier in the Revolution is one with the general history of the American soldier in action. Except perhaps at the Battle of Rhode Island, in which the Rhode Island regiment of predominantly Negro composition took part, the colored soldier of the Revolutionary War does not stand out as a racial entity.

I have tried to present a group portrait rather than a study of individuals. If, however, an often related story has not been included, it may be simply because it is not true. The female combatant and former schoolteacher Deborah Sampson who, disguised as a man, served for a year and a half in the Fourth Massachusetts Regiment, was not a Negro. Other episodes which I have discarded seem to owe their existence mainly to local legend. Such is the story, told in the Joseph Walker family of Virginia, about slave cook Dinah who, on a June morning in 1781, prepared such a succulent fried chicken breakfast for British officer Banastre Tarleton and his staff, and served it in such leisurely fashion, that a messenger had time to ride to Charlottesville and carry the warning that Tarleton's mounted force was on its way to seize Governor Jefferson and capture the state legislature. Still other tales have been omitted because the supporting evidence is weak. It is doubtful, for example, that a Negro slave, Pompey, guided the assaulting parties commanded by Anthony Wayne at Stony Point. Similarly, the contention that at Bunker Hill the shot that killed marine officer John Pitcairn was fired by former slave Peter Salem must be handled cautiously.

Another difficulty which arises in dealing with the Negro past stems from the nature and inherent limitations of the source material. It is not easy to know what Negroes were thinking; they were not articulate in a literary sense. Unlettered, they put very little down on paper. If they are to be understood, it must be primarily by what they did. Hence, especially in the pages of this work which deal with the Negro acting on his own volition, my approach has been to state the facts about his activities, indicate the documentary sources, and as far as possible avoid conjecture as to his unrecorded thought.

A final problem has been the determination of Negro identity. Since most of the participants in the Revolutionary War were racially anonymous, on what basis may a person be identified as a Negro? In this work I have designated an individual as a Negro only when the source specifically states it or where the source is referring only to Negroes. I make only one assumption: if the first or last name of a person was "Negro," he was not likely to be white. And although there are certain names largely confined to Negroes, I have not assumed that persons with such names were necessarily colored. Thus, although three of the Americans on the sloop *Charming Polly,* captured by the British on May 16, 1777, bore the typically Negro names of William Cuff, Prince Hall, and Cuff Scott (and all came from Massachusetts coastal towns where Negro seamen were common), I have not assumed that they were Negroes. Similarly, although the owner of the famed Fraunces Tavern, scene of Washington's farewell to his soldiers on December 4, 1783, was called "Black Sam," more conclusive evidence than the adjective "black" may be needed to establish a Negro identity. Many Negroes had only one name, whereas few whites did; yet a person with but one name cannot be classified with certainty on that basis alone.

* * *

In making this study I have had many benefactors. I am grateful to the John Simon Guggenheim Foundation for a generous fellowship which freed me for a year. To the Social Science Research Council, I am indebted for a military policy grant extending over the summers of 1955 and 1957. Morgan State College readily gave me a leave of absence.

I owe much to the staffs of research libraries: in Boston the Massachusetts Historical Society, the Boston Athenaeum, the Boston Public Library, and the Massachusetts State House; at Harvard University the Houghton and Widener libraries; in New York the New-York Historical Society and the New York Public Library, its 42nd Street center and its Schomburg Collection branch in Harlem; in Philadelphia the Pennsylvania Historical Society and the American Philosophical Society; in Virginia the University of Virginia at Charlottesville and the Virginia State Library at Richmond; in Chicago the Newberry Library and the Chicago Historical Society; and at the University of Michigan, the William L. Clements Library. My obligations in Washington, D. C., include the National Archives, the Moorland Foundation Collection at Howard University, headed by Mrs. Dorothy Porter, with her extensive knowledge of Negro bibliography, and the Library of Congress, especially the Manuscripts Division personnel.

I have had the good fortune to be located in Baltimore with its own good libraries, notably the Enoch Pratt Free Library, the Peabody Library, and those of Johns Hopkins University and the Maryland Historical Society. The staffs of these libraries have been most graciously helpful. To the library personnel at Morgan State College I have compounded a long-standing debt for their "second-mile" assistance in arranging inter-library loans and in permitting me the fullest use of Morgan's own Negro materials.

My deepest gratitude goes to Mr. Howard H. Peckham, historian of the Revolutionary War and Director of the William L. Clements Library. Mr. Peckham read seven of the chapters, making penciled comments and calling attention to points to be checked. This study is much freer of flaws for his preliminary reading. I am greatly indebted to the readers to whom the original manuscript was sent and, above all, to the editorial staff of the Institute, for many good suggestions as to style, organization, and content.

THE NEGRO IN THE AMERICAN REVOLUTION

CHAPTER I

UNCERTAIN TRUMPET

"O, not in vain did Attucks fall."

From a poem read at a "Centennial Entertainment
Given by the Excelsior Charitable Organization of
Colored Ladies of Boston."

The sky was clear. The moon shed its calm light upon the
frosted housetops, but on the fifth of March 1770 there was no
quiet in the streets of Boston, storm center of a brewing revolt.
If the evening's climax was unplanned, the ingredients of violence were nonetheless present. Foremost was the anger of the
citizens of Boston at two British regiments quartered in the
town. To the colonists these soldiers were trespassers whose
only purpose was to aid in the enforcement of unpopular laws.
For seventeen months the soldiers and the jeering crowds had
kept up a running series of noisy disputes, sometimes punctuated
by fist fights. The resentment of the populace, a standing invitation to disorder, had now gathered a full head of steam.
Boston was at the mercy of a mishap, and it came shortly after
nine o'clock on the first Monday evening in March.

A small crowd had gathered around a soldier stationed at
the Custom House on King Street, accusing him of using the
butt of his musket on a boy who had made slurring remarks
about a British officer. Pelted with a volley of snow balls and
broken ice, the solitary sentinel loaded his gun, backed up the
steps, and called for help. From the British twenty-ninth regiment a rescuing file of eight came on the trot, followed quickly
by Captain Thomas Preston, the officer of the day. The crowd,
now swollen to more than fifty men, grew rowdier; it flung
another barrage at the British reinforcements and taunted the
troops with shouted insults: "You lobster," "You bloody-back,"
"You coward." Then the town fire bell was sounded, and
"numerous bodys immediately assembled in the streets." Some

who poured into the square carried fire bags and buckets, not knowing they were answering a false alarm; others came "armed, some with musquets, but most with clubs, bludgeons and such like weapons."[1]

The restraint of the soldiers finally gave way when one of them received a blow, which threw him off-balance and knocked his gun to the ground. In an act blended of panic, resentment, self-defense, and a belief that above the din they had heard the voice of Captain Preston ordering them to fire, the soldiers discharged their weapons.[2] Eleven civilians were hit. Three lay motionless, killed immediately; eight were wounded, two of them mortally. The coming Revolutionary War had its martyrs. "If there had ever been any intention in the Colonies to rebel, what a fair opening had been made," wrote a resident of the city, "the military, without the least provocation, slaughtering the unarm'd defenceless and innocent citizens."[3]

John Adams later observed that the men who lost their lives that night were "the most obscure and inconsiderable that could have been found upon the continent."[4] His remark had some justification. Crispus Attucks, "the first to defy, and the first to die," was a Negro of obscure origin, with some admixture of Indian blood.[5] Presumably he had been a slave, for he

1. "That the party which went to protect the sentinel was assaulted all agree; but there is great contrariety in the evidence as to the degree of violence in the assault, one side saying it was only with snow balls and the other with brickbats and clubs or sticks." Thomas Hutchinson to Thomas Gage, Boston, Apr. 1, 1770, Randolph G. Adams, "New Light on the Boston Massacre," American Antiquarian Society, Proceedings, New Ser., 47 (Worcester, Mass., 1937), 298; Gage to Lord Hillsborough, Apr. 10, 1770, Clarence E. Carter, ed., The Correspondence of General Thomas Gage, 2 vols. (New Haven, 1931-33), I, 249.

2. "Captain Thomas Preston's Account of the Boston Massacre, March 13, 1770" in Merrill Jensen, ed., American Colonial Documents to 1776 (New York, 1955), 752; in David C. Douglass, ed., English Historical Documents, IX (London, 1955), 752.

3. William Palfrey to John Wilkes, Mar. 13, 1770, Massachusetts Historical Society, Proceedings, 1st Ser., 6 (Boston, 1863), 483. Hereafter cited as Mass. Hist. Soc., Proc.

4. Adams to James Burgh, Dec. 28, 1774, Charles Francis Adams, ed., The Works of John Adams, 10 vols. (Boston, 1850-56), IX, 352.

5. Line from "Crispus Attucks," by John Boyle O'Reilly in A Memorial of Crispus Attucks, Samuel Maverick, James Caldwell, Samuel Gray and Patrick Carr, from the City of Boston (Boston, 1889), 53; on shaky evidence, J. B. Fisher asserts that Attucks was a full-blooded Natick Indian, the terms mulatto and Indian having been used interchangeably in colonial times. "Who Was Crispus Attucks?" American Historical Record, 1 (Phila., 1872), 531-33.

hailed from Framingham, Massachusetts, where in 1750 William Brown of that city had advertised for his runaway man, "a mulatto fellow, about 27 years of age, named Crispus, 6 feet 2 inches high, short, curl'd hair, his knees nearer together than common."[6] Attucks's obscurity prior to the Boston Massacre was in dramatic contrast to his role on that occasion. On that evening he had gone to a "victualling house" kept by Thomas Simmons. While at supper he heard the fire bell ring and quickly went out to join the gathering crowd. On the way to King Street, he stepped to the fore of a crowd of twenty or thirty men, many of whom brandished sticks or clubs gathered from butcher's stalls and wood piles. He carried "a large cordwood stick."[7] Becoming more noisy and numerous with each step, the crowd made its way to King Street and confronted Captain Preston and his hastily summoned rescue squad. Then it was that a British soldier, Hugh Montgomery, was struck.

Who dealt the blow and thereby touched off the firing? It was not Attucks, according to colonial propagandist Samuel Adams, since "he was leaning upon a stick when he fell, which certainly was not a threatening posture." Adams based his assertion on the testimony of John Danbrooke, who testified before the Court of Inquiry.[8] Another eye-witness, Andrew, slave of Oliver Wendell, a Boston selectman, told a different story, the one that has more generally been accepted:

The People seemed to be leaving the soldiers, and to turn from them when there came down a number from Jackson's corner, huzzaing and crying, damn them, they dare not fire, we are not afraid of them. One of these people, a stout man with a long cord wood stick, threw himself in, and made a blow at the officer;

6. For a reproduction of this *Boston Gazette* advertisement see George Livermore, *An Historical Research Respecting the Opinions of the Founders of the Republic on Negroes as Slaves, as Citizens, and as Soldiers* (Boston, 1862), 115. This advertisement was first discovered in 1859 by C. H. Morse of Cambridgeport, Mass., who sent a transcript to *The New England Historical and Genealogical Register.* In an accompanying note, Morse said that he learned from a grandson of Brown's that the latter had had a slave named Crispus. *New Eng. Hist. and Gen. Reg.,* 13 (Boston, 1859), 300.

7. Ruth Anna Fisher, "Manuscript Materials Bearing on the Negro in the British Museum," *Journal of Negro History,* 27 (1942), 86; Henry Alonzo Cushing, ed., *The Writings of Samuel Adams,* 4 vols. (New York, 1904-08), II, 119; testimony of James Bailey, in Frederic Kidder, *History of the Boston Massacre* (Albany, 1870), 29.

8. Cushing, ed., *Writings of Samuel Adams,* II, 119. Kidder, *Boston Massacre,* 142.

I saw the officer try to ward off the stroke; whether he struck him or not I do not know; the stout man then turned around, and struck the grenadier's gun at the captain's right hand, and immediately fell in with his club, and knocked his gun away, and struck him over the head; the blow came either on the soldier's cheek or hat. This stout man held the bayonet with his left hand, and twitched it and cried, kill the dogs, knock them over. This was the general cry; the people then crowded in.

When the court asked the identity of the "stout man," Andrew replied, "I thought, and still think, it was the mulatto who was shot."[9]

Whatever Attucks actually did that night, his prominent role in the Boston Massacre owed much to John Adams, who as counsel defending the British soldiers, chose to make him the chief target. Adams informed the trial jury that it was Attucks who "appears to have undertaken to be the hero of the night; and to lead this army with banners, to form them in the first place in Dock square, and march them up to King Street with their clubs." It was Attucks "whose very looks was enough to terrify any person," who "had hardiness enough to fall in upon them, and with one hand took hold of a bayonet, and with the other knocked the man down." It was Attucks "to whose mad behavior, in all probability, the dreadful carnage of that night is chiefly to be ascribed."[10]

Attucks's one impulsive act wrote his name in the annals of American history, for patriots did not allow the Boston Massacre to be forgotten. Its anniversary was duly observed each year in a public ceremony, which took on a ritualistic pattern. Bells would toll during the day, and at night lighted transparencies depicted the soldiers and their victims, giving a substance of sorts to the "discontented ghosts, with hollow groans," summoned to solemnize the occasion. The highlight of the evening was a stirring address by a leading citizen which, as the

9. *Ibid.*, 205. Partial support of Andrew came from James Bailey who, when asked which way Montgomery fired when he recovered his gun, testified that he imagined it was toward the mulatto, *ibid.*, 139. Presumably, Montgomery would most likely have aimed at his assailant.

10. *Ibid.*, 257-58. Adams's concluding statement on Attucks indicated that he doubtless felt it necessary to appeal to the emotions of the jury: "And it is in this manner, this town has been often treated; a Carr from Ireland, and an Attucks from Framingham, happening to be here, shall sally out upon their thoughtless enterprises, at the head of such a rabble of negroes, &c., as they can collect together . . . ." *Ibid.*, 258.

contemporary historian David Ramsay observed, "administered fuel to the fire of liberty, and kept it burning with an incessant flame."[11] The propaganda value of the Boston Massacre cannot be minimized, for despite the just acquittal of Captain Preston and his squad, the initial impression of foul play was never effaced. "No previous outrage had given a general alarm, as the commotion on the fifth of March, 1770," wrote Mercy Warren, sister of James Otis. It "created a resentment which emboldened the timid" and "determined the wavering."[12]

The lives of the five men who died on the occasion were nothing compared with military losses in the Revolution. But as John Fiske remarked in 1889 while speaking at the dedication of the Crispus Attucks monument on the Boston Common, "it will not do to measure history with a foot-rule."[13]

* * *

The pioneer Negro historian, George Washington Williams, assumed that Attucks was a true martyr, who died for a principle. He found it "significant indeed that a Negro was the first to open the hostilities between Great Britain and the colonies,—the first to pour out his blood as a precious libation on the altar of a people's rights."[14] This point of view rests, of course, upon inference. It could be said that Attucks was simply an unruly spirit who was looking for trouble. Certainly he was a man of large physical stature, and it appears that he had once been a runaway slave. Still, it is hard to believe he could have lived in Boston and not have been influenced by the general feeling against Britain. He must often have heard that taxation without representation was tyranny, and perhaps such slogans had given him a sense of personal grievance. The libertarian credos of the patriotic movement may have led him to conceive a dissatisfaction with the existing social order. In

11. *Boston Town Records, 1770 through 1777* (Boston, 1887), 48. Arthur M. Schlesinger, *Prelude to Independence: The Newspaper War on Britain, 1764-1776* (New York, 1958), chapter head, chap. V; phrase from Joseph Warren's speech, in *Orations Delivered at the Request of the Inhabitants of the Town to Commemorate the Evening of the Fifth of March, 1770* (Boston, 1785), 64; David Ramsay, *A History of the American Revolution,* 2 vols. (London, 1793), I, 91.

12. Mercy Warren, *History of the American Revolution,* 3 vols. (Boston, 1805), I, 93.

13. *A Memorial of Crispus Attucks,* 84.

14. George Washington Williams, *History of the Negro Race in America* (New York, 1882), 364.

arguing that the writs of assistance endangered liberty, James Otis had "asserted the rights of Negroes" in his celebrated oration of February 1761—perhaps Attucks knew this.[15] At any rate, there is no reason to question his patriotism; probably no less than his companions in the riot, Attucks was motivated by principle.

What vision moved Attucks can only be surmised. But that he should have joined the mob that assailed the British soldiers that night is not singular. Negroes were not wholly excluded from the patriotic movement, and in nearly every province a few of them were to be found in the ranks of the colonial militia, where their employment was a practice of long standing.[16]

Although general policy in early America was to exclude Negroes from militia service, manpower shortages often outweighed the reluctance to give the Negro a gun; hence official attitudes did not always mirror actual practice. A case in point is the French and Indian War in which both northern and southern colonies were driven to employ colored men. A few illustrative instances may be noted. In Granville County, North Carolina, under date of October 8, 1754, a muster of Colonel William Eaton's company lists five Negroes and two mulattoes, a muster of Captain John Glover's company lists three Negroes and that of Captain Osborn Jeffreys lists five Negroes.[17] And in Virginia, General Edward Braddock wrote from Williamsburg in 1755: "There are here numbers of mulattoes and free Negroes of whom I shall make bat men, whom the province are to furnish with pay and frocks."[18]

Among northern colonies, New York made extensive use of the Negro.[19] So did Connecticut; colored men served in

15. The quoted phrase is from John Adams. Adams, ed., *Works of John Adams*, X, 315.

16. On this topic see Benjamin Quarles, "The Colonial Militia and Negro Manpower," *Mississippi Valley Historical Review*, 45 (1959), 643-52.

17. Walter Clark, ed., *State Records of North Carolina, 1777-1790*, 16 vols. (1895-1905), XXII, 370-72. Hereafter cited as Clark, ed., *State Rec. of N. C.* After the war, the customary precautions were resumed; by an act of 1768 overseers of six slaves or more were to be fined if they appeared at musters. Luther L. Gobbel, "The Militia in North Carolina in Colonial and Revolutionary Times," *Historical Papers of the Trinity College Historical Society*, 12 (Durham, 1916), 42.

18. Edward Braddock to Robert Napier, Mar. 17, 1755, Stanley Pargellis, ed., *Military Affairs in North America, 1748-1765* (New York, 1936), 78.

19. For the names of Negroes serving in New York companies, with such descriptive data as date of enlistment, age, birthplace, occupation, stature,

twenty-five of her militia companies.[20] In Rhode Island James Richardson of Stonington, advertising in May 1763 for his Negro servant, reported him as having served as a soldier earlier that year.[21] The town of Hingham, Massachusetts, recruiting men in 1758, placed two Negroes, Primus Cobb and Flanders, among the thirty-six privates in Captain Edward Ward's company.[22] Despite the laws, Negroes were enlisted for military service.

* * *

Use of Negroes in the colonial militia established a pattern which was followed in the first months of the war with England. In July 1775 the Continental Congress recommended that all able-bodied men in each colony form themselves into regular companies of militia. Congress did not mention Negroes, and they may not have been among the "minute men" and militia units of Massachusetts which drilled during the fall and winter preceding Lexington and Concord. But when in the spring the crisis approached and there was a call for volunteers, colored men presented themselves and were accepted.

They took part in the first military engagement of the Revolution as the British marched to destroy the military supplies at Concord and returned on April 19, 1775, to Boston. For the British this was, in the words of General Henry Clinton, "an unfortunate excursion."[23] Going and coming, the British met armed opposition from militiamen all along the line of march.

One of the Negroes taking part in the battle of Lexington

militia company, and officer who did the enlisting, see "Muster Rolls of New York Provincial Troops, 1755-1764," New-York Historical Society, *Collections*, Publication Fund Ser., 24 (New York, 1892), 60, 182, 284, 364, 385, 398, 402, 406, 418, 420, 426, 427, 440, 442, 498. Hereafter cited as N.-Y. Hist. Soc., *Coll.* One Negro, Solomon Jolly, is designated as free; the others, presumably, were slaves.

20. *Rolls of Connecticut Men in the French and Indian War* (Connecticut Historical Society, *Collections,* 9, 10 [1903-05]), I, 322, II, 437. Hereafter cited as Conn. Hist. Soc., *Coll.* The figure 25 as the number of companies is derived from a page check of the regimental and militia affiliations of the Negroes listed in the indexes (barring duplications) of these two volumes.

21. "Eighteenth Century Slaves as Advertised by Their Masters," *Journ. of Negro Hist.,* 1 (1916), 200.

22. *History of the Town of Hingham, Massachusetts,* 3 vols. (Hingham, 1893), I, 265.

23. William B. Willcox, ed., *The American Rebellion: Sir Henry Clinton's Narrative of his Campaigns, 1775-1782* (New Haven, 1954), 13.

and Concord was Peter Salem who served in Captain Simon Edgel's Framingham company of minutemen.[24] Peter's owners, the Belknaps of Framingham, had given him his freedom so he could enlist. From South Precinct in Braintree came Pompy, a private in Seth Turner's company, and numbered in Thomas White's Brookline company was "Joshua Boylston's Prince."[25] Other Negroes marching in the alarm on April 19 included Cato Stedman and Cato Bordman of Captain Samuel Thatcher's Cambridge company, which entered the hostilities at Lincoln, and Cuff Whittemore and Cato Wood of Captain Benjamin Locke's Arlington company, which attacked at the same point.[26] Seeing action at both places was Pomp Blackman, later to serve in the Continental army. One of the fifty-one casualties on the American side was Prince Estabrook, a Negro from West Lexington. Estabrook was in Captain John Parker's company, the first to enter the fray.[27]

At Boston two months later, on June 17, came the Battle of Bunker Hill, another British effort to prevent local armies from developing a posture of strength and again a morale booster for the Americans. Here too, Negroes fought with the provincial forces. Former slave Peter Salem saw action for the second time.[28] Seasor and Pharaoh, both of whom on May 3 had en-

24. *Massachusetts Soldiers and Sailors of the Revolutionary War,* 17 vols. (Boston, 1896-1908), XII, 743. Hereafter cited as *Mass. Soldiers and Sailors.*

25. *Ibid.,* XII, 520, 788.

26. Frank W. Coburn, *The Battle of April 19, 1775* (Lexington, Mass., 1912), 41, 76.

27. *Ibid.,* 76; *Mass. Soldiers and Sailors,* II, 110; *John C. Warren Collection to Serve as Materials for an Account of the Battle of Lexington and Concord* (New York Public Library); Coburn, *Battle of April 19, 1775,* 6. Perhaps it was a Negro other than Prince of whom a British officer spoke: "As soon as the troops had passed Charlestown Neck the Rebels ceased firing. A Negro . . . was wounded near the houses close to the Neck, out of which Rebels fired to the last." "Description of the Battle of Lexington by Lieutenant Mackenzie of the Royal Welsh Fusileers," Mass. Hist. Soc., *Proc.,* 2nd Ser., 5 (1890), 394.

28. *Mass. Soldiers and Sailors,* XIII, 743. On Salem see David E. Phillips, "Negroes in the American Revolution," *Journal of American History,* 5 (1911), 143-46. The story that Salem fired the shot that felled British officer John Pitcairn is not easy to substantiate. For various accounts of questionable accuracy, see "Extracts from Dr. Belknap's Notebooks," Mass. Hist. Soc., *Proc.,* 1st Ser., 14 (1876), 93; Samuel Swett, *Historical and Topical Sketch of Bunker Hill Battle* (Boston, 1818), 75; Livermore, *Historical Research Respecting Negroes,* 119. Supporters of this story point out that the celebrated John Trumbull painting of the Battle of Bunker

listed in Colonel James Scamman's York County "Regiment of Foot," were among those present as the officers rode through the American lines admonishing the men to preserve their scarce powder by holding their fire until they were close enough to the enemy to see the whites of their eyes. Another Negro participant at Bunker Hill was Barzillai Lew of Chelmsford, a cooper turned fifer. Although then only thirty years old, Lew had fought in the French and Indian War, having seen thirty-eight weeks of service in 1760 as a Pepperell enlistee in a Massachusetts company commanded by Thomas Farrington. Another Negro at Bunker Hill was Cuff Whittemore who "fought to the last," receiving a ball through his hat. He picked up a British officer's sword lying loose on the field, a trophy he later turned into cash.[29]

Particularly noteworthy was the conduct of Salem Poor. His bravery was so exceptional as to warrant a petition on his behalf to the General Court, signed by fourteen Massachusetts officers. Dated December 5, 1775, the petition stated "that a negro called Salem Poor, of Col. Frye's regiment, Capt. Ames' company, in the late battle at Charlestown, behaved like an experienced officer, as well as an excellent soldier." It would be tedious, stated the officers, to go into detail concerning Poor's conduct: "We only beg leave to say, in the person of this said negro centers a brave and gallant soldier. The reward due to so great and distinguished a character, we submit to Congress." Poor later served at Valley Forge and White Plains.[30]

Hill conspicuously shows a Negro with a gun. Trumbull, however, was four miles away, and his canvas was executed in London seven years after the event. On this subject see E. H. Silver, "Painter of the Revolution," *American Heritage,* 9 (1958), 51; also, *Proceedings of the Bunker Hill Memorial Association* (Boston, 1911), frontispiece and p. 57; Samuel Abbott, "John Trumbull, the Painter of the Revolution," *ibid.,* 59-60. For a detailed study of the battle with a mass of primary sources, see "Bunker's Hill," *The Historical Magazine,* 3 (Boston, 1868), 321-440. Perhaps it should be noted that at the Bunker Hill Monument one may see on display the "Peter Salem Gun."

29. Nathan Goold, *History of Colonel James Scamman's Thirtieth Regiment of Foot* (Portland, Me., 1899), 41, 63; *Mass. Soldiers and Sailors,* IX, 725; "Record of Service in the Colonial Wars of Barzillai Lew" (typescript copy of statement from the Secretary of the Commonwealth of Massachusetts), Carter G. Woodson Papers, Library of Congress; Samuel Swett, *Notes to His Sketch of Bunker-Hill Battle* (Boston, 1825), 24.

30. Revolutionary Rolls Collection, Massachusetts Archives (State House, Boston), CLXXX, 241. Hereafter cited as Mass. Arch. *Mass. Soldiers and Sailors,* XII, 561.

After the action at Bunker Hill, neighboring towns such as Plymouth and Andover sent their minutemen or militia to assist in the siege of Boston; a sprinkling of colored men were included. From New Hampshire came three Negroes in one of the companies of Colonel John Nixon's regiment, which made camp on Winter Hill in September 1775. Their previous occupation listed as "husbandman," these three recruits were "effective able bodied men," noted muster master Samuel Hobart, "but they are slaves—Inlisted with the Consent of their Masters." Another New Hampshire company stationed at Winter Hill in late 1775 included two Negroes.[31]

"In the regiments at Roxbury," wrote General John Thomas, commander of one of the two brigades comprising the American right wing at Boston, "we have some Negroes; but I look on them, in General, Equally Serviceable with other men, for Fatigue & in action; many of them have proved themselves brave."[32] Another high ranking officer, writing a day earlier, spoke of the number of Negroes in the armies assembled around Boston. "There are in the Massachusetts Regiments some Negroes," reported William Heath. "Such is also the case with the Regiments from the Other Colonies, Rhode Island has a number of negroes and Indians, Connecticut has fewer negroes, but a number of Indians. The New Hampshire regiments have less of both."[33]

The Eighth Connecticut Regiment which took its post at Roxbury had two Negroes. Four Negroes served in two Connecticut companies—Captain John Steven's and Captain Aaron Austin's—sent early in 1776 to Boston "to reinforce the Northern armies." A Negro serving in another Connecticut company was killed at Lechmere Point, "by the bursting of a shell which fell into the fort." Of the fifteen privates of Captain John Steven's West Hartford company, ordered on January 23, 1776, to join the army in Canada, one was a Negro named Jack. In New York City on March 17, 1776, there were eleven Negroes in Captain Benjamin Egbert's fifty-nine man company of the 22nd Beat.[34]

31. Isaac W. Hammond, ed., *Revolutionary War Rolls and Documents* (Manchester, 1889), 8, 24.

32. Thomas to John Adams, Oct. 24, 1775, John Adams Papers, Mass. Hist. Soc.

33. William Heath to John Adams, Oct. 23, 1775, *ibid.*

34. *Connecticut Military Record, 1775-1848* (Hartford, 1889), 85, 90;

In Virginia, where the militia law of July 1776 opened the service to all free male persons, a Negro served with the local militia in the Battle of Great Bridge in December 1775. In this action the British attempted to seize the bridge which spanned the Elizabeth River, some twelve miles below Norfolk. With the defending colonial troops was free Negro William Flora of Portsmouth, the last sentinel to leave his post as the enemy approached. Flora withdrew "amidst a shower of musket balls," returning fire eight times.[35] Another Negro credited with a share in the victory was a well-instructed slave (property of the father of future Chief Justice John Marshall) who, according to Colonel William Woodford, crossed into the British lines and duped the English officers into believing that the Great Bridge fort was lightly manned and the men in low spirits.[36]

* * *

The early use of Negro soldiers did not continue; within ten months after Lexington and Concord a pattern of exclusion had developed. The reasons were many. Most Negroes were slaves, whose enlistment violated the property rights of their masters, and there was no intention of allowing the army to become a refuge for runaway slaves. The dominant reason, however, was fear. A slave with a gun was an open invitation to trouble. As early as 1715 a group of Carolina patentees had expressed it quite well: "there must be great caution used [in

"Rolls and Lists of Connecticut Men in the Revolution," Conn. Hist. Soc., Coll., 8 (1901), 35, 36; Royal R. Hinman, Historical Collection of the Part Sustained by Connecticut During the War of the Revolution (Hartford, 1842), 558; "Journal of Bayze Wells of Farmington, in the Canada Expedition, 1775-1777," Conn. Hist. Soc., Coll., 7 (1899), 259; Calendar of Historical Manuscripts Relating to the War of the Revolution in the Office of the Secretary of State, 2 vols. (Albany, 1868), I, 267.

35. William Waller Hening, ed., The Statutes at Large: Being a Collection of All the Laws of Virginia . . . , 13 vols. (Richmond, 1809-23), IX, 27. Hereafter cited as Hening, Statutes of Va. "The Battle of Great Bridge," Virginia Historical Register and Literary Companion, 4 (Richmond, 1853), 5. For a sketch of Flora, see Luther P. Jackson, Virginia Negro Soldiers and Sailors in the Revolutionary War (Norfolk, 1944), 16-19. Hereafter cited as Jackson, Va. Negro Soldiers and Sailors. On November 24, 1783, Flora had a balance of pay due him of nearly $250. Pay Lists, 1781-1789: United States Army, Virginia Line, Ford Collection, New York Public Library.

36. Woodford to the Virginia Convention, Dec. 10, 1775, "The Woodford, Howe, and Lee Letters," Richmond College Historical Papers, 1 (Richmond, 1915), 119. Also Richard Kidder Meade to Everard Meade, Dec. 19, 1775, "Two Letters of Richard Kidder Meade," Southern Literary Messenger, 25 (Richmond, 1857), 24.

the military employment of Negroes] lest our slaves when armed might become our masters."[37]

As the war with England became imminent, this sense of apprehension grew stronger in areas of heavy Negro concentration. In Maryland in late April 1775, a delegation visited Governor Robert Eden requesting arms and ammunition to put down any uprisings by slaves. Persuaded almost against his will, Eden furnished 400 stands of arms to four counties.[38] In South Carolina, the Council of Safety issued warnings two months later against "instigated insurrections by our negroes." In neighboring North Carolina the climate of fear was intensified by the widely held belief that the British had decreed that every Negro who put his master to death would come into possession of his master's plantation.[39] The latent distrust of the slave seems to have been deliberately exploited by Southern patriots as a means of arousing animosity toward the British and of coercing those who were lukewarm or timid about breaking with England. Whatever its inspiration, such propaganda was effective in stilling any inclination to make a warrior of the Negro.

The reluctance to employ colored soldiers materialized in the formation of the Continental army in June 1775. A military establishment which represented the thirteen colonies had to reflect the sentiment of all its components. "Many northern blacks were excellent soldiers," wrote Samuel Swett, "but southern troops would not brook an equality with whites."[40] Thus, the federal army tended to be more selective than the local militia or the state levy; those in charge of the nation's armed forces were responsive to the wishes and fears of citizens up and down the seaboard, as well as the backwoodsmen who were trekking into the Western regions between the Appalachian divide and the Mississippi.

With such considerations in mind, the national military es-

37. "Agent for Carolina and Merchants Trading Thither" to Board of Trade, July 18, 1715, William L. Saunders, ed., *Colonial Records of North Carolina, 1662-1766,* 10 vols. (Raleigh, 1886-90), II, 197.

38. John T. Sharf, *History of Maryland,* 3 vols. (Baltimore, 1879), II, 179.

39. "Journal of the Council of Safety for South-Carolina," South Carolina Historical Society, *Collections,* 2 (1858), 40. Hereafter cited as S. C. Hist. Soc., *Coll.* E. W. and C. M. Andrews, eds., *Journals of a Lady of Quality* (New Haven, 1923), 199.

40. Swett, *Notes to His Sketch of Bunker-Hill Battle,* 25.

tablishment quickly made its decision. On July 10, 1775, the adjutant general of the American army, Horatio Gates, instructed recruiting officers that they should not enlist, among others, "any deserter from the Ministerial army, nor any stroller, negro, or vagabond."[41] The Continental Congress was not quite ready to order the exclusion of blacks, and on September 26 rejected a resolution, presented by Edward Rutledge of South Carolina, requiring the discharge of all Negroes—free as well as slave— from the army.[42] But this did not deter the military men. Two weeks later, on Sunday, October 8, at a council of war at Cambridge attended by eight generals and called to decide upon the number of men needed to continue the siege of Boston, the question of enlisting free Negroes and slaves was discussed. The officers agreed on a policy of exclusion for both groups, the recommendation being unanimous concerning slaves.[43]

Within the next month this policy was twice re-affirmed by orders from headquarters at Cambridge. On October 31 the quartermaster general was directed to supply clothes to all those who would re-enlist, "Negroes excepted, which the Congress do not incline to inlist again." Twelve days later a decree was issued forbidding recruiting officers to sign up "Negroes, Boys unable to bear Arms nor Old men unfit to endure the Fatigues of the Campaign." By this time headquarters had already posted an order to seize and confine any Negro found "straggling" about the camp at Cambridge, or any of the roads or villages near the Roxbury or Cambridge encampments.[44]

Free Negro soldiers were vexed at this official policy and carried their protest to headquarters at Cambridge. Washington was sympathetic toward their complaints and on December 30, 1775, ordered recruiting officers to re-enlist free Negroes, adding that he intended to lay the matter before Congress. On

41. Peter Force, ed., *American Archives, . . . a Documentary History of . . . the North American Colonies*, 4th Ser., 6 vols., 5th Ser., 3 vols. (Washington, 1837-53), 4th Ser., III, 1385. Hereafter cited as *Amer. Arch.*

42. "Diary of Richard Smith in the Continental Congress, 1775-1776," *American Historical Review*, I (1896), 292.

43. *Amer. Arch.*, 4th Ser., III, 1040.

44. John C. Fitzpatrick, ed., *The Writings of George Washington from the Original Manuscript Sources, 1745-1799*, 39 vols. (Washington, 1931-44), IV, 21, 57, 86. Hereafter cited as Fitzpatrick, ed., *Writings of Washington*. See also "Orderly Book Kept and Signed by John Polley . . . at Gen'l Artemas Ward's Headquarters, Roxbury, Sept. 19—Dec. 31, 1775," Clements Library, University of Michigan.

the following day he wrote to its president, John Hancock, pointing out that free Negro soldiers were "dissatisfied at being discarded." He had given them permission to re-enter the service, he continued, but would put a stop to it if Congress disapproved. Washington's letter was referred to a committee which on January 16, 1776, recommended that free Negroes who had already served might be re-enlisted, but no other colored volunteers would be accepted. Slaves were already being excluded under military order and on February 21, 1776, instructions from headquarters reaffirmed this policy.[45]

The individual states were not long in adopting the Negro exclusion policies of the central government. Indeed Massachusetts preceded Congress and the federal high command in considering a ban on black enlistments. On May 20, 1775, the Committee of Safety, the state's executive branch, recommended that no slave be admitted into the Massachusetts army "upon any consideration whatever;"[46] but the legislature withheld its approval. John Adams, writing in alarm from Philadelphia to General Heath on October 5, 1775, asked whether there was any truth to the widespread allegations that in the Massachusetts regiments "there are great numbers of boys, old men, and negroes." Were there, inquired Adams, "more of these in proportion in the Mass—Regiments, than in those of Connecticut, Rhode Island, and New Hampshire."[47]

Massachusetts soon cleared up the matter. On January 22, 1776, a militia act was passed excluding Negroes, Indians and mulattoes. Later that year the General Court, in an act to raise troops for the Continental army, ordered that non-whites could not take up arms, nor could whites "procure any person to do it in their room."[48]

45. *The Orderly Book of Colonel William Henshaw, October 1, 1775, through October 3, 1776* (Worcester, Mass., 1881), 65; *Amer. Arch.*, 4th Ser., IV, 485; W. C. Ford and Gaillard Hunt, eds., *Journals of the Continental Congress, 1774-1789,* 34 vols. (Washington, 1904-37), IV, 60. Hereafter cited as Ford, ed., *Journ. of Cont. Cong.* Fitzpatrick, ed., *Writings of Washington*, IV, 342; *Boston Gazette*, Feb. 3, 1777.

46. *Amer. Arch.*, 4th Ser., II, 762; *The Journals of Each Provincial Congress of Massachusetts in 1774 and 1775* (Boston, 1838), 302.

47. Adams to Heath, Oct. 5, 1775, "The Heath Papers, 1775-1779," Massachusetts Historical Society, *Collections,* 7th Ser., 4 (1904), pt. 2, 3-4. Hereafter cited as Mass. Hist. Soc., *Coll.*

48. *The Acts and Resolves of the Province of Massachusetts Bay, 1769-1780,* V (Boston, 1886), 445, 596.

The example of Massachusetts was followed by the other New England states. At a meeting on October 23, 1775, attended by George Washington, three official representatives from Congress—Thomas Lynch, Jr., from South Carolina, Benjamin Harrison from Virginia, and Benjamin Franklin from Pennsylvania—discussed Negro enlistment with civilian authorities of Massachusetts, Rhode Island, and Connecticut. The conclusion reached was to reject all Negroes, bond or free.[49] New Hampshire followed the example of the other New England states. On April 12, 1776, her Committee of Safety requested all males above twenty-one to sign a declaration pledging themselves to oppose British hostilities with arms; lunatics, idiots, and Negroes were excepted. Six months later the legislature barred Negroes and Indians from the state armies.[50]

In the middle tier of states there was a similar policy of Negro and slave exclusion. In Pennsylvania non-whites were exempted, in April 1776, from a decree imposing a fine on able-bodied men who "did not meet and exercise in order to learn the Art Military." In Delaware the Council of Safety, on January 13, 1776, warned recruiting officers against signing up apprentices "or indebted Servants"—the latter presumably included slaves. This order was re-emphasized six weeks later in the official "instructions for enlisting men in the service of the Delaware Government."[51] In New Jersey early in 1776, the Shrewsbury Committee of Observation ordered that all Negroes with guns or other weapons be required to turn them in "until the present troubles are settled."[52] In New York the militia act of April 1, 1775, stipulated that "all bought servants during their Servitude shall be free from being listed in any Troop or Company within this Colony."[53] The ruling undoubtedly embraced slaves.

49. *Amer. Arch.*, 4th Ser., III, 1161.
50. Albert S. Batchellor, ed., *Miscellaneous Revolutionary Documents of New Hampshire* (Manchester, 1910), 1-2; *An Act for forming and regulating the Militia within the State of New-Hampshire* (Exeter, 1776), 28.
51. *Pennsylvania Gazette* (Philadelphia), Feb. 26, 1777; Leon de Valinger, Jr., ed., "Council of Safety Minutes," *Delaware History*, 1 (1946), 75; "Colonel John Haslet's Regiment," *Delaware Archives*, 1 (Public Archives Commission of Delaware, Wilmington, 1911), 33.
52. "Proceedings of the Committee of Freehold and Shrewsbury," New Jersey Historical Society, *Proceedings*, 1 (Newark, 1846), 192, 195. Hereafter cited as N. J. Hist. Soc., *Proc.*
53. *The Colonial Laws of New York: 1664 to the Revolution*, 5 vols. (Albany, 1894-96), V, 738.

Below the Potomac in the war's early stages all was quiet about the use of the Negro as a soldier. Virginia still left a door ajar for the free Negro; otherwise in the heavily Negro populated Southern states the enlistment laws were carbon copies of colonial statutes confining military service to whites.

* * *

Negro exclusion had by the summer of 1776 become the policy on local, state, and continental levels. But even before the year came to a close there was a re-opening of the question. One of the reasons for the willingness to reconsider the barring of Negroes was the British policy of welcoming them. This cordial invitation from His Majesty's officers to Negroes was to be initiated in Virginia.

CHAPTER II

"LORD DUNMORE'S ETHIOPIAN REGIMENT"

"This measure of emancipating the negroes
has excited an universal ferment."

William Eddis, Annapolis, January 16, 1776

In American patriotic tradition the first full-fledged villain
to step from the wings as the Revolutionary War unfolded was
John Murray, Earl of Dunmore.[1] Like other royal governors in
office as the crisis reached its height, the crown's representative
in Virginia would have been a marked man no matter how
circumspect his behavior. Dunmore, lacking in diplomatic skills,
was destined to furnish the colonists with a convenient hate-
symbol. The act for which he incurred the greatest infamy was
one which in Negro circles cast him in the role of liberator.
This was Dunmore's proclamation inviting slaves to leave their
masters and join the royal forces.

Issued as of November 7, 1775, on board the *William* in
the harbor at Norfolk, the proclamation announced that in order
to defeat "treasonable purposes" the Governor was declaring
martial law. Colonists who refused "to resort to his Majesty's
standard" were to be adjudged traitors. Then came the words
which were destined to be quoted far and wide: "and I do hereby
further declare all indented servants, Negroes, or others, (ap-
pertaining to Rebels,) free, that are able and willing to bear
arms, they joining His Majesty's Troops, as soon as may be,
for the more speedily reducing the Colony to a proper sense of
their duty, to His Majesty's crown and dignity."[2]

1. The following chapter is adapted from an article of mine appearing in
the *William and Mary Quarterly*, 3rd Ser., 15 (October, 1958), 494-507.
2. Original broadside, in University of Virginia library. For a facsimile
which Patrick Henry circulated, and which differs a little in punctuation
from the original, see Francis L. Berkeley, Jr., *Dunmore's Proclamation of*

Dunmore's proclamation had its expected effect. "The colonists," wrote a contemporary, "were struck with horror"; the "Poet of the American Revolution" implored the heavens to deliver the colonies from the "valiant" Dunmore and "his crew of banditti" ("who plunder Virginians at Williamsburg city").[3] Taking alarm, the Continental Congress on December 2, 1775, instructed its committee for fitting out armed vessels to engage ships of war to capture or destroy the Governor's fleet, and General Washington was urged to take such measures against his lordship as would "effectually Repel his violences and secure the peace and safety of that Colony." Two days later the Congress recommended to Virginia that she resist Dunmore to the utmost.[4]

The apprehension over Dunmore's proclamation was grounded initially in the fear of its unsettling effect on the slaves, but ultimately in the fear of a servile insurrection—that nightmarish dread in communities where the whites were outnumbered. A policy that would strike off their shackles would obviously have a marked appeal to the inhabitants of slave row. Moreover, there had been recent evidence that the Virginia bondmen were responsive to the offer of freedom.

Emancipation (Charlottesville, 1941), frontispiece. See also *Amer. Arch.,* 4th Ser., III, 1385.

3. Ramsay, *History of the American Revolution,* I, 234; Fred Lewis Pattee, ed., *The Poems of Philip Freneau,* 3 vols. (Princeton, 1902-07), I, 140. "Hell itself could not have vomitted anything more black than this design of emancipating our slaves," wrote a Philadelphia correspondent to a friend abroad. *Morning Chronicle and London Advertiser,* Jan. 20, 1776, quoted in Margaret W. Willard, ed., *Letters on the American Revolution, 1774-1776* (Boston, 1925), 233. It was the judgment of Edward Rutledge that the proclamation tended "more effectually to work an eternal separation between Great Britain and the Colonies,—than any other expedient, which could possibly have been thought of." Rutledge to Ralph Izard, Dec. 8, 1775, in A. I. Deas, ed., *Correspondence of Mr. Ralph Izard,* 2 vols. (New York, 1844), I, 165.

4. Ford, ed., *Journ. of Cont. Cong.,* III, 395, 403; John Hancock to George Washington, Dec. 2, 1775, Edmund C. Burnett, ed., *Letters of Members of the Continental Congress,* 8 vols. (Washington, 1921-36), I, 267. The army commander shared the apprehension of Congress. "If," he wrote to a Virginia delegate, "that man is not crushed before spring, he will become the most formidable enemy America has; his strength will increase as a snow ball by rolling: and faster, if some expedient cannot be hit upon, to convince the slaves and servants of the impotency of his designs." George Washington to Richard Henry Lee, Dec. 26, 1775, in R. H. Lee, *Memoir of the Life of Richard Henry Lee* (Philadelphia, 1825), II, 9. Compare Washington to Joseph Reed, Dec. 15, 1775, in Fitzpatrick, ed., *Writings of Washington,* IV, 176.

Dunmore himself had furnished such evidence. For at least eight months prior to the formal proclamation, the Governor had seriously considered the idea of enlisting the slaves. His reasons were plain. Rebellious planters who contemplated a resort to arms would be deprived of their workers and would be compelled to return to their homes to protect their families and their property. Moreover, the slaves would help fill the ranks of military laborers for His Majesty's forces. Such human *potential de guerre* was badly needed, since Dunmore could expect little help from British headquarters in Boston.[5] Raising the slaves against their masters was such an obvious tactic that from the beginning the crown supporters and their sympathizers had contemplated inciting disaffection among Negroes in the South.[6]

Dunmore let it be known late in April 1775 that he might be driven to set up the royal standard, adding that if he did, he believed that he could count "all the Slaves on the side of Government."[7] On May 1 the Governor wrote to the Earl of Dartmouth expressing confidence that, once supplied with arms and ammunition, he would be able "to collect from among the *Indians,* negroes and other persons" a force sufficient to cope with the Virginia patriots.[8] Two weeks later, Gage in a letter to Dartmouth touched

5. General Thomas Gage wrote to Dunmore on Sept. 10, 1775: "I can neither assist you with Men, arms or ammunition, for I have them not to spare; should you draw upon me I have not the Cash to pay your Bills." Sir Henry Clinton Papers, Clements Lib. Hereafter cited as Clinton Papers. For England's continuing great difficulty in getting manpower see Edward E. Curtis, *The Organization of the British Army in the American Revolution* (New Haven, 1926), 51-80.

6. "Although Virginia and Maryland are both very populous," wrote Governor Joshiah Martin of North Carolina to Dartmouth on June 30, 1775, "the Whites are greatly outnumbered by the Negroes, at least in the former; a circumstance that would facilitate exceedingly the Reduction of those Colonies who are very sensible of their Weakness arising from it." Clinton Papers.

7. "Deposition of Dr. William Pasteur. In Regard to the Removal of Powder from the Williamsburg Magazine," in "Virginia Legislative Papers (from originals in Virginia State Archives)," *Virginia Magazine of History and Biography*, 13 (July 1905), 49.

8. Dartmouth to Dunmore, Aug. 2, 1775, *Amer. Arch.*, 4th Ser., III, 6. In this passage Dartmouth repeats the contents of a letter from Dunmore dated May 1. Later that year Dunmore concocted a plan to raise the tribes, as Gage phrased it, "on the back Parts of the Province of Virginia, to be joined by such inhabitants and Indians as may be at, and about Detroit." Gage to Guy Carleton, Sept. 11, 1775, Gage Manuscripts, American Ser., Clements Lib. This so-called "Connolly Plot" is briefly described in Isaac S. Harrell, *Loyalism in Virginia* (Philadelphia, 1926), 35-37.

on Dunmore's proposal: "We hear," wrote the British commander, "that a Declaration his Lordship has made, of proclaiming all the Negroes free, who should join him, has Startled the Insurgents."[9]

In late April a group of slaves, scenting freedom in the air, went to the Governor's house and volunteered their services. Not quite ready for an open break with the patriots, Dunmore had them dismissed. But a decision could not be long delayed. On June 8, 1775, the Governor took the decisive step of quitting Williamsburg and taking asylum aboard the man-of-war *Fowey* at Yorktown, a move he had been turning over in his mind since May 15. "I have thought it best for his Majesty's Service," he wrote, "to retire from amidst such hostile appearances around me." The House of Burgesses, taking note of the Governor's flight, assured him that his personal safety was in no danger, but pointedly noted its displeasure that "a Scheme, the most diabolical, had been meditated, and generally recommended, by a Person of great influence, to offer Freedom to our Slaves, and turn them against their Masters."[10]

Realizing that there was no turning back, but not as yet willing to declare his policy, Dunmore seized any means at hand to add black reinforcements to his tiny force of 300 white soldiers, seamen, and loyalist recruits. In early August the officers of the volunteer companies in Williamsburg informed the Convention that the "Governour's Cutter had carried off a number of Slaves belonging to private gentlemen."[11] Small sloops, which the Crown employed primarily to intercept intracolonial shipments of powder, invited slaves aboard. "Lord Dunmore sails up and down the river," wrote a Norfolk correspondent on October 28, 1775, to a friend in England, "and where he finds a defenceless place, he lands, plunders the plantation and carries off the negroes."[12]

9. Gage to Dartmouth, May 15, 1775, Gage MSS, English Ser., Clements Lib.

10. "Deposition of John Randolph in Regard to the Removal of the Powder," in "Virginia Legislative Papers," *Va. Mag. of Hist. and Biog.*, 15 (Oct. 1907), 150; Dunmore to Gage, May 15, 1775, Gage MSS, American Ser., Clements Lib.; John Pendleton Kennedy, ed., *Journals of the House of Burgesses of Virginia, 1773-1776* (Richmond, 1905), 256.

11. "Proceedings of the Virginia Convention, August 3, 1775," *Amer. Arch.*, 4th Ser., III, 373.

12. *Morning Chronicle and London Advertiser*, Dec. 22, 1775, quoted in Willard, ed., *Letters on the American Revolution*, 271-72. The number of

Ready at last to come out into the open, Dunmore was concerned only with his timing. An apparently auspicious moment came in mid-November 1775, when a skirmish took place at Kemp's Landing on the Elizabeth River. In this action the colonial militia was routed and its two commanding colonels were captured. Entering the village in triumph, Dunmore, on November 14, ordered the publication of the proclamation he had drafted a week earlier on board the *William*. The final break had come—the Governor had set up his standard and had officially called upon the slaves to join him.

Tidewater Virginia took alarm as rumors spread that slaves were stampeding to the British.[13] However the stampede, if it occurred, did not go very far. Before any substantial slave migration to Dunmore could get under way, the Governor suffered a decisive defeat at arms. This occurred on December 9 at Great Bridge, a fortified span across the Elizabeth River some ten miles below Norfolk which dominated the land approach to the town. Dunmore had believed an attack was impending and had rashly decided to take the offensive. His force of 600 was severely repulsed, suffering 61 casualties, including 3 dead officers. Forced to retreat after twenty-five minutes of combat, Dunmore's troops hurried back to Norfolk. Feeling that he could no longer hold the city and fearing a retaliatory attack, the Governor spiked his twenty pieces of cannon and ordered his followers aboard the vessels in the harbor. He was never to regain a foothold on the Virginia mainland.

The military preparation of the colonists was matched by their promptness in adopting "home front" measures to prevent slaves from joining the Governor. Newspapers lost no time in publishing the proclamation in full, as information and as a warning. To deter runaways, local patrols were doubled, highways were carefully watched, and owners of small craft were required to exercise vigilance. Since Dunmore's action had come as no surprise, the Virginians had had time to put

slaves reaching Dunmore before he issued his proclamation is indeterminate; "some accounts make them about 100; others less." Edmund Pendleton and others to Virginia Delegates in Congress, Nov. 11, 1775, Lee Family Manuscripts, University of Virginia Library, Charlottesville.

13. "Letters mention that slaves flock to him in abundance, but I hope it magnified." Edmund Pendleton to Richard Henry Lee, Nov. 27, 1775, *Amer. Arch.,* 4th Ser., IV, 202.

the colony in a "tolerable state of defense."[14]   Adjacent Maryland, through its Council of Safety, ordered a military force
to station itself in St. Mary's County "and guard the shores
from thence to the river Powtowmack, to prevent any servants,
negroes, or others from going on board the Fowey ship of war."[15]

To vigilance the colonists added psychological warfare. The
Virginia Gazette published a letter from a subscriber urging that
Negroes be warned against joining Dunmore.. Slaves should
be told that the English ministry, in refusing to stop the slave
trade, had proved a far greater enemy to Negroes than their
American masters, and that if the colonists were defeated, their
slaves would be sold in the West Indies. They should be told,
too, that Dunmore was cruel to his own black servitors. And,
finally, slaves should be urged to place their expectation on a
better condition in the next world. If this information had
been spread widely, the correspondent observed, "not one slave
would have joined our enemies."[16]

A week later the *Gazette* carried another letter in similar
vein. Colonists were advised to inform slaves that Dunmore
proposed to free only those who would bear arms for him,
leaving the aged and infirm, the women and children, to bear
the brunt of the shorn master's anger. Moreover, under the
English flag the slaves would be much worse off than under Virginia masters, "who pity their conditions, who wish in general
to make it as easy and comfortable as possible, and who would
willingly, were it in their power, or were they permitted, not
only prevent any more negroes from losing their freedom, but
restore it to such as have already unhappily lost it." Contrast
this benevolent disposition with that of British masters, the
Gazette warned, who would sell the runaways to the sugar islands. "Be not then, ye negroes, tempted by this proclamation
to ruin your selves."[17]

Official action was not long in coming. The Virginia Convention on December 8 appointed a committee to prepare an

14. Ramsay, *American Revolution,* I, 234.

15. Journal and Correspondence of the Maryland Council of Safety, Aug.
29, 1775, to July 6, 1776; William H. Browne, *et al.,* eds., *Archives of Maryland*
(Baltimore, 1883—in progress), XI, 511-12. Hereafter cited as *Arch. of Md.*

16. *Virginia Gazette* (Williamsburg), Nov. 17, 1775. Hereafter cited as
Va. Gaz.

17. *Ibid.,* Nov. 24, 1775.

answer to Dunmore's proclamation. Five days later, when the committee made its report, it was directed to draw up a declaration stating that runaways to the British would be pardoned if they returned in ten days; otherwise they would "be liable to such punishment as shall be directed by the Convention." The following day, with the committee's report at hand, the delegates issued a declaration of policy. Beginning with a reminder that the time-honored penalty for a slave insurrection was death without benefit of clergy, the document stated that Negroes who had been "seduced" to take up arms were liable to punishment. But in order that they might return in safety to their duties, they would be pardoned if they laid down their arms forthwith. The proclamation concluded with a request to "all humane and benevolent persons in the colony" to convey to the slaves this "offer of mercy." To insure a wide circulation, the proclamation was published as a broadside.[18]

The Virginians supplemented techniques of persuasion and sweet reasonableness with means forthright and punitive. In early December the Convention decreed that slaves taken in arms were to be sold to the foreign West Indies; the sale money, minus expenses, was to go to their masters.[19] Somewhat less severe was the fate of captured runaways who had failed in attempts to reach the king's forces. Such slaves, if their masters were patriots, were merely returned to their home plantations, often after serving a term of imprisonment, although their masters might be ordered to "convey them to some interior part of the Country as soon as may be."[20] Slaves of British sympathizers were put to work in the lead mines,[21] a practice which became customary in Virginia for the duration of the war. Distrusting all Negroes who had joined the Gov-

18. *Proceedings of the Convention of the Delegates in the Colony of Virginia* (Richmond, 1816), 63; Virginia Broadsides, LIV, Univ. Va. Lib.
19. Hening, ed., *Statutes of Va.*, IX, 106.
20. Such was the language used by the Virginia Council to William Kirby (July 12, 1776) concerning his slave, Frank. H. R. McIlwaine and Wilmer L. Hall, eds., *Journals of the Council of State of Virginia*, 3 vols. (Richmond, 1931-32, 1952), I, 67.
21. On Dec. 14, 1775, the Convention ordered the Committee of Safety to employ captive slaves "in working the Lead Mine in the County of Fincastle, for the Use of this Colony," *Amer. Arch.*, 4th Ser., IV, 85. Shortly afterward four would-be followers of Dunmore who were captured at Accomac were ordered "sent up the country and employed in some publick works." *Ibid.*, VI, 1553.

ernor, the Convention recommended that military officers "seize and secure" even those who came bearing flags of truce.[22]

The death penalty was used sparingly. In Northampton County the court passed such a sentence on a group of thirteen slaves who had seized a schooner at Hungers Creek and sailed into the bay, their destination the James River. Overtaken by a whale boat, they were captured and sentenced to execution. But the Northampton Committee of Safety sent word to Williamsburg inquiring whether the punishment should not be mitigated since the seizure of the boat was more "intended to effect an escape to Dunmore than any other Design of committing a felony."[23] The fate of these particular slaves is uncertain, but the intervention of the Northampton Committee reflects a general reluctance to inflict the death penalty. Whenever it was carried out, as in the case of two runaways who mistook an armed vessel of the Virginia navy for a British man-of-war, it was used mainly "as an example to others."[24]

Despite preventive efforts, whether an appeal to common sense or a resort to legal reprisals, many slaves made their way to the British, spurred in part by loyalist propaganda which promised them good treatment from the Governor. Some two hundred "immediately joined him," and within a week after the proclamation, three hundred. "Numbers of Negroes and Cowardly Scoundrels flock to his Standard," wrote a member of the provincial Committee of Safety.[25]

Since Dunmore had no base on the mainland after mid-December 1775, the Negroes who sought his sanctuary were

22. *Ibid.*, VI, 1524.

23. James Kent and William Henry to Maryland Council of Safety, Feb. 28, 1776, *Arch. of Md.*, XI, 191; Northampton Committee of Safety to General Committee of Safety, Apr. 23, 1776, "Va. Leg. Papers," *Va. Mag. of Hist. and Biog.*, 15 (1908), 407.

24. *Va. Gaz.*, Apr. 13, 1776.

25. Northampton Committee of Safety to Continental Congress, Nov. 25, 1775, to General Committee of Safety, Apr. 23, 1776, "Va. Leg. Papers," *Va. Mag. of Hist. and Biog.*, 14 (1907), 251, 15 (1908), 407; Andrew Sprowel to Peter Paterson, Nov. 19, 1775, *ibid.*, 14 (1907), 387; John Page to Thomas Jefferson, Nov. 24, 1775, Julian P. Boyd, ed., *The Papers of Thomas Jefferson* (Princeton, 1950—), I, 265. Dunmore would have every reason to welcome runaways, but perhaps his reception of them fell short of the report, circulated in the *Virginia Gazette*, that on the evening the Governor's forces landed on Gwynn's Island, they amused themselves "with a promiscuous ball, which was opened, we hear, by a certain spruce little gentleman, with one of the black ladies." *Va. Gaz.*, May 31, 1776.

water-borne. Two weeks after the proclamation a group of slaves came down the James in a thirty-foot vessel, bound for the fleet off Norfolk, but they were captured near Surry. Shortly afterward seven Negroes broke out of a Northampton jail and "went off in a pettinger," bound for the British ships.[26] Colonel Landon Carter of the Sabine Hall plantation made a diary notation of the break for the open water executed by ten of his retainers:

26 Wednesday, June 1776. Last night after going to bed, Moses, my son's man, Joe, Billy, Postillion, John, Mullatto, Peter, Tom, Panticove, Manuel & Lancaster Sam, ran away, to be sure, to Ld. Dunmore, for they got privately into Beale's room before dark & took out my son's gun & one I had there, took out of his drawer in my passage all his ammunition furniture, Landon's bag of bullets and all the Powder, and went off in my Petty Auger [pettiauger] new trimmed, and it is supposed that Mr. Robinson's People are gone with them, for a skow they came down in is, it seems, at my landing. These accursed villians have stolen Landon's silver buckles, George's shirts, Tom Parker's new waistcoat & breeches.[27]

The Negroes who reached the British were generally able-bodied men who could be put to many uses.[28] It was as soldiers, however, that Dunmore envisioned them, and from the beginning he enlisted them in his military forces. By early December he was arming them "as fast as they came in." Negro privates took part in a skirmish at Kemp's Landing in which the colonials were routed; indeed, slaves captured one of the two commanding colonels.[29] In the encounters preceding the action at Great Bridge, two runaways who were taken prisoner testified that the garrison was manned by thirty whites and ninety Negroes, and that "all the blacks who are sent to the fort at the great

26. *Va. Gaz.*, Jan. 10, 1776; *Maryland Gazette* (Annapolis), Feb. 22, 1776. Hereafter cited as *Md. Gaz.* "Pettinger" and "pettiauger" (below) are corruptions of the Spanish *piragua*, "a dugout," "a two-masted, flat-bottomed boat."

27. "Diary of Col. Landon Carter," *Wm. and Mary Qtly.*, 1st Ser., 20 (1912), 178-79.

28. Two women, however, were among a party of nine slaves who were seized in mid-December after putting out to sea in an open boat in an attempt to reach Norfolk. *Pennsylvania Gazette* (Phila.), Dec. 20, 1775. Hereafter cited as *Pa. Gaz.*

29. Dunmore to Sec. of State for Colonies, Dec. 6, 1775, Virginia: Official Correspondence, Peter Force-George Bancroft transcripts, Lib. Cong.; Edmund Pendleton to R. H. Lee, Nov. 27, 1775, *Amer. Arch.*, 4th Ser., IV, 202.

Bridge, are supplied with muskets, Cartridges &c strictly ordered to use them defensively & offensively."[30] By the first of December the British had nearly three hundred slaves outfitted in military garb, with the inscription, "Liberty to Slaves," emblazoned across the breast of each. The Governor officially designated them "Lord Dunmore's Ethiopian Regiment."[31]

The first and only major military action in which Dunmore's forces engaged was the battle of Great Bridge.[32] Of the Governor's troops of some six hundred men, nearly half were Negroes. Of the eighteen wounded prisoners taken by the Virginians in this rout, two were former slaves. One of them, James Anderson, was wounded "in the Forearm—Bones shattered and flesh much torn." The other one, Casar, was hit "in the Thigh, by a Ball, and 5 shot—one lodged."[33] After the fiasco at Great Bridge, the Governor was forced to operate from his ships. Taking aboard the hardiest of his Negro followers and placing them under officers who exercised them at small arms, he sanguinely awaited recruits.

Dunmore's use of Negroes also embraced maritime service. On the six tenders sent by the Governor to cannonade Hampton in late October 1775, there were colored crewmen, two of whom were captured when the Virginians seized the pilot boat *Hawk Tender*.[34] To man the small craft that scurried in and out of

30. William Woodford to Edmund Pendleton, Dec. 5, 1775, "The Woodford, Howe, and Lee Letters," *Richmond College Hist. Papers*, 1 (1915), 113. Added Woodford, "The bearer brings you one of the Balls taken out of the cartirages found upon the negro Prisoners, as they were extremely well made." *Ibid.*, 112.

31. *Md. Gaz.*, Dec. 14, 1775; Dunmore to Sec. of State for Colonies, Dec. 6, 1775, Virginia: Official Correspondence, Force-Bancroft transcripts.

32. For eyewitness accounts of the action at Great Bridge, see Willard, ed., *Letters on the American Revolution*, 234-35, 244-45; Thomas McKnight to Rev. Dr. McKnight, on board the *King's Fisher*, Dec. 26, 1775, Miscellaneous Collection, Clements Lib.; H. S. Parsons, "Contemporary English Accounts of the Destruction of Norfolk in 1776," *Wm. and Mary Qtly.*, 2nd Ser., 13 (1933), 219-24; Richard Kidder Meade to Theodorick Bland, Jr., Norfolk Town Camp, Dec. 18, 1775, Charles Campbell, ed., *The Bland Papers* (Petersburg, Va., 1840-43), I, 38; "The Woodford, Howe, and Lee Letters," *Richmond College Hist. Papers*, 1 (1915), 96-163 *passim;* William Woodford to Edmund Pendleton, Dec. 10, 1775, *Md. Gaz.*, Dec. 21, 1775, Jan. 4, 1776. For Dunmore's account see Dunmore to Sec. of State for the Colonies, Dec. 13, 1775, Virginia: Official Correspondence, Force-Bancroft transcripts, Lib. Cong.

33. Woodford to Pendleton, Dec. 10, 1775, "The Woodford, Howe and Lee Letters," *Richmond College Hist. Papers*, 1 (1915), 118.

34. John Page to Thomas Jefferson, Nov. 11, 1775, Boyd, ed., *Papers of Jefferson*, I, 257.

the river settlements, harassing the plantations, the British depended largely on ex-slaves, particularly as pilots. Joseph Harris, a runaway, served as pilot of the *Otter*, having come to Captain Matthew Squire with the highest recommendation from a fellow naval officer. "I think him too useful to His Majesty's service to take away," wrote the latter, because of "his being well acquainted with many creeks in the *Eastern* Shore, at *York, James* River, and *Nansemond,* and many others," and "accustomed to pilot."[35] Two citizens on the Isle of Wight advised the chairman of the Virginia Committee of Safety to go slow on discharging "a Negro fello, named Caesar," who was not only "a very great Scoundrel" but also "a fello' they can't do well without being an Excellent pilot."[36]

Another service performed by Dunmore's black followers was foraging. The Governor's supply of provisions, particularly fresh foods needed constant replenishment, and the Virginia leaders understandably would not permit the British to send men ashore to make purchases. "Back settlers" who might have been willing to supply his lordship with provisions had no means of conveying them, and Dunmore fell back upon the foraging abilities of his Negro recruits. Marauding parties of predominantly ex-slave composition preyed on the countryside, nightly descending upon plantations and making off with the choice livestock. One foraging party, captured while on its way to the Eastern Shore, was made up of "one white and sixteen blacks."[37]

Allegedly one of the services of Negroes to Dunmore was germ spreading. That the charge of germ warfare was propaganda-laden did not make it less potent in arousing indignation. The accusation was that Dunmore had inoculated two Negroes and sent them ashore at Norfolk to spread the smallpox. The charge was ironic in view of the fate of the Negroes who fled to the British. The majority of them died of disease. Late in

35. George Montague to Matthew Squire, July 20, 1775, *Amer. Arch.*, 4th Ser., II, 1692.

36. Thomas Pierce and Thomas Smith to Edmund Pendleton, Dec. 17, 1775, "Miscellaneous Colonial Documents," *Va. Mag. of Hist. and Biog.*, 19 (1911), 267.

37. "Extract of a letter to a gentleman in Scotland, dated Norfolk, Virginia, February 17, 1776," *Amer. Arch.*, 4th Ser., IV, 1166; Archibald Cary to R. H. Lee, Dec. 24, 1775, in Robert K. Brock, *Archibald Cary of Ampthill* (Richmond, 1937), 161.

March the Governor informed his superior in England that the recruiting of the black regiment "would have been in great forwardness had not a fever crept in amongst them, which carried off a great many very fine fellows." He added that on advice of local physicians, he had concluded that the trouble came from overcrowding aboard ship and the lack of clothing, against both of which provision had now been made.[38]

Nevertheless the plague persisted, killing off the Negroes and the Governor's hopes alike. Writing to Germain in June, Dunmore confessed defeat. The fever, he explained, was malignant, and had "carried off an incredible number of our people, especially blacks." Had this not happened he would have had 2,000 Negro followers. He was separating the sick from the well, he wrote, and would try to keep the two groups from intermingling.[39] The Governor's efforts were unavailing, it seems, for by early June 1776 there were not more than "150 effective Negro men," although each day the black corps was augmented by six to eight arrivals.[40]

Failure to arrest the smallpox and the harassment by the Virginia and Maryland militia finally brought an end to his lordship's stay in Chesapeake waters. In May 1776, faced with the likelihood of heavy losses from disease, the fleet moved from their exposed quarters at Tucker's Mills near Portsmouth and took shelter on Gwynn's Island near the mouth of the Rappahannock. Nowhere were Dunmore and his "floating Town"[41] allowed peace; "we no sooner appear off the land, than signals are made from it," he wrote, "and if we come to

38. *Va. Gaz.*, June 15, 1776; Dunmore to George Germain, Mar. 30, 1776, *Amer. Arch.*, 5th Ser., II, 159-60.

39. Dunmore to Germain, June 26, 1776, *ibid.*, II, 162. Dunmore's policy of isolation seems to have prevented the smallpox from decimating the white troops. The monthly return of the 14th Regiment of Infantry, signed by Capt. Sam Leslie, lists a total of 128 men (with breakdowns as to rank) for Mar. 1, 1776, a total of 126 men for Apr. 1, 1776, and a total of 122 for May 1, 1776. "Monthly Return of a Detachment of His Majesty's 14th Regiment of Infantry, off Norfolk, Virginia, 1 March 1776," "Monthly Return . . . 1 April 1776," and "Monthly Return . . . 1 May 1776," in Clinton Papers, Clements Lib. In addition to the factor of isolation, the mortality of the Negro soldiers may have been due to their performing most of the garrison and fatigue duties; at Gwynn's Island the entrenchments were guarded "chiefly by the black regiment." *Va. Gaz.*, June 1, 1776.

40. Entry of June 10, 1776, Andrew Snape Hamond Diaries, 1775-77, Univ. Va. Lib. Andrew Snape Hamond, Captain of the *Roebuck,* was the commanding officer in Virginia waters.

41. *Ibid.*, May 19, Aug. 5, 1776. The descriptive phrase is Hamond's.

anchor within cannon-shot of either shore, guns are immediately brought to bear upon us."[42] Early in July the British, after suffering an attack upon their shipping, took refuge on St. George's Island in the Potomac. By the end of the month the disease-ridden corps, lacking suitable drinking water and despairing of re-enforcements, prepared to leave. Dismantling, burning, or running aground 63 of their 103 vessels, they sailed out of the Potomac on August 6, seven of the ships bound for Sandy Hook and the others setting a southward course for St. Augustine and the Bermudas. With the departing fleet went some three hundred Negroes—the healthiest—who were going northward, destined for further military service. Dunmore's schemes had come to an inglorious end.[43]

Perhaps not more than a total of eight hundred slaves had succeeded in reaching the British;[44] perhaps one-eighth of these had come with their loyalist masters. But Dunmore's proclamation undoubtedly had an indirect effect on thousands of other slaves, quickening their hopes for freedom. Perhaps it was only the imagination of newspaper editors that spawned such stories as that of a colored mother in New York naming her child after his lordship,[45] or of a Negro in Philadelphia jostling whites on the streets and telling them to wait until "lord Dunmore and his black regiment come, and then we will see who is to take the wall."[46] But whether fact or fabrication, such reports re-

42. Dunmore to George Germain, July 31, 1776, *Amer. Arch.*, 5th Ser., II, 166.

43. A. S. Hamond Diaries, Aug. 6, 1776, Univ. Va. Lib. Dunmore himself went to New York, arriving on Aug. 14, *Journals of Lieut.-Col. Stephen Kemble*, N.-Y. Hist. Soc., *Coll.*, Publication Fund, 16 (1884), 84. Dunmore remained convinced of the soundness of his plan to arm Negroes, reviving it even after Yorktown. See Percy Burdelle Caley, Dunmore: Colonial Governor of New York and Virginia, 1770-1782 (unpubl. Ph.D. diss., University of Pittsburgh, 1939), 887-93. See also chapter IX below.

44. Dunmore's Negro followers were computed in general terms: *e.g.*, ". . . came in a great number of Black Men from the Rebels." Logs of *Roebuck and Fowey*, in Greenwich Museum, England, entry of June 27, 1776. Photostat in A. S. Hamond MSS, Univ. Va. Lib.

45. Taking due note, the *New York Journal* carried an occasional poem, copied in the *Va. Gaz.*, May 25, 1776:

> Hail! doughty Ethiopian Chief!
> Though ignominious Negro Thief!
> This Black shall prop thy sinking name,
> And damn thee to perpetual fame.

46. *Ibid.*, Supplement, Dec. 29, 1775.

flect the expectant attitude that Dunmore engendered among colored people along the Chesapeake. It made no difference that he had offered freedom only to the bondmen of his enemies,[47] and that as governor he had withheld his signature from a bill against the slave trade; to those who whispered his name in slave quarters he was in truth the "African Hero" he was derisively dubbed by a Virginia patriot.[48]

* * *

If Dunmore was viewed by one group as a tyrant and by another as a liberator, this was but another paradox in a war that abounded in paradox. The Negro who fled to the Governor was actuated by the same love of liberty for which the colonists avowedly broke with the mother country. To the slave, his lordship's proclamation was an invitation to the fellowship of the free, and thus conformed with the times. But there were additional and more tangible signs and revelations of changes to come.

47. John King, runaway slave of a loyalist, was ordered discharged from the *King's Fisher*. Logs of *Roebuck* and *Fowey*, Feb. 23, 1776, photostats, A. S. Hamond MSS, Univ. Va. Lib.

48. R. H. Lee to Thomas Jefferson, July 21, 1776, James C. Ballagh, ed., *The Letters of Richard Henry Lee*, 2 vols. (New York, 1912-14), I, 210.

CHAPTER III

THE NEGRO AND THE RIGHTS OF MAN

Does it follow that it is right to enslave a man because he is black? Will short curled hair, like wool . . . help the argument? Can any logical inference in favour of slavery be drawn from a flat nose, a long or short face?

James Otis

The roots of the American Revolution lay in the colonial past; similarly, the movement to ameliorate the lot of the Negro had its origin in the late colonial period. Among the forces making for Negro betterment just prior to the outbreak of the war, three are especially notable: the activities of reformers, the efforts of Negroes themselves, and public antipathy toward the slave trade.

Anti-slavery sentiment in America was almost as old as American slavery itself. The initial opposition to human bondage came from such groups as the Quakers and the Puritans, who were actuated by religious and moral impulses.[1] But during the closing years of the colonial period, abolitionist sentiment increasingly found its basis in the philosophical doctrines of the eighteenth-century Enlightenment, notably the concept of the natural and inalienable rights of man. To be free was a natural right, which slavery violated.

Whether inspired by religious principle or ideals of natural rights, reformers became increasingly vocal on the eve of the Revolution. Perhaps the most active New Englander to enter the lists was the Reverend Samuel Hopkins, pastor of the First Congregational Church of Newport, Rhode Island, who in 1770 turned his attention to the anti-slavery cause. Endeavoring to convert his neighbors and friends, Hopkins made

1. Mary S. Locke, *Anti-Slavery in America* (Boston, 1901), 9-32.

house-to-house canvasses, urging masters to liberate their servants. In one instance a slaveholding friend of Hopkins asserted
that his bondman was quite satisfied with his lot, whereupon
Hopkins asked permission to question him. In answer to the
clergyman's kindly put inquiries, the slave said that he was
happy and that he had a good master. When asked whether
he would be more happy if he were free, the slave quickly replied, "O yes, Massa,—me would be much more happy!" His
owner, impressed, emancipated him on the spot.[2]

A pioneer Back-to-Africa enthusiast, Hopkins believed that
much good would result from sending American Negroes to
the Guinea Coast as missionaries carrying the Christian gospel.
In April 1773 he approached fellow clergyman Ezra Stiles,
later president of Yale, with the proposal. Stiles was favorably
inclined, suggesting that thirty or forty Negroes should be
selected and trained for the enterprise. It was decided to begin
the experiment with two colored communicants of Hopkins's
own church who were good prospects: free Negro John Quaumino, and Bristol Yamma, a slave. Yamma had raised almost
enough money to buy himself, lacking only $50.[3]

At Hopkins's request, Stiles summoned Quaumino in order
to "examine his abilities." After hearing him read aloud from
St. John's Gospel and the Psalms, Stiles reported that the
young Negro had read the pages "not freely, yet distinctly,"
charitably adding that "he has but little time for reading; seldom any but Lord's days." The two colored candidates for
missionary work in Africa had "good common natural abilities,"
he concluded, "but are of slender acquaintance as to Letters."[4]

Undismayed, Hopkins proceeded to raise funds for buying
Yamma's freedom, educating him and Quaumino, and recruiting others. He donated $100 himself, and with Stiles wrote
a circular letter to churches in Massachusetts and Connecticut.[5]
Late in November 1774, with blessings of Hopkins, his two
Negro protégés left Newport for Princeton where they were
to reside at the College of New Jersey and receive instruction

2. Samuel Hopkins, *Timely Articles on Slavery* (Boston, 1854), 5.
3. Franklin B. Dexter, ed., *The Literary Diary of Ezra Stiles,* 3 vols. (New York, 1901), 362.
4. E. A. Park, ed., *The Works of Samuel Hopkins, D. D.,* 3 vols. (Boston, 1854), I, 130; Dexter, ed., *Diary of Ezra Stiles,* I, 365.
5. Lorenzo J. Greene, *The Negro in Colonial New England* (New York, 1942), 279. For the circular letter see Park, ed., *Works of Hopkins,* I, 131-32.

from President John Witherspoon. Leaving no stone unturned, the zealous Hopkins wrote to John Adams in December 1775 inquiring about the propriety of asking the Continental Congress for money to assist in sending the two Negroes to Africa.[6] By April 1776 Hopkins and Stiles could report encouraging progress. They had received over $500 in contributions, and had selected two additional missionary candidates; one was a relative of Quaumino's, and the other was Salmar Nubia, a member of Stiles's Second Congregational Church. Moreover, Yamma and Quaumino were doing well. They had "spent one winter at Princeton" where they "have made such proficiency, and in such a measure qualified for the mission proposed, that they would enter upon it directly, were there opportunity to send them to Africa."[7] The whole experiment. however, was arrested by the outbreak of the war.

Another notable anti-slavery worker who, like Hopkins, was moved by religious impulses, was the Quaker schoolmaster, Anthony Benezet. Perhaps the foremost anti-slavery propagandist of his day, Benezet was "a compiler, reprinter, and distributor" of reform books and pamphlets. It was one of Benezet's publications that led the Englishman, Thomas Clarkson, into a lifetime of anti-slavery dedication; it was one of Benezet's books which touched on the conscience of Patrick Henry, drawing from him the confession that even though he held slaves he could not justify the practice, since it was "repugnant to humanity. . . inconsistent with the Bible," and destructive to liberty. Benezet wrote hundreds of personal letters in the cause of abolition, addressing some of them to such notables as the queens of England, France, and Portugal.[8]

Benezet sought to prepare Negroes for freedom by giving them an education under Christian auspices. He was the leading figure in the operation of the racially mixed Quaker school founded in Philadelphia in 1770. Five years later this school

6. Dexter, ed., *Diary of Ezra Stiles*, I, 486; Hopkins to Adams, Dec. 29, 1775, Adams Papers, Mass. Hist. Soc.
7. This optimistic report was incorporated in a second circular letter, Park, ed., *Works of Hopkins*, I, 134-36.
8. Thomas E. Drake, *Quakers and Slavery in America* (New Haven, 1950), 62; Patrick Henry to Robert Pleasants, Jan. 18, 1773, George S. Brookes, *Friend Anthony Benezet* (Phila., 1937), 443; Edward Bettle, "Negro Slavery as Connected with Pennsylvania," Historical Society of Pennsylvania, *Memoirs*, I (Phila., 1826), 385.

had six whites and forty Negroes in attendance; its existence was founded in the simple Quaker dictum "that by a religious care to discharge our duty to these oppressed people they may receive much benefit."[9] For two years the school was held in Benezet's own house.

"Anthony Benezet stood alone a few years ago, in opposing negro slavery in Philadelphia; and now three-fourths of the province, as well as of the city, cry out against it," wrote Benjamin Rush in 1773. With the hopeful outlook of the true reformer, he continued: "A spirit of humanity and religion begins to awaken, in several of the colonies in favour of the poor Negroes."[10] The writer of these lines, like Benezet a Philadelphian, was destined for a long, distinguished, and versatile career as a public servant, but he was never too busy to espouse the cause of the Negro. In 1773 he put himself in the forefront of the anti-slavery ranks with the publication of "An Address to the Inhabitants of the British Settlements in America upon Slave-keeping" which, in his words was "designed to shew the iniquity of the slave trade."[11] He was one of the sponsors of "The Society for the Relief of Free Negroes Unlawfully Held in Bondage," which was formed early in 1775 at the Sun Tavern in Philadelphia—the first organization in America to cut across denominational lines in working for the colored people. Rush's detestation of slavery was attested by his refusal of 1,000 guineas a year to practice medicine in Charleston, South Carolina; he was unwilling, he said, to live in a place "where wealth has been accumulated only by the sweat and blood of Negro slaves." It is notable, also, that in his long years of practice, Rush never charged a fee for administering to his Negro patients of slender means.[12]

Rush sent many of his optimistic reports on anti-slavery activity to Granville Sharp, a Quaker well known on both sides of the Atlantic for his role in the abolition of slavery in England. Sharp's reputation had been made by the Somerset case, which

9. *A Brief Sketch of the Schools for Black People and Their Descendants Established by the Religious Society of Friends in 1770* (Phila., 1867), 13.

10. Rush to Granville Sharp, May 1, 1773, L. H. Butterfield, ed., *Letters of Benjamin Rush*, 2 vols. (Princeton, 1951), I, 81.

11. George W. Corner, *The Autobiography of Benjamin Rush* (Princeton, 1948), 83.

12. Rush to Barbeu Dubourg, Apr. 28, 1773, Butterfield, ed., *Letters of Rush*, I, 77; Rush to Mrs. Rush, Oct. 4, 1793, *ibid.*, II, 716.

concerned a slave, James Somerset, who had been taken to London in November 1769 by his Boston master. In October 1771 Somerset made an unsuccessful attempt to escape. As punishment he had been sentenced to deportation to dreaded Jamaica, when Sharp, long a foe of slavery, became his counsel. Chief Justice Mansfield hoped that the case could be settled out of court since he was hesitant to render a verdict that would free some fourteen thousand slaves in England, destroy the property rights of the masters, and raise the question of caring for newly emancipated Negroes. Sharp, however, pressed for a decision. His attorneys argued that the air of England was too free for a slave to breathe in. On June 22, 1772, Mansfield reluctantly ordered that "the black must be discharged."[13]

Negroes in England had followed the case with deep interest. "Since the commencement of the suit now pending in the court of King's Bench relative to the freedom of a Negro servant," wrote a London correspondent to the *Virginia Gazette,* "the spirit of Liberty had diffused itself so far amongst that species of people that they have established a club near Charing Cross where they meet every Monday night for the more effectual recovery of their freedom."[14] Three days after the decision, a group of 200 Negroes "with their ladies" held a public entertainment in Westminster "to celebrate the triumph of their Brother Somerset." Lord Mansfield's "health was echoed round the room," and the evening's festivities concluded with a ball.[15]

In the thirteen colonies neither governors, legislatures nor the courts took official notice of the Mansfield decision, but it was not without influence on American thinking. The decision confirmed the abolitionist views expressed by reformers; it stimulated requests for legislative action against slavery, and hastened its downfall in New England.[16]

An Englishman of considerably more liberal views than Lord

13. Emory Washburn, "Somerset's Case, and the Extinction of Villenage and Slavery in England," Mass. Hist. Soc., *Proc.,* 1st Ser., 7 (1864), 323. Sharp commented: "This judgment would have done Lord Mansfield honour had he not all along seemed inclined to the other side of the question." Sharp to Benezet, Aug. 21, 1772, Brookes, *Benezet,* 419.

14. *Va. Gaz.,* May 7, 1772.

15. *Ibid.,* Sept. 3, 1772.

16. Samuel G. Arnold, *History of the State of Rhode Island and Providence Plantations,* 2 vols. (Providence, 1878), II, 331-32.

Mansfield was Thomas Paine, who arrived in Philadelphia in November 1774 carrying a letter of introduction from Benjamin Franklin. He also brought with him the great gift of his vigorous prose and a love of liberty that embraced all races and conditions of men. Familiar with the writings of Benezet and Rush, Paine wrote his first published essay in the cause of abolition. Entitled "African Slavery in America," it appeared in the March 8, 1775, *Postscript to the Pennsylvania Journal and Weekly Advertiser.* Its opening words suggest its tone and style: "That some desperate wretches should be willing to steal and enslave men by violence and murder for gain, is rather lamentable than strange. But that many civilized, nay, christianized people should approve, and be concerned in the savage practice, is surprising."[17] Less than a year later Paine published *Common Sense,* which had a phenomenal success in swaying American public opinion. In it Paine spoke a language which to Negroes, slaves or free, had a meaning of its own: "O! ye that love mankind! . . . O! receive the fugitive, and prepare in time an asylum for mankind."[18]

* * *

In the America of the late colonial period, the Negro himself was quick to respond to the temper of the times. In the decade before Lexington and Concord, Negroes had not been idle in seeking freedom. One method was to go to court, charging their masters with restraining them of their liberty. Such a case in November 1766, in which a mulatto woman sued for her freedom, found in John Adams an interested onlooker. He had not witnessed such a case up to that time, "though I have heard there have been many."[19] Late in 1769, in a suit brought against John Swain by slave Boston, the Nantucket Court of Common Pleas gave the Negro whaleman his freedom.[20] In the fall of 1773 Caesar Hendrick charged Richard Greenleaf of Newburyport with "detaining him in slavery." The jury freed Caesar, awarding him damages and cost.

17. Moncure D. Conway, *The Writings of Thomas Paine,* 3 vols. (New York, 1894-96), I, 1, 4-9.
18. Conway, *Writings of Paine,* I, 100-1.
19. Adams, ed., *Works of Adams,* II, 200. For this Jenny Slew case see George H. Moore, *Notes on the History of Slavery in Massachusetts* (New York, 1866), 112-14.
20. *Ibid.,* 117; Drake, *Quakers and Slavery,* 88. On this general topic see Locke, *Anti-Slavery in America,* 80-81.

A year later a Negro belonging to Caleb Dodge of Beverly was similarly successful in a court action.[21] Although freedom suits were invariably won by the complaining party,[22] the procedure had its drawbacks. It was expensive, even though in some instances Negroes pooled their own meager funds to assist the plaintiff in meeting the court and legal fees.[23] The procedure was slow. It was also individual— the verdict in these suits did not extend beyond the parties immediately involved. Unlike the Mansfield decision these cases established no broad principle of universal freedom.[24] Hence, "suits for service" gave way to another technique, that of petition.

In Massachusetts in January 1773 a group of "many slaves" asked the General Court to grant them relief. They called attention to their privations: "We have no property! we have no wives! we have no children! no city! no country!" On June 25, 1773, the legislature appointed a "Committee on the Petition of Felix Holbrook, and others; praying to be liberated from a State of Slavery." Three days later this committee recommended that the petition be tabled until the next session. Thereupon the Negroes visited Governor Thomas Hutchinson to enlist his support of their request; he told them his instructions made it impossible for him to assist them.[25]

In May of the following year the slaves sent another petition to the Governor and the legislature, describing themselves as "a Grate Number of Blacks . . . who . . . are held in a state of slavery within the bowels of a free and christian Country." They were, they said, a free born people who had never forfeited that blessing by any compact or agreement. Some of them "were stolen from the bossoms of our tender Parents and from a Populous, Pleasant and plentiful country and brought hither to be made slaves for Life in a christian land." Six weeks later,

21. Moore, *Slavery in Massachusetts*, 118-19.
22. "I never knew a jury by a verdict, to determine a negro to be a slave. They always found him free." John Adams to Jeremy Belknap, Mar. 21, 1795, "Queries Relating to Slavery in Massachusetts," Mass. Hist. Soc., *Coll.*, 5th Ser., 3 (1877), 402.
23. "Judge Tucker's Queries Respecting Slavery, with Doctor Belknap's Answers," Mass. Hist. Soc., *Coll.*, 1st Ser., 4 (1795), 202.
24. Moore, *Slavery in Massachusetts*, 115-16, 119-24.
25. Herbert Aptheker, ed., *A Documentary History of the Negro People in the United States* (New York, 1951), 6; Moore, *Slavery in Massachusetts*, 135; "Judge Tucker's Queries," Mass. Hist. Soc., *Coll.*, 1st Ser., 4 (1795), 202.

in a follow-up supplication, they asked not only for their freedom but for "some part of the unimproved land, belonging to
the province, for a settlement, that each of us may there sit down
quietly under his own fig tree."[26] In response to this petition
the legislature again debated "the state and circumstances of
the Negro slaves in this province." The vote finally taken simply
stipulated that "the matter now subside."[27]

* * *

In the late colonial period the states and the Continental
Congress took steps against the foreign slave trade. Such action
was based on a variety of motives, arising not only from the
impact of the philosophy of freedom, but also from the over-
stocked condition of many of the American slave markets.

In Massachusetts agitation against the slave trade began
ten years before the outbreak of the Revolutionary War. On
May 26, 1766, the town of Boston instructed its representatives to the legislature—James Otis, Thomas Cushing, Samuel
Adams and John Hancock—to "move for a law, to prohibit
the importation and purchasing of slaves." These instructions
were reaffirmed at the town meeting on March 16, 1767.[28] In
the same month a bill against the slave trade was introduced
in the House of Representatives, but was lost in shuttling
between the House and the Council. In 1771 the legislature
passed such a bill but Governor Hutchinson withheld his signature. Three years later much the same procedure was repeated;
on March 8, 1774, the General Assembly enacted a measure
prohibiting the importation of Negroes, and on the following
day the Assembly was unexpectedly prorogued.[29]

The traffic suffered a marked decline in other New England
states. In New Hampshire no legislation was necessary; there
were only 479 slaves in that province in 1775. The institution
had never struck any roots. Connecticut in 1774 adopted "An
Act for prohibiting the Importation of Indian, Negro or Molat-

26. "Negro Petitions for Freedom," Mass. Hist. Soc., *Coll.,* 5th Ser., 3
(1877), 432, 434-35.

27. *The Journals of Each Provincial Congress of Massachusetts in 1774
and 1775,* 29.

28. *Boston Town Records, 1758 to 1769,* 183, 200.

29. Moore, *Slavery in Massachusetts,* 28, 131, 138-9; "Queries Relating to
Slavery in Mass.," Mass. Hist. Soc., *Coll.,* 5th Ser., 3 (1877), 388.

to Slaves."[30] In the same year Rhode Island restricted the slave trade, the assembly prefacing its act with a ringing declaration that "those who are desirous of enjoying all the advantages of liberty themselves, should be willing to extend personal liberty to others." The act stipulated that any Negro or mulatto brought into the colony would immediately become free. The effect of the act was partially nullified, however, when the assembly provided that if traders were unable to dispose of their slaves in the West Indies, they might bring them to Rhode Island with the understanding that they would be re-exported within a year.[31] It was difficult, as a later New England historian observed, for "ethics to prevail over commerce" in a province whose economy was materially involved in the slave trade.[32]

In the agricultural middle colonies the trade was on the decline before the war broke out. Pennsylvania killed it by means of a prohibitive tax; in February 1773 a duty of £20 was imposed on every imported slave. In New Jersey the following year the lower house proposed a high tax similar to that of Pennsylvania, but the Council rejected it.[33]

In the South, as the war approached, three colonies took action against slave importation: Virginia and North Carolina in August 1774, and Georgia less than a year later.[34] This action by the planting colonies was not primarily an expression of humanitarian sentiment; it was rather a phase of the general non-importation program by which the colonies sought to secure the repeal of objectionable parliamentary legislation.

It was the same motive, among many other considerations, that led the Continental Congress in October 1774 to pledge the states to a discontinuance of the slave trade after December

30. W. E. B. DuBois, *The Suppression of the African Slave-Trade* (New York, 1896), 30.
31. *Ibid.*, 222.
32. William B. Weeden, *The Economic and Social History of New England,* 2 vols. (Boston, 1890), II, 764.
33. J. T. Mitchell and Henry Flanders, eds., *Statutes at Large of Pennsylvania, from 1682-1801* (Harrisburg, 1896-1908), 330-32. DuBois, *Sup. of the African Slave-Trade,* 25.
34. H. Niles, *Principles and Acts of the Revolution* (Baltimore, 1882), 199; Stephen B. Weeks, "Anti-Slavery Sentiment in the South," Southern Historical Association, *Publications,* 2 (1898), 106; "Proceedings of the First Provincial Congress of Georgia, 1775," Georgia Historical Society, *Collections,* 5, pt. 1 (1901), 6. Hereafter cited as Ga. Hist. Soc., *Coll.*

1, 1774. This prohibition was reaffirmed on April 6, 1776, when Congress voted that no slave be imported into any of the thirteen united colonies.[35]

* * *

With the outbreak of the Revolutionary War the movement to better the lot of the Negro was accelerated. More weight was given to the contention that slavery was dangerous to the public peace and safety; it was feared that slaves would be more minded to revolt than ever. Also, particularly above the Potomac, the economic and utilitarian argument against slavery —that it was not profitable—was more strongly voiced. Finally, the ideals of the Revolution had an effect; the theories set forth to justify economic and political freedom from England could scarcely leave domestic institutions untouched. A master-slave society was repugnant to the revolutionary spirit and to the beliefs in the human freedoms which were its heart.

This spirit of liberty, of so much significance to the unfree, was nowhere better expressed than in the Declaration of Independence. As originally presented to Congress by the Committee of Five, among them Thomas Jefferson, the document included a sharp condemnation of the slave trade. George III, ran the indictment, "has waged cruel war against human nature itself, violating its most sacred rights of life and liberty in the persons of a distant people who never offended him, captivating and carrying them into slavery in another hemisphere, or to incur miserable death in their transportation thither." This clause was stricken from the final draft since it gave offense to some of the Southern delegates (and a few from the North); the successful attack for its deletion was led by twenty-six-year-old Edward Rutledge from Charleston.[36] The growing humanitarian sentiment against slavery therefore found no direct expression in the Declaration of Independence; indeed, the only reference to slavery was the indirectly stated charge that George III had fomented domestic insurrection in America. In *Common Sense* Paine had bluntly accused England of stirring up the Negroes "to destroy us,"[37] but in the Declaration, Jef-

35. Ford, ed., *Journ. of Cont. Cong.*, I, 77, IV, 258. On the whole point of the colonial motivation to prohibit the slave trade on the eve of the war, see DuBois, *Sup. of the African Slave-Trade*, 41-42.

36. For a vivid account of the fate of the slave trade charge against George III see Cornel Lengyel, *Four Days in July* (New York, 1958), 174-77, 245-48.

37. Conway, *Writings of Paine*, I, 100.

ferson dared not be specific and spell out the domestic insurrection charge. To have done so would have called attention to American slavery—an embarrassing topic in a document whose keynote was human freedom. Despite its omissions and evasions, however, the Declaration of Independence held a great appeal for those who considered themselves oppressed. "All men are created equal," ran the magic words. Perhaps the congressmen who adopted the document intended that the word "equal" was to be narrow and qualified in interpretation. Perhaps the words were not meant to apply to slaves, since men in bondage were not considered constituent members of society. Perhaps the great phrases which assert that among the rights every man is born with are life, liberty, and the pursuit of happiness were intended to be an expression of ideals rather than a plan of social action. Yet the Declaration of Independence would remain a battle cry for freedom. "It did, indeed, at last become very hard for us to listen each year to the preamble to the Declaration of Independence and still remain the owners and users and catchers of slaves," wrote Moses Coit Tyler.[38] And if Jefferson himself did not fully sense this when he drafted the document, he would come to a fuller realization some years later when Benjamin Banneker, a Negro mathematician and astronomer, would write him a long letter asking him to reconcile his "created equal" language with his practice of "detaining by fraud and violence so numerous a part of my brethren, under groaning captivity."[39]

* * *

The Negro was not slow in responding to the revolutionary spirit of the opening passages of the Declaration of Independence. New hope came to slaves as the words "liberty" and "independence" became common currency. Giving a personal interpretation to the high-sounding slogans which justified the break with England, they redoubled their efforts for emancipation.

New England's slaves particularly took heart. Unlike the mildly worded supplications of pre-war days, their petitions now took on a note of impatience. In a petition dated January 13, 1777, a group of Massachusetts Negroes stated that they

38. Moses Coit Tyler, *The Literary History of the American Revolution.* 2 vols. (New York, 1897), I, 517.
39. Aptheker, ed., *Documentary History of the Negro People,* 25.

had long awaited a favorable response to entreaty after entreaty. Every principle which impelled America to break with England, they said, "pleads stronger than a thousand arguments in favor of your humble petitioners." A life of slavery was "far worse than Nonexistence."[40] Late in 1779 a group of nineteen Negroes in Portsmouth, New Hampshire, urged the state to pass a law whereby they might regain their liberty "and that the name of slave may not more be heard in a land gloriously contending for the sweets of freedom." The petitioners pointed out that they were not complaining of any mistreatment from their masters, but "we would wish to know . . . from what authority they assume to dispose of our lives, freedom and property."[41]

In the spring of 1779 a group of Connecticut slaves petitioned the state legislature for their liberty, condemning slavery in the same breath. They not only "groaned" under their own burdens, ran their plea, but they contemplated with horror "the miserable Condition of Our Children, who are training up, and kept in Preparation, for a like State of Bondage and Servitude."[42] In Connecticut a few petitions came from Negroes whose masters had fled to the British. In October 1779 Pomp, belonging to a Norwalk Tory, sent a request to the legislature praying to be set free. A month later eight slaves of William Browne of Salem, Connecticut, "Great Prince, Little Prince, Luke, Cesar, and Prue and her three children,—all friends to America," asked the General Assembly for their freedom. "We hope," they stated, "that our good mistress, the free State of Connecticut, engaged in a war with tyranny, will not sell good honest Whigs and friends of freedom and independence, as we are." An individual request was sent in by Belinda who alleged that, although she had been serving her master for more than forty years, her labors had not brought her any comfort or security. She begged freedom for herself and her "poor daughter."[43]

* * *

40. Revol. Rolls Coll., Mass. Arch., CCXII, No. 132.
41. Isaac W. Hammond, "Slavery in New Hampshire," *Magazine of American History*, 21 (1880), 63.
42. "Negro Petitions for Freedom," Mass. Hist. Soc., *Coll.*, 5th Ser., 3 (1877), 432.
43. Charles J. Hoadly, ed., *The Public Records of the State of Connecticut*, 3 vols. (Hartford, 1894-1922), II, 427-28; Livermore, *Historical Research Respecting Negroes*, 116-17; William C. Nell, *The Colored Patriots of the American Revolution* (Boston, 1855), 52.

Three of the best-known Negroes in Revolutionary America—Prince Hall, Paul Cuffe, and Phillis Wheatley, all of Massachusetts—took a personal role in the agitation. Born in Barbados, Hall had come to America in 1765 and by industry and private study had become fairly well-to-do by the time of the war. Free himself, he made it a point to sign slave petitions for emancipation. Three months before seeing action at the Battle of Bunker Hill, Hall was initiated with fourteen other Negroes into the Masonic order by a British military lodge then garrisoned in Boston.[44]

Paul Cuffe was a captain of ships constructed in his own yards. In February 1780 Cuffe, barely twenty-one years old, got up a petition, signed by six others, which was offered to the Massachusetts legislature. It asked that Negroes be relieved from paying taxes, since they had "no voice or influence in the election of those who tax us."[45] A year later Cuffe and his brother requested the selectmen of Dartmouth to give free Negroes and mulattoes the same voting privileges enjoyed by the whites of the town.[46]

Sharing the general hopes of all who had known oppression was the most conspicuous Negro of her brief day, Phillis Wheatley, who had been brought to America while still a little girl. Given every opportunity by the Wheatley family in Boston, she published her first poem in 1770, which was followed three years later by a book of verse, *Poems on Various Subjects, Religious and Moral*. By 1774, although not more than twenty years old, she enjoyed an international reputation; Voltaire knew of her, and referred to her "very good English verse."[47] Her stanzas, patterned after Pope, were "echoes of the English classicists," but they were not without their racial and personal elements. In a composition dedicated to the Earl of Dartmouth, whom she had met in London, young Phillis praises liberty, condemns tyranny, then proceeds to account for her own sentiments:[48]

44. "Judge Tucker's Queries," Mass. Hist. Soc., *Coll.*, 1st Ser., 5 (1795), 210.
45. Aptheker, ed., *Documentary History of the Negro People*, 15.
46. Mass. Arch., CLXXXVI, No. 134.
47. Edward D. Seeber, *Anti-Slavery Opinions in France During the Second Half of the Eighteenth Century* (Baltimore, 1937), 57.
48. Arthur P. Davis, "Personal Elements in the Poetry of Phillis Wheatley," *Phylon*, 13 (1953), 191-98; Phillis Wheatley, *Poems on Various Subjects, Religious and Moral* (London, 1773), 74.

> Should you, my lord, while you peruse my song,
> Wonder from whence my love of Freedom sprung,
> . . . .
> I, young in life, by seeming cruel fate
> Was snatch'd from Afric's fancy'd seat:
> . . . .
> Such, such my case. And can I then but pray
> Others may never feel tryannic sway?

An occasional poet, Phillis composed a tribute to Washington upon his appointment as commander-in-chief of the army. In the letter which accompanied the poem, Phillis expressed the hope that "your Excellency" would meet with all possible success "in the great cause you are so generously engaged in." Her lines reach the level of panegyric:

> Thee, first in place and honours,—we demand
> The grace and glory of thy martial band.
> Fam'd for thy valour, for thy virtues more,
> Here every tongue thy guardian aid implore![49]

Washington took some months to acknowledge these lines. On February 10, 1776, he sent the poem to Joseph Reed, adding that the latter might find it amusing. His first impulse, Washington said, was to publish it, but thinking he might be considered vain, he had "laid it aside."[50] Nearly three weeks later Washington wrote to his eulogist, thanking her and adding that he would have had the verse published as a "striking proof of your great poetical talents," but had not done so lest his motives be misconstrued. He would be happy to see her, ran his concluding sentence, if she should ever come to Cambridge or near his headquarters.[51]

49. It has generally been assumed that this poem first appeared in the *Pennsylvania Magazine, of American Museum* in Apr. 1776, during Tom Paine's editorship. See, for example, Vernon Loggins, *The Negro Author* (New York, 1931), 21. However, in the *Virginia Gazette* for Mar. 30, 1776, one may find Phillis's letter and poem plus a covering letter to the editor.

50. Washington to Reed, Feb. 10, 1776, Fitzpatrick, ed., *Writings of Washington*, IV, 323.

51. Washington to Wheatley, Feb. 28, 1776, *ibid.*, IV, 360-61. Benson Lossing says that Phillis had a half-hour's visit with Washington and his staff at army headquarters at Cambridge a few days before the British troops left Boston. Lossing, *Pictorial Field Book of the Revolution*, 2 vols. (New York, 1860), I, 556. Whether such a meeting took place is open to question. Equally speculative is the degree of acquaintance between the young poet

The pen of a Wheatley, the protest of a Cuffe, and the petition of a Belinda were not without influence above the Potomac. As the war dragged on, the advocates of freedom for the slave found a more receptive public. Among the New England states, Massachusetts was the readiest to let slavery die. In June 1777, in response to a Negro petition, the Massachusetts legislature drafted a bill for "preventing the practice of holding persons in Slavery." A committee was appointed to prepare a letter to the Continental Congress asking whether such an enactment by Massachusetts might imperil the friendly relations among the states.[52] However, the committee's report, made on the following day, was "ordered to lie."[53]

Slavery in Massachusetts, however, had but a short lease on life. It was dealt a blow by an interpretation which the state courts gave to its constitution. The Massachusetts constitution of 1780, borrowing from the Virginia Bill of Rights and the Declaration of Independence, stipulated that "all men are born free and equal." This phrase seemed to be given a literal interpretation in the celebrated Quok Walker case.

In April 1781 twenty-eight-year-old Walker had run away from his master, Nathaniel Jennison, a Worcester County farmer. The latter brought suit against John Caldwell, a neighbor, who

and America's greatest naval hero. From aboard the *Ranger,* John Paul Jones dispatched this undated note to Captain Hector McNeill at Boston: "I am on the point of sailing—I have to write to you—pray be so good as to put the Inclosed into the hands of the Celebrated Phillis, the African Favorite of the Muse and of Apollo—should she reply. I hope you will be the bearer." Phillips Russell, *John Paul Jones, Man of Action* (New York, 1927), 22.

52. *A Journal of the Honorable House of Representatives of the State of Massachusetts-Bay in New-England* (Boston, 1777), 25. For this letter see "Remarks of Charles Dean, Esq.," Mass. Hist. Soc., *Proc.,* 1st Ser., 10 (1869), 332-33.

53. Moore, *Slavery in Massachusetts,* 182. Most likely no letter was ever sent. In preventing this bill from going into effect, John Adams did an effective behind-the-scenes job. He wrote to James Warren on June 22, 1777: "We have had a bill before us for freeing the Negroes, which is ordered to lie, lest if passed into an Act it should have a bad effect on the Union of the Colonies. A letter to Congress on the subject was proposed and reported, but I endeavoured to divert that, supposing it would embarrass and perhaps be attended with worse consequences than passing the Act." *Warren-Adams Letters,* 2 vols., Mass. Hist. Soc., *Coll.,* 73-74 (1917-25), I, 335. Fifteen days later, Adams had this to say: "The bill for freeing the Negroes, I hope will sleep for a Time. We have Causes enough of Jealousy Discord and Division, and this Bill will certainly add to the Number." *Ibid.,* 339.

had given Walker asylum and employment. Stating his damages at £1,000, Jennison charged Caldwell with enticing Walker away. In turn, Walker brought suit against Jennison for assault and battery; Jennison, having discovered Walker's whereabouts ten days after his flight, had gone there and beaten him with the handle of a whip.[54]

As revealed by the brief prepared by Levi Lincoln, later United States attorney-general under President Jefferson, the lawyers for Walker and Caldwell based their main plea on the general principles of freedom. Two lines from Lincoln's brief illustrate this approach:

> Mr. Stearns says the custom and usage of the
> country consider slavery as right.
> Objt. Custom and usages against reason and
> right, Void.[55]

The master, Jennison, lost his suit against Caldwell, and he lost the suit brought against him by Quok Walker. In the verdicts the Supreme Judicial Court seemed to concur in the opinion that the "born free" clause of the state constitution was to be regarded as an authoritative expression of the law rather than as a high-sounding but legally meaningless rhetorical flourish. By 1783, when the judiciary passed down its final decision in the Jennison case, slavery in Massachusetts was in its death throes.

No other New England state took such forthright antislavery action during the war. In New Hampshire the assembly twice debated the freedom petition sent in by slaves but on June 9, 1780, postponed the matter "to a more convenient opportunity."[56] In Connecticut the legislature in 1779 set at liberty a Negro slave, Pomp who had petitioned for his freedom, his master having "absconded to the enemy."[57] In the same year,

54. For an exposition on this case see Moore, *Slavery in Massachusetts,* 200-23; for a penetrating contemporary examination see William O'Brien, "Did the Jennison Case Outlaw Slavery in Massachusetts?" *Wm. and Mary Qtly.,* 3rd Ser., 17 (1960), 219-41.

55. "Brief of Levi Lincoln in the Slave Case Tried 1781," Mass. Hist. Soc., *Coll.,* 5th Ser., 3 (1877), 440.

56. Hammond, "Slavery in New Hampshire," *Mag. of Amer. Hist.,* 21 (1860), 64.

57. Hoadly, ed., *The Public Records of the State of Connecticut,* II, 427-28. For Pomp's petition see Aptheker, ed., *Documentary History of the Negro People,* 13.

however, the petition of eight slaves of another Tory master was granted by one house of the legislature but not the other. The following year a gradual emancipation bill passed the upper chamber but got no further.[58] In August 1775 the Quaker merchant, Moses Brown, led the movement to prod the Rhode Island legislature into acting on an emancipation measure, but his recommendation did not bear fruit until nine years later. The only Rhode Island legislation against slavery during the war, apart from the partial abolition of the slave trade described earlier, was an act which prohibited selling a slave out of the state without his consent.[59]

The middle states had their anti-slavery advocates. In New Jersey Governor William Livingston asked the assembly in 1778 to pass a manumission law, stating that slavery was "utterly inconsistent with the principles of Christianity and humanity; and in Americans who have almost idolized liberty, peculiarly odious and disgraceful."[60] In New York Gouverneur Morris, against slavery but fearing immediate emancipation, sought in 1777 to persuade his colleagues in the legislature to instruct the framers of the state constitution to insert into that document a pledge of future liberation. But his colleagues, even more apprehensive than Morris, labeled the proposal "inexpedient," and would give it no further consideration.[61]

To Pennsylvania, with its Quaker background, went the distinction of becoming the first state to abolish slavery. In November 1778 the Council requested the lower chamber to prepare a bill for manumitting infant Negroes born of slaves,[62] but a matter of protocol between the two houses prevented the

58. Livermore, *An Historical Research Respecting Negroes,* 150; Jeffrey R. Brackett, "The Status of the Slave, 1775-1789," in J. Franklin Jameson, ed., *Essays in the Constitutional History of the United States* (Boston, 1889), 297.

59. *Amer. Arch.,* 4th Ser., III, 453; J. R. Bartlett, ed., *Records of the Colony of Rhode Island and Providence Plantations in New England (1636-1792),* 10 vols. (Providence, 1856-65), VIII, 618.

60. Henry S. Cooley, *A Study of Slavery in New Jersey,* in Johns Hopkins University Studies in History and Political Science, 14th Ser., Nos. IX, X (Baltimore, 1896), 23.

61. For Morris's proposal and its reception see "Historical Notes on Slavery in the Northern Colonies and States," *Historical Magazine,* 10 (1866), 238. See also Jared Sparks, *The Life of Gouverneur Morris,* 3 vols. (Boston, 1832), I, 125; and A. H. Payne, "The Negro in New York Prior to 1860," *Howard Review,* 1 (1923), 29.

62. *Pennsylvania Packet* (Phila.), Nov. 28, 1778.

passing of an act until March 1, 1780. This historic measure was designed to "extend a portion of that freedom to others which has been extended to us." This act did not provide for immediate and outright emancipation; its approach was gradualist. It freed nobody who was then a slave. Henceforth, however, when children of slaves reached twenty-eight years old, they would become free.[63]

The revolutionary spirit of freedom had a marked influence upon America. Just prior to the war this spirit, fanned by humanitarians like Anthony Benezet, found expression in slave petitions for freedom. But sympathy for the Negro was enlivened by the moving prose of the Declaration of Independence, and the wartime fruits of that enlivened sentiment were the curtailment of the slave trade and a movement toward slave manumission, particularly above the Mason-Dixon line. Emancipation measures did not go unopposed, and even when adopted, as in Pennsylvania, their opponents were adept in finding loopholes in the law.[64] But slaves in Pennsylvania and elsewhere found another avenue to freedom—in military service.

63. Mitchell and Flanders, eds., *Statutes at Large of Pennsylvania*, X, 67-70.

64. For these loopholes see Edward R. Turner, *The Negro in Pennsylvania, 1619-1861* (Washington, 1911), 80-81.

CHAPTER IV

POLICY REVERSAL ABOVE
THE POTOMAC

"The rebel clowns, oh! what a sight!
Too awkward was their figure.
'Twas yonder stood a pious wight.
And here and there a nigger."

Frank Moore, *Songs and Ballads of the
American Revolution*

Ordinarily a military officer would be pleased to receive a letter from a civilian who declared himself "ever ready under your honors command to fight against all Enemys of the Honble. United States in defense of Liberty and the Rights of Mankind." But in this instance there were strings attached. Charles, the writer of the letter, was a slave who with his wife and daughter had fled from a Long Island master only to be seized by a sergeant in one of General Edward Hand's regiments and sold back into slavery. Charles would enlist, he said, if he would thereby obtain his freedom and that of his family.[1] Another freedom-minded Negro expressed a somewhat similar sentiment to General John Sullivan. When that commanding officer told his slave that they were starting for the army in order to fight for liberty, the slave remarked "that it would be a great satisfaction to know that he was indeed going to fight for *his* liberty."[2]

Hundreds of slaves were ready to bear arms in exchange for freedom. The names they gave themselves reflect their expectations. The forty-eight Negroes in a Connecticut regiment included Jeffery Liberty, Pomp Liberty, Sharp Liberty, Cuff Liberty, Dick Freedom, Ned Freedom, Cuff Freedom, Peter Free-

1. *The Unpublished Letters of Major-General Edward Hand of Pennsylvania* (New York, 1907), 30.
2. Nell, *Colored Patriots,* 119-20.

man, Jube Freeman, and Prinnis Freeman. A private in the Fifteenth Regiment of the Massachusetts Line took the shortest possible surname of emancipation, announcing himself as Juperter Free.[3]

Opportunities to exchange military service for freedom increased with every passing month. Above the Potomac, the policy of enlisting Negroes, especially free Negroes, met with decreasing opposition as the war continued, for after the first year it was difficult to raise volunteer forces. Even with the promise of pay raises and substantial bounties, men avoided military service. Many free Negroes, therefore, covertly took the place of whites. Recruiting officers in Massachusetts, who by the summer of 1779 received $10.00 a head for every man they signed up, were not overly squeamish about enlisting Negroes.[4] Colored recruits were enlisted by officers who received their commissions for bringing a certain number of volunteers into camp.

When Congress in 1777 began to fix troop quotas for the states, the use of colored men gained many supporters. Northern state legislatures might continue to pass laws prohibiting the enrollment of Indians and Negroes,[5] but muster masters calmly ignored the law, at least as it concerned Negroes. Faced by manpower requests for Washington's army, state recruiting officers were inclined to send Negroes whenever available. The practice spared a like number of white men for the state or county military forces, which were usually inducted for short terms and local assignments.

3. Frank Landon Humphreys, *The Life and Times of David Humphreys*, 2 vols. (New York, 1916), I, 192; "Revolutionary Muster Rolls," 2 vols., N.-Y. Hist. Soc., *Coll.,* 47 (1916), I, 192.

4. "The greater the number of recruits mustered by an officer the larger his bounty." Arthur J. Alexander, "How Maryland Tried to Raise Her Continental Quotas," *Maryland Historical Magazine,* 42 (1947), 185.

5. In 1778, 1779, and 1780, the Massachusetts legislature exempted Indians, Negroes and mulattoes from military service in acts raising troops for specific assignments in defense of the state. *Acts and Resolves, Public and Private of the Province of the Massachusetts Bay* (Boston, 1869-1922), *1777-1778,* 470, *1779-1780,* 33, 398. In 1779 the New Jersey militia was restricted to whites. *Laws of the State of New Jersey* (Newark, 1800), 436. Delaware in 1782 likewise restricted military service to white males. *Laws of the Government of New-Castle, Kent, and Sussex, upon Delaware* (Wilmington, 1783), 611.

For the very sparing use of Indians see Andrew M. Davis, "The Employment of Indian Auxiliaries in the American War," *English Historical Review,* 2 (1887), 709-28.

In order to fill their Continental army quotas, individual towns in New Hampshire and Massachusetts appointed committees to hire men to enlist. These committees were often told to get them as cheaply as possible. Since Negroes came relatively cheap and had little status, they were easy game, and the committees were seldom deterred by a man's color. In New Hampshire the town of Barrington enlisted five Negroes, all of whom received a bounty of £20 currency, plus a mileage allowance of 16s., 8d. Other New Hampshire towns furnishing Negroes were Newmarket, Epping, Exeter, Northwood, Stratham, Durham, and Kingstown.[6]

In Massachusetts fourteen Negroes served for the town of Lancaster, one of whom died in service. Bearing arms for Plymouth for designated periods of three years each were six black recruits. In April 1778 the town of Medford enlisted Prince Hall despite his slight build and short stature, paying him a bounty of $100 currency in two installments.[7] Hingham's recruiting committee procured Plato McLellan and Jack—the latter lost his life at Morrisania.[8] The town of Andover engaged Cato Freeman, his bounty officially stipulated as "freedom in three years."[9]

In tapping the reserve of black manpower, the New England state governments soon followed the lead of the towns, and Negro recruitment became prevalent after 1777. Among these states, however, there were differences worth noting. The enlistment of Negroes aroused little controversy or concern in New Hampshire. Slaves and free Negroes unobstrusively filtered into the state levies, generally signing up for three years and

6. Isaac W. Hammond, ed., *Revolutionary War Rolls of the State of New Hampshire*, 4 vols. (Manchester, 1887-89), I, 10, 11, 12, 102, 618, II, 618, III, 845. For a copy of town's "Enlistment Document" see *ibid.*, III, 288.

7. Henry S. Nourse, *The Military Annals of Lancaster, Massachusetts, 1740-1865* (Lancaster, 1889), 237; William T. Davis, *History of the Town of Plymouth* (Phila., 1885), 93; Revolutionary Rolls, LXXII, Nos. 257, 258, Mass. Arch.

8. *History of the Town of Hingham*, I, 312, 314. Serving also for Hingham were Caesar Blake and Caesar Scott who may have been Negroes but were not designated as such. *Ibid.*, 320, 321.

9. "Return of Recruits Unfit for service Sent by the State of Massachusetts Since January 1, 1781, mustered out by Baron Steuben, June 1782," George Washington Papers, CCI, No. 21, Lib. Cong. Hereafter cited as Washington Papers.

receiving the same bounty as whites. In Connecticut and Massachusetts, however, Negro recruitment became a public issue.

Connecticut gave official consideration to recruiting slaves in May 1777, when a specially appointed legislative committee recommended that they be allowed to enlist in the Continental battalions being raised in the state, provided they could raise enough money, by their bounty bonus or otherwise, to satisfy their masters. A slave who wished to enlist "shall be allowed to do so." He would then be appraised in money value by the town selectmen. His bounty would go to his master, who would also receive "one-half of the annual wages of such slave during the time he shall continue in said service."[10] This measure was defeated in the state senate.

While rejecting the specific procedure outlined in the defeated bill, the legislature nevertheless passed two acts designed to spur Negro recruitment. The first act exempted from the draft any two men who could procure an able-bodied substitute. The substitute could be of any hue or status. In October 1777 a second law did away with the responsibility of a manumittor for the subsequent support of a former slave—[11] hitherto a master who freed a slave had still been liable for his support. Slave-owners were thus encouraged to give freedom to slaves as a condition for their serving as substitutes: the master not only secured exemption from the draft but release from future liability for maintenance.

Massachusetts was a bit more forthright on Negro recruitment, although at first she backed into it. Requested to furnish fifteen regiments for the Continental army, the legislature in 1777 passed two resolutions exempting none but Quakers from military service. By implication Negroes were included among persons liable to be drafted. By April 1778 the state resolved any ambiguity by legally sanctioning the enlistment of Negroes. At the same time the legislature turned down a request from Thomas Kench, an artillery captain, who proposed to raise a detachment whose commissioned officers and orderly sergeant would be white, followed by "three sergeants black, four corporals black, two drums and fifes black, and eighty-four rank and file." Kench had observed that such a regiment would spur

10. Livermore, *An Historical Research Respecting Negroes*, 146.
11. Hoadly, ed., *The Public Records of the State of Connecticut*, I, 415.

its Negroes "to outdo the white men in every measure that the fortune of war calls a soldier to endure."[12] Although Kench's proposal was rejected,[13] the legislature had appointed two committees, one from each house, to study the slave-soldier measure recently passed in Rhode Island. Early in 1778 that state had authorized the formation of a battalion of slaves, the move having been initiated by Rhode Island officers in the Continental army. Since the state's two existing battalions in the Continental army camped at Valley Forge were greatly undermanned, these officers proposed that the battalions be combined and the superfluous officers permitted to return to their home state to receive and train a force of recruits. The proposed recruits were to include Negroes, if not to be exclusively confined to them. On January 1, 1778, General James Mitchell Varnum sent the officers' proposals to General Washington, who in turn forwarded them to Nicholas Cooke, governor of the state. In his covering letter the Commander-in-Chief expressed the hope that Cooke would "give the officers employed in this business all the assistance in your power."[14]

When the legislature convened at its February session, Cooke placed the slave enlistment proposal before it. The discussion was spirited. Six deputies protested against the measure, doubting whether there were enough Negroes in the state "who would have an inclination to inlist, and would pass muster." Moreover, there was an inconsistency, they said, in assigning slaves to defend the liberties of America—an inconsistency which would expose patriots to the kind of British ridicule that "we so liberally bestowed upon them on account of Dunmore's regiment of blacks." The scheme was expensive, since the state would be obliged to purchase the slaves, and the masters would likely be dissatisfied, both as to the sum allowed them as compensation and the apparent permission given to the slave to seek enlistment upon his own initiative.[15]

The deputies who protested against recruiting slaves had no suggestions, however, as to where white recruits could be found, and with no other choice before it, the legislature in late Feb-

12. Revolutionary Rolls, CXCIX, No. 80, Mass. Arch.
13. *Journal of the House of Representatives,* 243.
14. For the two letters see Bartlett, ed., *Records of the Colony of Rhode Island,* VIII, 640, 641.
15. *Ibid.,* VIII, 360.

ruary 1778 passed the slave enlistment act. It provided that upon passing muster a slave would be declared free. His master would be paid a sum according to his worth, a sum which was to be paid by the state, which in turn expected reimbursement from Congress. "The number of slaves in this State is not great," Governor Cooke informed Washington, "but it is generally thought that three hundred and upward will be enlisted."[16]

The military employment of Negroes went farthest in New England. Among the middle states only New York took forthright action. In order to raise two regiments the legislature on March 20, 1781, provided that a land grant bounty would be given to any person who delivered his able-bodied slave (or slaves) to a warrant officer. The slave was to serve for three years, or until "regularly" discharged.[17]

Of the Southern states Maryland alone authorized slave enlistments. Hard pressed after 1777 to supply troops for the state and Continental service, Maryland decided to abandon its time-honored opposition to arming the Negro. By the summer of 1780 militia colonels were welcoming the colored man. "Our recruiting business in this County goes on much worse than I expected," wrote Richard Barnes of St. Mary's to Governor Lee. "The greatest part of those that have enlisted are free Negroes & Mulattoes, all of which from what I have been informed will not amount to more than fifteen."[18] Another colonel in the same county asked the Governor to think twice before sending down a warrant for the execution of a Negro under sentence of death since "he is young and healthy and would make a fine Soldier."[19]

Reading the changing times, the state legislature in October 1780 ordered that "any able-bodied slave between 16 and 40 years of age, who voluntarily enters into service, and is passed by the lieutenant, in the presence and with the consent and agreement of his master, may be accepted as a recruit." In the following spring, still short by 1,340 men, Maryland reached out for the non-slave Negro. On May 10, 1781, the legislature

16. *Ibid.*, 358-60; Cooke to Washington, Feb. 23, 1778, Jared Sparks, ed., *Correspondence of the American Revolution: Being Letters of Eminent Men to George Washington*, 4 vols. (Boston, 1853), II, 78. Hereafter cited as Sparks, ed., *Letters to Washington.*
17. *Laws of the State of New York* (Poughkeepsie, 1782), 179.
18. Richard Barnes to Governor Lee, July 23, 1780, *Arch. of Md.*, XLV, 24.
19. Zachariah Forrest to Lee, Apr. 17, 1781, *ibid.*, XLVII, 196.

decreed that all free men, "although blacks or mulattoes," were thenceforth subject to the draft.[20]

Three weeks later the lawmakers pondered the idea of raising a regiment of 750 slaves. A bill was proposed stipulating that a person having six or more slaves between the ages of fourteen and fifty-five must furnish one slave if the latter consented to enlist for the war's duration.[21] "I wish the regiment would be raised. I am of the opinion that the Blacks will make excellent soldiers—indeed experience proves it," wrote Major Edward Giles of Harford County to his close friend, General Otho H. Williams. "As to the danger of training them to Arms— tis the Child of a distempered Imagination. There are some people who are forever frightening themselves with Bugbears of their own Creation."[22]

In early June the bill seemed likely to pass,[23] but four weeks later a change of attitude had set in. "The Assembly is up and abandoned the Design of raising a Regiment of Blacks," wrote the Council to General Lafayette in answer to his recommendation of an officer to take command of the proposed colored companies.[24]

Perhaps the chief reason for the rejection of the slave regiment act was the planters' fear of economic loss. "I hope none of our negroes will enlist—the price if paid . . . is not equal to the value of a healthy, strong, young negro man," Charles Carroll wrote to his father in early June when the bill's prospects were good.[25] Whatever the reasons, Maryland was willing to take slave soldiers only in limited numbers and refused to constitute them as a distinct military unit.

Virginia drew the line against slave enlistments in any form. James Madison, one of the state's representatives in the Continental Congress, favored liberating some slaves and making soldiers of them, taking the safeguard of "having white officers

20. *Laws of Maryland Passed at a Session of the Assembly in the Year One Thousand and Seven Hundred and Eighty* (Annapolis, 1781), Oct. Sess., chap. 43, Sect. IV; *Arch. of Md.,* XVIII, 375.

21. Charles Carroll (of Carrollton) to Charles Carroll, June 4, 1781, Carrollton Manuscripts, Maryland Historical Society.

22. Giles to Williams, June 1, 1781, Otho Holland Williams Papers, Md. Hist. Soc.

23. John Cadwalader to Washington, June 5, 1781, Sparks, ed., *Letters to Washington,* III, 331.

24. Council to Lafayette, July 3, 1781, *Arch. of Md.,* XLV, 494.

25. Carroll to Carroll, June 4, 1781, Carrollton MSS.

and a majority of white soldiers." But the Virginia legislature, although scraping for military manpower late in 1780, refused to listen to such suggestions. The Negro scheme is laid aside," wrote Madison's intimate friend, Joseph Jones, from Richmond. It was "considered unjust, sacrificing the property of a part of the community to the exoneration of the rest."[26]

Although unwilling to call upon slaves, Virginia went so far as to lift the ban on free Negroes. As early as July 1775 the Virginia Convention, meeting at Richmond, opened the militia to "all free male persons, hired servants and apprentices above the age of sixteen and under fifty." This measure had one unforeseen consequence—a number of slaves signed up, passing themselves off as free men. To clarify the law the Assembly on May 6, 1777, stipulated that henceforth it would be unlawful to enlist any Negro or mulatto unless he could produce a certificate of freedom signed by his county's justice of the peace. By implication free Negroes were made eligible for military duty, and by an act passed the same day, they were allowed to serve as drummers, fifers or pioneers.[27]

*   *   *

Wherever Negroes, free or slave, were taken into military service, their employment was an adjunct to the substitution system. Generally, throughout the United States, a draftee could avoid service by producing someone to serve in his place. Men who employed substitutes incurred no charges of "draft-dodging," or questions about their valor. The substitute system favored the man of means, but it did not evoke the storm of criticism which it aroused in the Civil War.

The system was sanctioned by law. Connecticut, seeking to raise its continental quota, passed a law on May 2, 1777, exempting from active service any two men who could procure one able-bodied recruit to enlist for three years.[28] Maryland, too, passed a substitution law in 1777.[29] Delaware did not go

26. Madison to Joseph Jones, Nov. 28, 1780, Gaillard Hunt, ed., *The Writings of James Madison*, 9 vols. (New York, 1900-10), I, 107; Jones to Madison, Dec. 8, 1780, Worthington Ford, ed., *Letters of Joseph Jones, 1777-1787* (Washington, 1889), 63.

27. Hening, ed., *Statutes of Va.*, IX, 27, 268, 280.

28. *Connecticut Courant* (Hartford), Mar. 17, 1778.

29. Alexander, "How Maryland Tried to Reach Her Continental Quota," *Md. Hist. Mag.*, 42 (1947), 192.

as far as some of her sister states; her substitution law of 1777 limited the recruiting of servants or apprentices to those whose terms of servitude had no longer than two years to run.[30] Despite Delaware's restrictions, much unauthorized servant enlistment went on in that state and elsewhere. Particularly in Pennsylvania, where a man summoned to the militia did not have to appear in person, the temptation to send a servant or an apprentice was not always easy to resist. In states like Massachusetts and Virginia, where slaves were not permitted to enlist, more than one master weighed the idea of representing his slave as a free man in order to get him on the rolls as a substitute. A man summoned to service saw nothing wrong in employing a Negro. In September 1777 Elkanah Watson of Plymouth furnished "Dolphin Negro" for thirty days' service in Rhode Island.[31] In May 1778 Jonathan Giddings of New Fairfield, Connecticut, hired a colored man as his substitute for the duration of the war.[32] Cudjo, a Newark slave, served as a Continental soldier for his master, Benjamin Coe; another New Jersey draft choice, Casper Bergen, purchased slave Samuel Sutphin to do his service stint.[33] In New York David Belknap, summoned to Fort Montgomery, sent his slave who, after "faithfully performing his duty," died as a prisoner of war.[34] In April 1778, in Maryland's Anne Arundel County, Negro Anthony was enlisted for Thomas Johnson, Jr. In the same county two other draftees jointly engaged free Negro Abram Brissington whom they "delivered to John Enwright for Pulaski's Company."[35] In North Carolina slave Ned Griffin was produced

30. *Pennsylvania Gazette,* May 28, 1777.
31. In Rhode Island some draftees, in desperation, furnished as substitutes prisoners of war stationed in the state, making it necessary, on Feb. 12, 1778, to legislate against the practice. *Connecticut Courant,* Mar. 17, 1778; Davis, *History of Plymouth,* 91.
32. "Lists and Returns of Connecticut Men in the Revolution, 1775-1783," Conn. Hist. Soc., *Coll.,* 12 (1909), 122.
33. Simeon F. Moss, "The Persistence of Slavery and Involuntary Servitude in a Free State," *Journal of Negro History,* 35 (1950), 301; Irving S. Kull, ed., *New Jersey: A History* (New York, 1930-36), II, 733.
34. *Historical Magazine,* 2 (1867), 44.
35. Margaret R. Hodges, comp., *Unpublished Revolutionary War Records of Maryland,* 6 vols. (Md. Hist. Soc., 1939), II, 205. Negro substitution was practiced in Virginia. For an example, see W. P. Palmer *et al.,* eds., *Calendar of Virginia State Papers,* 11 vols. (Richmond, 1875-93), V, 260. Hereafter cited as *Cal. of Va. State Papers.*

as a substitute by William Kitchen, a deserter who had been caught.[36]

When Congress early in the war entertained the notion of enlisting Negroes, the idea was overridden, as we have seen, by the objection of Southern delegates. Although the states recruited Negroes to meet their Continental troop quotas, they acted without the formal sanction of Congress.[37] Neither Congress nor the Continental army commanders voiced any disapproval. By the summer of 1776 Washington and his generals had learned the hard facts of life and were taking whatever the states sent; any reluctance remaining in Congress had been overcome by the need to reinforce the Continental army. At the federal level there was little opposition to using Negro soldiers; in fact, Congress by the spring of 1779 was ready to take the unprecedented step of recommending slave enlistment. Hitherto restrained by a regard for the sensibilities of slave-owners and, of necessity, by a deference to states' rights, Congress was forced into decisive action by the British occupation of Savannah and the opening of a second enemy campaign to subjugate the South. On March 29, 1779, Congress recommended to South Carolina and Georgia that they "take measures immediately for raising three thousand able-bodied negroes." These would be formed into separate battalions with white commissioned and non-commissioned officers. Owners of the slaves were to be compensated by a sum of not more than a thousand dollars for "each active able-bodied negro man of standard size, not exceeding thirty-five years of age." The enlisted slaves would receive no bounty or pay, but would be clothed and subsisted at government expense. If they served "well and faithfully" to the end of the war, they would be freed and receive fifty dollars.[38]

On the same day these resolutions were adopted, Congress announced the selection of the candidate to go to South Carolina to enlist local support for the proposition.[39] The choice fell on young John Laurens, heretofore an aide-de-camp to General Washington, and now promoted to a lieutenant colonel. A more willing officer could not have been found; no man believed more

36. Aptheker, ed., *Documentary History of the Negro People*, 14.

37. William Ellery to William Greene, Apr. 4, 1780, Burnett, ed., *Letters of Members of Cont. Cong.*, V, 105.

38. Ford, ed., *Journ. of Cont. Cong.*, XXIII, 387-88.

39. *Ibid.*, 388.

in arming the slaves and no man had done more to bring it about than this devoted patriot.

Dedicated to human freedom since his studies at Geneva just before the war, Laurens on his return to America was deeply disturbed by slavery in his native land. His convictions were strengthened by the sympathetic attitude of his father, Henry Laurens, president of the Continental Congress. A former importer and commission merchant, the elder Laurens had by 1770 abandoned the slave trade; a landowner and planter, he had been most considerate about the welfare of his slaves.[40]"I am devising means for manumitting many of them and for cutting off the entail of slavery," he wrote to John in August 1775. Father and son shared beliefs on slavery which marked them as unusual among upper-class South Carolinians.[41]

Since the early months of the war Laurens had advocated giving slaves their freedom in exchange for military service. By the spring of 1778 his tone had become insistent: "It is a pity that some such plan as I propose could not be more extensively executed by public authority," he wrote his father from Valley Forge headquarters, "A well chosen body of 5,000 black men, properly officer'd to act as light troops . . . might give us decisive success in the next campaign."[42]

It was another year, however, before the generals and Congress were ready to act. In mid-March the elder Laurens, writing from Philadelphia to the Commander-in-Chief, expressed the belief that in four months the British could be driven out of Georgia if the patriot armies were strengthened by 3,000 blacks from South Carolina.[43] A week later a somewhat evasive reply came from Washington. The policy of arming the slaves was "a moot point, unless the enemy set the example." More-

40. "Be kind to Berom in his affliction," wrote Laurens to an overseer. David D. Wallace, *The Life of Henry Laurens* (New York, 1915), 66.

41. *Ibid.*, 446; E. T. H. Shaffer holds that one of the factors contributing to the relative obscurity of Henry and John Laurens in South Carolina history was their anti-slavery attitude, "The Rejected Laurens—A Carolina Tragedy," South Carolina Historical Association, *Proceedings* (Columbia, 1934), 21-23. A recent book presents John Laurens in a very favorable light, Sara Bertha Townsend, *An American Soldier: The Life of John Laurens* (Raleigh, N. C., 1958).

42. John Laurens to Henry Laurens, Feb. 2, 1778, William Gilmore Simms, *The Army Correspondence of Colonel John Laurens, with a Memoir* (New York, 1907), 117.

43. Henry Laurens to Washington, Mar. 16, 1779, Burnett, ed., *Letters of Members of Cont. Cong.*, IV, 107.

over, to arm some of the slaves would produce discontent among those remaining in servitude. But, concluded the Commander-in-Chief, "this is a subject that has never employed much of my thoughts. . . ."[44]

Washington was quite accurate in describing the plantation owners' chief reason for keeping the slave as he was. The prospect of advancement for slaves along any line might engender discontent among those who remained in slavery. In other respects, however, his reply to Laurens was less candid. Washington appears to assume that the Lord Dunmore scare had never taken place, and that the British had no thought of arming Negroes. Five months earlier, on October 15, 1778, in a letter to Andrew Lewis, he had referred to Britain's employment of Hessian, Indian, and Negro allies.[45] And although Washington lightly broke off the subject of Laurens's letter with the remark that he had never given much thought to arming the slaves, he himself had given his tacit approval some fourteen months earlier to General Varnum's proposal to arm slaves in Rhode Island. About the same time, the younger Laurens had written his father that Washington was "convinced that the numerous tribes of blacks in the southern parts of the continent, offer a resource to us that should not be neglected."[46]

That Washington had previously given the matter some considerable thought is indicated by a lengthy missive which Alexander Hamilton wrote from army headquarters to John Jay, then president of Congress, on March 14, 1779. Hamilton presented a carefully reasoned statement for slave enlistment. "The contempt we have been taught to entertain for the blacks, makes us fancy many things that are founded neither in reason nor experience." But, continued the twenty-two-year-old colonel, "the dictates of humanity and true policy, equally interest

44. Washington to H. Laurens, Mar. 20, 1779, Fitzpatrick, ed., *Writings of Washington*, XIV, 267.

45. Washington to A. Lewis, Oct. 15, 1778, *ibid.*, XIII, 80.

46. Laurens to H. Laurens, Feb. 2, 1778, Simms, *Correspondence of John Laurens*, 117. The military use of Negroes had engaged Washington's attention some twenty years previously. "I think it will be advisable to detain both Mulatto's and negroes in your Company," he wrote to Captain Peter Hogg during the French and Indian War, "and employ them as Pioneers and Hatchet-men." Washington to Hogg, Dec. 27, 1755, Fitzpatrick, ed., *Writings of Washington*, I, 259. Some months later Washington sent a message to Captain John McNeill: "You may tell Captain Hogg, that another equally good as the mulatto, will be agreeable." Washington to McNeill, July 21, 1756, *ibid.*, I, 407.

me in favor of this unfortunate class of men." A member of Washington's staff, Hamilton presumably had secured the General's approval to the substance of this official letter. It is significant, too, that even before Congress took action on Hamilton's request, young Laurens had been dispatched to South Carolina "to raise two, three, or four battalions of negroes."[47] Whatever the degree of Washington's interest or influence, young Laurens was overjoyed at the action of Congress in unanimously recommending slave soldiers to South Carolina and Georgia. Now he had official blessing, military and civilian, for his efforts to bring about the two-fold good of advancing the lot of "those who are unjustly deprived of the rights of mankind," and of re-enforcing "the defenders of liberty with a number of gallant soldiers."[48] Full of zeal the newly appointed lieutenant colonel hurried to his native state to press for approval of the plan.

Chivalrous, manly and gracious, handsome John Laurens could have won South Carolina over if anyone could, but he was foredoomed to failure. In a state which prior to the Revolutionary War had imported more than two thousand slaves a year for a twenty year span,[49] there was an understandable reluctance to arm the blacks. Laurens was soon given his answer. "I laid your Letter, respecting the black Levies, before the Council, yesterday," wrote Governor John Rutledge on May 26, 1779, "but they adhere to their former Sentiments on that Subject."[50] In the lower house the story was the same; the measure "was received with horror by the planters, who figured to themselves terrible consequences."[51] Indeed the Coun-

47. Henry Cabot Lodge, ed., *The Works of Alexander Hamilton,* 12 vols. (New York, 1904), IX, 161.

48. John Laurens to Henry Laurens, Jan. 14, 1778, Simms, *Correspondence of John Laurens,* 108.

49. O. M. Dickerson, *The Navigation Acts and the American Revolution* (Phila., 1951), 62.

50. Rutledge to John Laurens, May 26, 1779, Laurens Manuscripts, Lib. Cong.

51. R. W. Gibbes, ed., *Documentary History of the American Revolution,* 3 vols. (New York, 1883-87), II, 121. Hereafter cited as Gibbes, ed., *Doc. Hist. Amer. Rev.* "Their order to take 3,000 Negroes into their service, gives great Disgust to the Southern Colonies," gloated the loyalist Chief Justice of New York. William Smith to the Earl of Carlisle, June 8, 1779, Benjamin F. Stevens, ed., *Facsimiles of Manuscripts in European Archives Relating to America, 1773-1783,* 26 vols. (London, 1889-95), I, No. 123. Hereafter cited as Stevens, ed., *Facsimiles.*

cil was indignant enough to consider a proposal to send a flag of truce to British General Augustine Prevost, then threatening Charleston, offering to take South Carolina out of the war.[52] Laurens was not the kind to give up. To his friend Thomas Bee, a member of the Continental Congress, he expressed the hope that the Southern delegates would "second the recommendation of Congress for raising a corps of blacks in South Carolina and Georgia."[53] He promised Alexander Hamilton that he would not cease his efforts to press for Negro soldiers "while there remains the smallest hopes of success." To this end he intended to stand for election to the lower house. "Oh that I were a Demosthenes! The Athenians never deserved a more bitter exprobation than our countrymen."[54]

Young Laurens was not able to give his undivided efforts to his project; the field of battle and an appointment as special minister to France claimed his attention. But during his absence from his native state, his project did not die. General Benjamin Lincoln, noting in November 1779 that South Carolina had only 750 men fit for active duty, repeatedly urged Governor Rutledge to enlist slaves. "My own mind," he wrote from Charleston in March 1780, "suggests the utility and importance of the measure as the safety of the town makes it necessary."[55]

By 1781 the plea for the recruitment of black soldiers had found a proponent with a more powerful influence in national affairs than either Lincoln or Laurens. This was Rhode Island's able Nathanael Greene, sent to the South late in 1780 to reorganize the Continental forces located there. As usual, manpower was in short supply. "What a Herculean task we have," he wrote to Lafayette, "to contend with a formidable enemy with a handful of men."[56]

52. John Fiske, *The American Revolution*, 2 vols. (Boston, 1891), II, 172.

53. Laurens to Bee, Nov. 6, 1781, Laurens MSS, Lib. Cong.

54. Laurens to Hamilton, Charleston, 1779, John C. Hamilton, ed., *The Works of Alexander Hamilton*, 7 vols. (New York, 1850-51), I, 115. Hamilton was less sanguine: prejudice and private interest, he said, would prove "too powerful for public good." Hamilton to Laurens, Sept. 1779, Laurens MSS, Lib. Cong.

55. Lincoln to Washington, Nov. 7, 1779, Sparks, ed., *Letters to Washington*, II, 345; Livermore, *An Historical Research Respecting Negroes*, 178.

56. Greene to Lafayette, June 23, 1781, Photostat, Greene Manuscripts, Clements Lib. For Greene's pressing need for men see Clara Goldsmith Roe,

Even after Yorktown, Greene did not feel secure. He feared that the British army would be re-enforced and would overrun South Carolina. Expecting no assistance from either Virginia or North Carolina, he turned to the one remaining source—the Negro. On December 9, 1781, from his headquarters at the Round O, he dispatched a message to South Carolina's governor. Greene minced no words. There were not enough whites in the state, he wrote, to raise a force in any other way than by slave enlistment, especially since "the natural strength of this country in point of numbers appears to consist much more in the blacks than in the whites." If the British found they had to contend with Negroes as well as whites they would think twice before "making further attempts upon this country." Greene then specified what Negro assistance he desired: four regiments, plus a corps of pioneers and a corps of artificers. Those who made up the soldier regiments should be given their freedom and treated like other arms-bearers; otherwise "they would not be fit for the duties expected of them."[57]

The popular Greene, one of Washington's best generals, was too important to be brushed aside. On December 18, Rutledge sent a reply: it would be a few days, he said, before he could get the opinion of the Council, whose members had gone to Martin's Tavern to attend the elections held there the previous day. A week later the Governor notified Greene that the Council had met on December 23 and decided that in view of the Assembly's previous rejection of slave enlistments the question should be referred to that body, which was scheduled to convene in a few weeks.[58]

Within a few days after the Assembly met, Greene wrote another lengthy letter to Rutledge, reiterating the necessity of raising black regiments. He added a warning: should a peace be negotiated on the basis of *uti possidetis,* South Carolina could never forgive herself for the loss of her lands now in British hands.[59] Three days later Greene informed Washington that

Major General Nathanael Greene and the Southern Campaign of the American Revolution, 1780-1783 (unpubl. Ph.D. diss., University of Michigan, 1943), 165-70.
57. Greene to Rutledge, Dec. 9, 1781, Greene MSS, Clements Lib.
58. Rutledge to Greene, Dec. 18, 24, 1781, *ibid.*
59. Greene to Rutledge, Jan. 21, 1782, *ibid.*

some of the South Carolinians favored his proposal, "but the far greater part of the people are opposed to it."[60]

Greene's hopes had been raised a little by the knowledge that John Laurens, back from Paris and now a member of the state legislature, would be on hand. Indeed the young officer was doing all Greene could have expected. "Laurens tried yesterday to carry in the house his favorite scheme of raising 2500 blacks," wrote a member of the Assembly. "Only himself, Ramsay, Mr. Ferguson & about 13 others joined in it."[61] Eleven days later Laurens made a second attempt. Although his proposal was "strongly urg'd in the Assembly and warmly debated," the question when put to a vote was defeated.[62] The action of the legislature accurately reflected the sentiments of most South Carolinians: "The prejudices against the measure," wrote Lewis Morris, who was stationed in the state, "are so prevailing that no consideration could induce them to adopt it."[63]

On the day the slave enlistment bill was rejected, the new governor, John Mathews, informed a small committee of the legislature that Greene had just received official notice of the departure of a British force from New York, its supposed destination South Carolina. It appeared that something must be done for the defense of the state. At nine o'clock the next morning the legislature entertained a bill to provide the army with corps of Negro skilled laborers, wagoners, laborers, sappers, miners, and servants.[64] On the same day Mathews wrote to Greene inviting him to make a formal application for such non-arms-bearing black assistance. Greene's answer came promptly: he could use to advantage "140 wagoners, 150 pioneers, 120 artificers, and 20 or 30 servants." Mathews quickly transmitted

60. Greene to Washington, Jan. 24, 1782, Sparks, ed., *Letters to Washington*, III, 467.

61. AEdanus Burke to Arthur Middleton, Jan. 25, 1782, John W. Barnwell, ed., "The Correspondence of Arthur Middleton," *South Carolina Historical and Genealogical Magazine, 26* (1925), 194.

62. Mordecai Gist to R. H. Lee, Feb. 10, 1872, "Letters Colonial and Revolutionary Selected from the Dreer Collection of the Historical Society of Pennsylvania," *Pennsylvania Magazine of History and Biography, 42* (1918), 82; A. S. Salley, Jr., ed., *Journal of the House of Representatives of South Carolina, January 8, 1782-February 26, 1782* (Columbia, 1916), 56.

63. Lewis Morris to Jacob Morris, Feb. 7, 1782, "Letters to General Lewis Morris," N.-Y. Hist. Soc., *Coll.*, Publication Fund Ser., 7 (1876), 499. For Greene's reason for the defeat of the bill see Greene to Washington, Mar. 9, 1782, Sparks, ed., *Letters to Washington*, III, 491.

64. Salley, ed., *Journal of South Carolina House of Representatives*, 57-58.

this request to the legislature, accompanying it with his earnest recommendation.[65] Despite the pressure exerted by military authority and the presumed urgency of the situation, the legislature could not be driven into taking the hateful step of making soldiers of slaves. Washington had expressed hope that Laurens's proposal would be adopted; nevertheless he was not surprised when his former aide-de-camp informed him that the voice of reason had been "drowned by the howlings of a triple-headed monster, in which prejudice, avarice and pusillanimity were united." The Commander-in-Chief had some consoling words: private interest, rather than public welfare "influences the generality of mankind." He feared that Laurens would have no better success in Georgia.[66]

Washington needed no crystal ball to forecast accurately Georgia's response. Laurens, however, was still hopeful. Believing that he had the encouragement of Governor Richard Howley, he threw himself into the task "with all the tenacity of a man making a last effort."[67] But Georgia proved no less adamant than her adjoining sister state. As on a similar occasion three years earlier when the legislature had rejected a motion to use slaves as soldiers, the Georgians turned thumbs down.

Young Laurens was spared a full knowledge of Georgia's intransigence. Two months after his optimistic letter to Washington he fell at an obscure point on the Combahee River while leading a charge against the alerted British in a skirmish as futile as his slave soldier scheme.

*   *   *

The Negro in South Carolina and Georgia who sought to bear arms in the American cause may have felt that the war was being waged for white freedom and black slavery. But outside the lower South, colored men saw action under the newly unfurled Stars and Stripes.

65. Mathews to Greene, Feb. 6, 1782, Greene to Mathews, Feb. 11, 1782, Greene MSS, Clements Lib.; Mathews to the Legislature, Feb. 12, 1782, Gibbes, ed., *Doc. Hist. Amer. Rev.*, III, 251.
66. Washington to Laurens, Feb. 18, Mar. 22, July 10, 1782, Fitzpatrick, ed., *Writings of Washington*, XXIV, 4, 88, 421; Laurens to Washington, May 19, 1782, Sparks, ed., *Letters to Washington*, III, 506.
67. Laurens to Washington, June 12, 1782, *ibid.*, III, 515.

CHAPTER V

ARMS-BEARERS FOR AMERICA

"Zechery Prince now Ded, Rec^d his freedom"

*Connecticut Revolutionary Lists
and Returns, 1775-1783*

Caesar, a slave belonging to Daniel Griswold of Connecticut, was declared free "on condition of Enlistment and faithfully serving out the time of Enlistment." James Robinson of Maryland was promised his freedom for service in the army, but his reward turned out to be deportation to the lower South where he was sold. Taking the name of William Ferguson and passing as a freeman, slave Toby in 1778 joined the Fourteenth Virginia Regiment, serving until the end of the war. Charlestown Edes signed his mark authorizing his wages as a soldier in the Fifteenth Massachusetts Regiment to be paid to his master, Isaiah Edes of Groton.[1] These four—Charlestown Edes, Toby, Robinson, and Caesar—illustrate the varying fate that befell slaves who became soldiers.

Like Caesar, who served his time in the Fifth Connecticut Regiment and was honorably discharged, most slave soldiers received their freedom with their flintlocks. Upon enlistment they were given certificates of manumission. In some instances a slave might be given his freedom in advance, but with the understanding that he would join the army.[2] Many slaves, how-

1. Charles M. Andrews, "Slavery in Connecticut," *Mag. of Amer. Hist.*, 21 (1889), 423; Elio Gasperetti, trans., "an Italo-American Newspaper's Obituary of a Negro Revolutionary War Veteran," *Negro History Bulletin*, 17 (1954), 58; Luther P. Jackson, "Negro Soldiers and Seamen in the American Revolution," *Journal of Negro History*, 27 (1942), 255; Samuel A. Green, "Slavery at Groton in Provincial Times," Mass. Hist. Soc., *Proc.*, 3rd Ser., 42 (1909), 200.

2. John M. Merriam, *Five Framingham Heroes of the American Revolution* (Framingham, 1925), 10.

ever, had only verbal promises. A man summoned to service would procure a slave substitute, assuring him that he would be rewarded with his freedom. In Virginia, where this practice was common, masters represented their slaves as free men to the recruiting officers, since bondmen were not permitted to bear arms.

A slave running away to enlist was an old story; a hundred years before Bunker Hill the New York legislature threatened to punish "grievously" anyone who "upon pretense of going to the wars against the Enemy do run away from his Master's service."[3] To the foot-loose slave the Revolutionary War beckoned like the North Star, and many succeeded in enlisting by passing themselves off as free men. In Rhode Island slave Prince enlisted in Christopher Greene's battalion and was mustered in; it took an order from the General Assembly to get him out of the army and back to his owners.[4] To the same legislature came a request from Colonel Israel Angell of the Second Rhode Island Regiment, stationed at Valley Forge, to authorize the purchase of "negro Tone," then serving in his regiment although the property of a Maryland master.[5] In Massachusetts, in September 1777, the Council ordered the muster master of Plymouth County to take back the bounty money paid for Jupiter Richardson, "the sd. Jupiter being claimed as a slave."[6]

As these examples suggest, it often required the intercession of high authority to procure the release of a slave once he was firmly inducted into the ranks. On one occasion, Captain Jonathan Hobby of the Third Massachusetts Regiment appealed to General Washington for assistance in recovering a Negro soldier formerly belonging to him. From army headquarters came a reply that a Court of Inquiry would look into the case. But Hobby could take little comfort from a follow-up note informing him that "the Commander in Chief does not think himself authorized to discharge the Sd Negro, unless another man is obtained by the State, or otherwise, to serve in his room."[7] Another

3. *The Colonial Laws of New York*, II, 161-62.
4. Sidney S. Rider, "The Rhode Island Black 'Regiment' of 1778," *Rhode Island Historical Tracts*, 1st Ser., No. 10 (Providence, 1880), 10. Hereafter cited as *R. I. Hist. Tracts*.
5. Israel Angell to Luke Griffith, Mar. 30, 1778, Louise L. Lovell, *Israel Angell* (New York, 1921), 120.
6. Revolutionary Rolls Coll., CLXXIII, No. 423, Mass. Arch.
7. Headquarters to Rufus Putnam, Feb. 2, 1783, Fitzpatrick, ed., *Writings of Washington*, XXVI, 90; Headquarters to Hobby, Feb. 7, 1783, *ibid.*, 108.

runaway slave-soldier request came to General Washington from
a former member of his staff, James McHenry, later secretary
of war under John Adams. Writing on behalf of Mary Dulany,
"one of the best old ladies in the world," McHenry asked that
an inquiry be made to assist her to "recover the Negroe man
in your army." Her slave Jacob had enlisted in November
1781 "in the Marquis's department," in a regiment "commanded
by Col. Voes, the Capt^{n's} name Bradford."[8]

One of these cases of a master trying to recover the services
of an enlisted slave aroused the ire of General Horatio Gates.
A doctor in Westfield, Massachusetts, Israel Ashley, had been
ordered out with the town militia, and had intended to furnish
his slave Gilliam as his substitute. The only complication was
that Gilliam, who had previously enlisted as Ashley's substitute
for a short term stint, had re-enlisted without his master's consent. Thereupon the draft-pressed Ashley asked Gates to have
Gilliam sent back to Westfield. Instead, the Commander of
the Eastern Department wrote a scathing letter to the Council.
Having learned a lot since that day in July 1775 when he had
instructed recruiting officers not to enlist colored men, Gates
gratuitiously informed that body that Massachusetts had neither
formulated a policy on slaves who enlisted without their masters' consent nor passed a law "on behalf of slaves who have
or will assist us in securing our freedom at the risk of their
own lives." In his opinion the state legislature should take
action in view of the "great number of soldiers in that class
in this department, and in your own troops."[9]

Masters not uncommonly enlisted slaves in order to get
the bounty of land. By a New Jersey law passed in May 1777,
a master who enlisted his servant would be paid a sum determined
by two freeholders and a county judge.[10] New York's act of
March 20, 1781, for the raising of two regiments for frontier
defense, stipulated that a master who delivered an able-bodied
slave to a warrant officer would receive a land bounty of 500
acres.[11]

8. Mary Dulany to McHenry, Jan. 16, McHenry to Washington, Feb.
2, 1783, Washington Papers, CCXV, No. 54.
9. Gates to Massachusetts Council, July 2, 1779, Revolutionary Rolls Coll.,
CCI, 138-40, Mass. Arch.
10. *Pa. Gaz.*, June 4, 1777.
11. *Laws of the State of New-York*, 179.

In South Carolina it was a common practice for a cash-minded master to turn his slave over to the army. For her slave's services in the Continental artillery in 1780 Ann Lauce was paid £55. Daniel Horry and John Delka received £50 and £170 respectively for a Negro apiece lost at the siege of Savannah while in Continental service.[12] Although contrary to South Carolina official policy, the use of slaves in semi-military capacities was winked at by commanding officers.

* * *

Although serving in racially mixed units, the Negro soldier was not without his distinctive points of difference. Except around Boston for a few months in the spring and summer of 1775, few Negroes saw service in the volunteer forces—units enlisted for a single campaign, whose members planned to serve only a few weeks and then depart for home with their privately owned muskets. And, as has been noted, relatively fewer Negroes than whites were enrolled in the militia with its short term enlistments of three months, six months, nine months, or a year. In every state a scattering of Negroes could be found in militia units engaged in such local defense duties as guarding the nearby coast, protecting the county's military stores, or manning its forts when an enemy raid threatened. But the Negro soldier was more likely to serve in the Continental line; as such he usually enlisted for a longer term, sometimes three years or the war's duration, and was prepared to go wherever ordered. Continental troops formed the backbone of the army, and bore the brunt of its major battles. While the militiaman's shortcomings have perhaps been unduly highlighted[13]—such an enlistee was often a civilian with a gun, who scarcely thought of himself as a soldier—a man in the Continental line was more likely to adopt a professional attitude toward his military occupation. In any case, by the summer of 1778 the Continental army was well sprinkled with blacks. An official return of

12. Wylma A. Wates, *Stub Entries to Indents, Books G—H* (Columbia, 1955), 66, 104.

13. For a reassessment see Robert C. Pugh, "The Revolutionary Militia in the Southern Campaign, 1780-1781," *Wm. and Mary Qtly.*, 3rd Ser., 14 (1957), 154-75. For a clearly presented analysis of the militia as contrasted with the Continental army, see John C. Miller, *Triumph of Freedom, 1775-1783* (Boston, 1948), 233-38. A succinct paragraph on the Revolutionary militia may be found in Department of the Army ROTC Manual, 145-20, *American Military History, 1607-1958* (Washington, 1959), 51.

Negroes, dated August 24, 1778, and signed by Adjutant General Alexander Scammell, totalled 755, scattered over fourteen brigades.[14] The detachment with the highest percentage was General Samuel Holden Parsons's brigade, which had 148 Negroes, most of them from Connecticut.

As these figures suggest, Negroes were comparatively numerous in the units raised in New England. As early as June 1776 Alexander Graydon, after noting the "miserably constituted bands" from the eastern provinces, singled out for praise the Marblehead companies of Colonel John Glover. But, added Graydon, "even in this regiment there were a number of negroes, which to persons unaccustomed to such associations, had a disagreeable, degrading effect."[15] At Ticonderoga a month later Captain Persifor Frazer of the Fourth Pennsylvania Battalion, unburdening himself to his wife, described the Yankee regiments as composed in part by "the strangest mixture of Negroes, Indians, and whites, with old men and mere children, which together with a nasty lousy appearance make a most shocking spectacle." Such troops were "sufficient to make one sick of the service."[16] Writing in similar vein in late July 1777 from Saratoga, soon to be the site of the great victory over John Burgoyne, General Philip Schuyler complained of the soldiers that had been furnished him. One-third of "the few that had been sent" were boys, old men or Negroes. The last named, continued Schuyler, "disgrace our arms." "Is it consistent with the Sons of Freedom," he asked, "to trust their all to be defended by slaves?"[17] General William Heath, in reply to an inquiry about the Massachusetts troops with the Northern army, commented that among them were "some men advanc'd in life, and some lads, and a number of negroes." The last named were generally able-bodied, wrote Heath, but he confessed that he was not pleased to see them mixed with whites.[18]

14. "Return of the Negroes in the Army, 24th Augt, 1778," Washington Papers, LXXXII (unpaged, unnumbered, but in chronological sequence in volume entitled "1778, Aug. 17-30").

15. Alexander Graydon, Memoirs of a Life (Harrisburg, 1811), 131.

16. "Some Extracts from the Papers of General Persifor Frazer," Pa. Mag. of Hist. and Biog., 31 (1907), 134.

17. Schuyler to Heath, July 28, 1777, Heath Papers, Mass. Hist. Soc., Coll., 7th Ser., 4 (1904), 135-36. See also Schuyler to Washington, July 14, 1777, Sparks, ed., Letters to Washington, I, 398.

18. Heath to Samuel Adams, Aug. 27, 1777, Heath Papers, Mass. Hist. Soc., Coll., 7th Ser., 4 (1904), 148.

The New England states, despite their relatively small Negro population, probably furnished more colored soldiers than any other section. In central Massachusetts in 1777 an observer reported that he ran across no regiment without "a lot of Negroes."[19] In Connecticut practically no town of any size failed to supply one or more Negroes for the Continental forces. Ten of Stratford's 114 soldiers were colored, as were 13 of Wallington's 132.[20] The Rhode Island First Regiment enrolled some two hundred Negroes.[21]

One of this last regiment's enlistees, Jack Sisson, had previously come to public attention by taking part in the daring capture of General Richard Prescott on July 10, 1777, at the General's headquarters near Newport. Sisson was one of nearly 40 volunteers, led by Colonel William Barton, who quietly threaded their way through waters patrolled by British guard boats. Arriving at Prescott's headquarters they first hoodwinked and then disarmed the sentinel and thereupon seized the astonished Prescott, hurrying him off only half dressed. Sisson, who steered one of the boats, was credited with breaking down Prescott's chamber door by thrusting his head against it.[22] This remarkable feat of taking a high ranking officer without the loss of a man or the discharge of a gun "elated the Army much," and delighted Americans in general.[23]

19. Lee N. Newcomer, *The Embattled Farmers: A Massachusetts Countryside in the American Revolution* (New York, 1953), 106.

20. "Lists and Returns of Connecticut Men in the Revolution, 1775-1783," Conn. Hist. Soc., *Coll.*, 12 (1909), 58, 59-60.

21. Lorenzo J. Greene, a student of this regiment, estimates that it enrolled from 225 to 250 Negroes. "Some Observations on the Black Regiment of Rhode Island in the American Revolution," *Journal of Negro History,* 27 (1952), 165. Greene's estimate seems sound. An official muster roll of each company taken during the five weeks from January 6, 1780, to February 10, 1780, lists a combined total of 152 privates. Benjamin Cowell, *Spirit of '76 in Rhode Island* (Boston, 1850), 186-89. It is logical to suppose that 75 additional Negroes served in these companies prior to and after the dates when these muster rolls were taken.

22. *Pennsylvania Evening Post* (Phila.), Aug. 7, 1777.

23. George Weedon to Arthur Lee, July 18, 1777, Lee Papers, Houghton Library, Harvard University. For this incident see J. Lewis Diman, "The Capture of Prescott," *R. I. Hist. Tracts,* No. 1 (1877), 11-44. Barton left a manuscript account of his own, "A Narrative of the Particulars relative to the capture of Major General Prescott, and his aide-de-camp, Major Barrington." Rhode Island Historical Society (Providence), Manuscripts, vol. III. That Prescott was seized only half clad gave rise to merriment on both sides of the Atlantic. J. Lewis Diman, "Ballads and Poetry of the

Outside New England the state which recruited most Negroes was Virginia.[24] Many of the men which the state drafted in the autumn of 1777 were free Negroes—"as it was thought that they could best be spared," wrote Governor Nelson to General Washington. With the principle of Negro expendability the Governor had no quarrel, but he thought it unjust to these black soldiers that "after they have risked their lives & perhaps may have contributed to save America, [they] will not be entitled to the priviledges of Freemen."[25]

* * *

The typical Negro soldier was a private, consigned as if by caste, to the rank and file. Even more than other privates, he tended to lack identity. Often he bore no specific name; he was carried on the rolls as "A Negro Man," or "Negor by Name," or "A Negro name not known," or "Negro Name unknown."[26] Rarely did he serve in the small corps of American cavalry. Free Negro John Banks of Goochland County, Virginia, saw two years of service as a cavalryman in Theodorick Bland's regiment, but Banks's case was exceptional.[27] The mounted service tended to be made up of men of property and reputation, and the Negro enlistee, as a rule, had neither.

A small number of Negroes saw service in the brigade of artillery regiments. One of these, Edward Hector, of the Third Pennsylvania Artillery, took part in the Battle of Brandywine

---

Capture of Prescott," *R. I. Hist. Tracts,* No. 1 (1877), 49 and following. One piece of doggerel has these stanzas:

But to get in they had no means
Except poor Cuffee's head,
Who beat the door down then rush'd in
And seized him in his bed.

Stop! let me put my breeches on
The general then did pray:
"Your breeches, massa, I will take,
For dress we cannot stay."

Samuel E. Barney, *Songs of the Revolution* (New Haven, 1893), 41-42.

24. The number of Virginia Negroes in the land and sea forces may have gone "beyond the five hundred mark," writes a careful investigator. Jackson, *Va. Negro Soldiers and Sailors,* vi.

25. Thomas Nelson, Jr., to George Washington, Nov. 21, 1777, Washington Papers, LXI, No. 7324 A&B.

26. "Lists and Returns of Connecticut Men in the Revolution, 1775-1783," Conn. Hist. Soc., *Coll.,* 12 (1909), 59, 80, 81, 138.

27. Jackson, *Va. Negro Soldiers and Sailors,* 29.

in September 1777. When the American army was pulled back, Hector disobeyed the order to abandon wagons. Making use of arms left on the field by fleeing soldiers, he protected his horses and his ammunition wagon, bringing them safely in. Fifty years later the Pennsylvania legislature gave him a $40.00 donation.[28]

Another Negro artilleryman who was belatedly rewarded by a state legislature was Austin Dabney of Burke County, Georgia. A former slave, Dabney was freed in order to enlist as his master's substitute. Dabney served in Colonel Elijah Clark's artillery corps and sustained a broken thigh at the Battle of Kettle Creek early in 1779. Forty years later the Georgia assembly passed an act for Dabney's relief, voting him 112 acres of land in recognition, somewhat tardily, of the "bravery and fortitude" he showed "in several engagements and actions" against the enemy.[29]

Unlike Dabney, the typical Negro served with the infantry. Often he was a non-arms-bearing infantryman, detailed for duty as an orderly or assigned to functions in support of combat operations. During the attempted seizure of Charleston in June 1776, one of the twelve fatalities in the second infantry regiment commanded by Colonel William Moultrie was "A Mullatto waiting boy." A return of the First South Carolina Regiment's prisoners of war at Haddrell's Point on November 10, 1780, lists ten Negroes as servants. When Colonel Peter Horry made a trip from Georgetown to Black Mingo early in April 1782 he took "one Dragon to wait on me," since "my negro man is at Santee."[30] Colored private John Harris of Dinwiddie, after seeing service in two Virginia regiments and taking part in

28. William Summers, "Obituary Notices of Pennsylvania Soldiers of the Revolution," *Pa. Mag. of Hist. and Biog.*, 38 (1914), 444.

29. Lucian Lamar Knight, *Georgia's Roster of the Revolution* (Atlanta, 1920), 65; *Acts of the General Assembly of the State of Georgia passed at Milledgeville, at an Extra Session in April and May 1821* (Milledgeville, 1821), 20-21. For information on Dabney, I am indebted to Edward P. Sweat. For a sketch of Dabney, see Sweat's "Social Status of the Free Negro in Antebellum Georgia," *Negro History Bull.*, 21 (1958), 131: also George W. Gilmer, *Sketches of the First Settlers of Upper Georgia* (New York, 1855), 212-13.

30. John Drayton, *Memoirs of the American Revolution*, 2 vols. (Charleston, 1821), I, 326; "A Return of the First South Carolina Regiment at Haddrell's Point, November 10, 1780," *S. C. Hist. and Gen. Mag.*, 7 (1906), 21; Horry to Francis Marion, Apr. 1, 1782, Gibbes, *Doc. Hist. of Amer. Rev.*, III, 286.

the fighting at Monmouth, was made orderly to young Major James Monroe,[31] later the fifth president of the United States. Upon his retirement from the service in 1782, General John Glover took with him to Marblehead his orderlies, Boston Black and Myron Wilson, despite the "pointed applications" of the commander-in-chief that the two Negroes remain in the Continental line.[32]

One of the few Negro body servants to emerge from the shadows was Jordon Freeman, who lost his life at the Battle of Groton Heights on September 6, 1781, in one of the war's most tragic incidents. This action took place when the British, attempting to delay Washington's impending encirclement of Cornwallis at Yorktown, sent a diversionary force under Benedict Arnold to seize the Connecticut port of New London. Led by Colonel William Ledyard, for whom Freeman was orderly, the town's defenders drew back to Fort Griswold on the Groton side of the Thames. The British suffered such heavy casualties that when the heavily out-manned Americans finally laid down their arms, the victors were in no mood to show mercy. Ledyard was stabbed with the sword he offered to a British officer, and this act was followed by the bayoneting and shooting of the surrendered men. One of the slain was Jordan Freeman; according to eye-witness George Middleton, Freeman was one of the two men responsible for the fatal spearing of British officer William Montgomery in the hand-to-hand fighting that ensued when the fort's walls were scaled. Another Negro killed on the American side was Lambo Latham, who was neither a member of the militia nor a Continental soldier, but an on-the-spot volunteer. Latham had insisted on following his employer, Captain William Latham, into Fort Griswold, where, according to Latham family tradition, Lambo "fought manfully by his master's side."[33]

31. Jackson, *Va. Negro Soldiers and Sailors*, 36.
32. Washington to Glover, Sept. 23, 1782, and Washington to Heath, Jan. 15, 1783, Fitzpatrick, ed., *Writings of Washington*, XXV, 197, and XXVI, 37. For information about Black and Wilson, I am indebted to "Notes on Negroes in Glover's Command," a communication sent to me from Professor George Billias, the authority on Glover.
33. Charles Allyn, *The Battle of Groton Heights* (New London, Conn., 1882), 91-92, 242. This book is a collection of contemporary accounts, American and British, of the storming of Fort Griswold. See also Frances Manwaring Caulkins, *The Stone Records of Groton* (Norwich, Conn., 1903).

Other than orderly duties, Negro soldiers were often assigned to such semi-domestic occupations as those of waiter and cook. In the tenth Pennsylvania infantry regiment, colored Levi Burns was listed as a waiter. James Coopers, a free Negro from Goochland County, fought as a soldier in the Second Virginia Regiment but also doubled as a waiter to its colonel.[34] On July 5, 1778, this general order was issued from Fort Arnold at West Point: "If there is any Negro man in the Levies . . . who understands cooking & can be well recommended, 'tis desired that he may be sent to Gen[l] Glover's Quarters."[35]

A typical assignment of Negro soldiers was that of drummer. In Captain Rufus Lincoln's company of the Seventh Massachusetts Regiment the drummer was Jabez Jolly of Barnstable, who, young as were drummers generally, was either eighteen or nineteen when he enlisted on December 9, 1779. William Nickens, who came from a Northern Neck, Virginia, family which furnished nine brothers and cousins for war service, served as a drummer for "three or four years."[36] In South Carolina a payroll of Captain Samuel Wise's First Company of Rangers for the month of September 1775 lists "Negro Bob (drummer)."[37]

American soldiers generally disliked assignment to the wagon, commissary or forage services, hence it was not unusual for Negroes to find themselves enrolled in these departments.[38] At Ticonderoga in June 1777 the quartermaster general, Udney Hay, took Negroes from each regiment and formed them into a detail of "constant fatiguemen." Within a few weeks after it had been recruited, the First Rhode Island Regiment had something else to do besides learning the manual of arms; "I

34. "Journals and Diaries of the War of the Revolution with Lists of Officers and Soldiers, 1775-1783," Samuel Hazard, et al., eds., *Pennsylvania Archives*, 138 vols., 2nd Ser., 15 (Harrisburg, 1893), 496. Hereafter cited as *Pa. Arch.* Jackson, *Va. Negro Soldiers and Sailors*, 33.

35. John Glover, Letters and Orderly Books, 1776-1781, transcripts, N. Y. Pub. Lib.

36. James M. Lincoln, ed., *The Papers of Captain Rufus Lincoln* (Cambridge, 1903), 199; Jackson, *Va. Negro Soldiers and Sailors*, 27. For a sketch of the Nickens family see *ibid.*, 24-28.

37. "Papers of the First Council of Safety of the Revolutionary Party in South Carolina, June—November, 1775," *S. C. Hist. and Gen. Mag.*, 2 (1901), 168.

38. Many of New Jersey's Negro soldiers were assigned to teamster brigades. William S. Stryker, *Official Register of the Officers and Men of New Jersey in the Revolutionary War* (Trenton, 1872), 858, 860, 861, 869.

sent Maj^r Ward with all the Blacks but 15 to Warwick Making fascines," wrote Colonel Greene on July 28, 1778.[39]

* * *

If the Negro soldier felt himself an object of discrimination, it does not seem to have been reflected in his behavior. To be a soldier, with all its discomforts and dangers, was likely to be a step forward, as the Negro saw it. His morale was not likely to be below average. A former slave or low-paid town laborer, he was likely to be inured to the multiple hardships and privations of army life. Negroes made the best of inferior materials and short supplies, it seems, "and were cheerful under difficulties." Baron von Closen, who visited White Plains headquarters on July 4, 1781, noted that the Negroes, a quarter of the army there assembled, were merry and confident.[40]

The Negro soldier was seldom beset by conflicts of interest. With fewer reasons for clinging to civilian life, he was less given to summoning up the excuses which a vexed chief of artillery heard so often: "my business will not permit me to go,"—"my wife expects to lye in,"—"I shall lose a very good bargain."[41] Another factor making for a Negro's acceptance of a soldier's lot was his resignation to a long period of service. As a rule, the colored man at arms did not have to face one of the greatest menaces to morale—the short term enlistment.[42] A short-termer often fretted from the day he entered the service until the day he was discharged; this longing to be mustered out was not nearly so prevalent among the Continental soldiers. In a register, dated August 1782, of the noncommissioned officers and privates of Captain Lincoln's Seventh Massachusetts Regiment who were entitled to honorary badges for length of terms in service, a Bristol County Negro, Cesar Perry, ranked

39. "The Trial of Major General St. Clair, August, 1778," N.-Y. Hist. Soc., *Coll.*, Publication Fund, 13 (1881), 109; Christopher Greene to John Sullivan, July 28, 1778, Otis G. Hammond, ed., *Letters and Papers of Major-General John Sullivan*, 3 vols. (Concord, N. H., 1930-39), II, 136.

40. Henry Belcher, *The First American Civil War, 1775-1778*, 2 vols. (New York, 1811), II; Evelyn M. Acomb, ed., *The Revolutionary Journal of Baron Ludwig von Closen, 1780-1783* (Chapel Hill, 1958), 89.

41. Henry Knox to Henry Jackson, Aug. 20, 1777, "Historical Manuscripts from the Public Library of the City of Boston," *More Books*, 2nd Ser., 7 (1902), 463.

42. Allen Bowman, *The Morale of the American Revolutionary Army* (Washington, 1943), 48-50.

first.[43] Many of the colored soldiers of the First Rhode Island Regiment saw service for five consecutive years.[44] Such a long period of enlistment was not uncommon among black arms-bearers.

One of the notorious features of the American military service was the high incidence of unofficial absence; one-third of the regular troops deserted at one time or another. Negroes were sometimes included among those who ran away. A return of deserters at Ticonderoga on June 9, 1777, listed a mulatto, Israel Newport. The slave, Fisherman, enlisted in a Rhode Island regiment by his master, lost no time in going over to the British. A list of fifteen deserters in Virginia in May 1779 included Charles Valentine of Surry, described as long in stature and one "who talks very smooth and is very merry when a little in liquor."[45] But Negroes were less inclined than white soldiers to walk off without official leave. They were not likely to have a farm that needed protection nor the kind of home that inspired homesickness. They had less to desert to.

Perhaps the factor which contributed most to sustaining the slave's morale was his motivation. Service in the American army was for him a way of gaining freedom. That freedom was a compelling inducement to those in bondage was a commonplace. Alexander Hamilton declared a recognized truth when he pointed out that giving slaves their liberty would win their loyalty and animate their courage. Nathanael Greene believed it would be pointless even to hire Negro laborers for the army unless they could be offered such terms as would engage their fidelity. Conversely, Washington opposed using slaves as teamsters since they were too prone to run away to the enemy, taking their horses with them.[46] Summing up the case for giving a slave his freedom upon enlistment, a Boston editor observed: "Our non-emancipated soldiers are irresistibly

43. Lincoln, *Papers of Captain Rufus Lincoln*, 144.

44. Greene, "The Black Regiment of Rhode Island," *Journal of Negro History*, 27 (1952), 170.

45. Bowman, *Morale of the Revolutionary Army*, 72; *Boston Gazette*, June 23, 1777; Rider, "The Black 'Regiment,'" *R. I. Hist. Tracts*, 1st Ser., No. 10 (1880), 57; *Va. Gaz.*, May 1, 1779.

46. Hamilton to John Jay, Mar. 14, 1779, Lodge, ed., *Works of Hamilton*, VII, 566; Greene to Mathews, Feb. 11, 1782, Greene MSS, Clements Lib.; Washington to the Committee of Congress with the Army, Jan. 28, 1778, Fitzpatrick, ed., *Writings of Washington*, X, 401.

tempted to defect to our foes."[47]   It was obvious that the best
way to prevent the Negro from going over to the British was
to give him sufficient inducement to fight for America.

The slave's motivation was unmistakable, but what brought
free Negroes into the army? In some cases they were drafted.
A Virginia Negro, John Harris, managed to quit military service after 1780 by supplying a substitute—a highly exceptional
case, since most free Negroes could not afford to pay someone
to do their fighting.[48] The free Negro who enlisted of his own
volition, however, was probably inspired by a complex of motives—a desire for adventure, a conviction of the justice of
America's cause, a belief in the high-sounding goals of the Revolution, but also the prospect of receiving a bounty. Money gifts
were generously given (or promised) to those who joined the
army. In the later years of the war, when most of the Negroes
were recruited, the badly depreciated currency bonuses were
superseded by land grants as soldier bait. A grant of 100 acres
to a private, such as Virginia gave, was a tempting offer in a
region where land determined one's social status no less than
his economic well-being.

*   *   *

Since Negro soldiers fought side by side with whites, rather
than in separate organizations, there was no battle in which
black Americans were conspicuous as a racial group. Perhaps
the Battle of Rhode Island in August 1778—the only engagement in that state between the British and the Americans—comes
nearest to being an engagement in which Negroes were distinctive as a group. But even in this instance Colonel Greene's
First Regiment, composed of Negroes, was but a fraction of
one of the six brigades which, aside from a corps of light troops,
made up General John Sullivan's forces.

The battle was in essence a skillfully executed retreat from
the northern end of the island of Rhode Island. The withdrawal
was necessary because a terrific sea storm had battered a French
squadron, under the Count d'Estaing, which had undertaken
to cooperate with the Americans. When the commanding officer,
John Sullivan, learned that no French aid was forthcoming and
that the British forces on the island were about to be heavily re-

47. *Boston Gazette,* Oct. 13, 1777.
48. Jackson, *Va. Negro Soldiers and Sailors,* 36.

enforced, he ordered a retreat to the mainland. Thereupon the British launched a general attack aimed at preventing the withdrawal so that British warships, then en route, could cut the Americans off. Colonel Greene's regiment with some 125 colored soldiers, of whom over 30 were free Negroes,[49] held one of the positions assaulted by the British-Hessian forces. When the enemy made three spirited charges against the American right wing, the First Regiment, ably led by Major Samuel Ward, held the ground in its sector. Meeting "a more stubborn resistance than they expected,"[50] the Hessians suffered heavy casualties. Knowing that a large majority of the men of the First Regiment were little more than raw recruits, having been in the army only three months, the British command doubtless expected that this unit would show weakness and yield, thus exposing a soft spot in the American defense. If this was the plan, it was a costly miscalculation. In nearly four hours of hard fighting, the colored soldiers held as firmly as the other patriot troops.

The upshot was a retreat in which the whole army and its equipment was brought safely to the mainland. The American forces sustained only 211 casualties, scarcely more than a fifth of those incurred by the enemy. Of the American casualties Greene's regiment had a total of 22, of which 2 were killed, 9 wounded, and 11 missing. None of the wounded was seriously injured.[51]

Many flattering phrases were lavished on Sullivan for the masterly executed withdrawal. Congress gave him a vote of thanks, as did Rhode Island and his home state, New Hampshire. In turn, Sullivan said some generous things about his troops and their officers. In the general chorus of praise the predominantly colored unit was not left out. The First Regi-

49. A "Return of Freemen enlisted for during the War, in 1st Rhode Island Battalion, Commanded by Col. Greene," lists 33 free Negroes. (Rhode Island Historical Society, Military Papers, IV.) The return is undated but was probably made in the summer of 1778.

50. Max von Eelking, "Military Operations in Rhode Island," R. I. Hist. Tracts, No. 6 (1878), 60.

51. "Return of Killed, Wounded and Missing in the Army of Sullivan in action of August 29, 1778," Washington Papers, LXXXII (in volume entitled, "1778, Aug. 17-30"); Samuel Ward to unspecified person, Aug. 30, 1778, John Ward, A Memoir of Lieut.-Colonel Samuel Ward (New York, 1875), 13.

ment, said Sullivan in orders issued on August 30, would be entitled to a proper share of the day's honors.[52]

Aside from the participation of the First Regiment in the Battle of Rhode Island, the only action in which a Negro unit was identifiable as such was the unsuccessful siege of Savannah in the autumn of 1779. A number of blacks and mulattoes made up part of the French troops under the Count d'Estaing. Conveyed by a mighty armada, the French had come to join forces with the Americans in an attempt to regain Savannah, held by the British since December of the preceding year. Sailing from the West Indies in mid-August, the French fleet had anchored off Savannah on September 1, and had landed on the Georgia coast ten days later.

D'Estaing's army, some 3,600 strong, included 545 Negroes recently raised at Santo Domingo and officially designated as "Volunteer Chasseurs." Numbered among these were future leaders in the revolt that brought Santo Domingo her independence at the turn of the century. Perhaps the youngest member of the entire expedition was Henri Christophe, who one day would become King of Haiti, but was then a bootblack and messboy, not yet out of his teens.

The French-American allies at first decided upon siege operations, but after supplies began to grow short and the scurvy and dysentery lists began to mount, D'Estaing decided to attack on October 9. Forewarned by informers, the British were ready. They rained such devastating fire on the allies that D'Estaing had no alternative except retreat. The British came out of their entrenchments, bent upon a rout of the allies. But the British counterattack was contained when the allied rear guard prevented any breakthrough; among the reserve corps which held the British was the black unit from Santo Domingo.[53]

The twice-wounded D'Estaing, his forces battered at Savannah as they had been storm-tossed off Rhode Island, was not disposed to tarry any longer in American waters. He decided to lift the siege and re-embark. With the departing French fleet went the "Volunteer Chasseurs," their role in the American Revolution ended.   *   *   *

52. "Extracts from Orderly Book of the Massachusetts Regiment Under the Command of Colonel John Jacobs," in "The Centennial Celebration of the Battle of Rhode Island," *R. I. Hist. Tracts,* No. 6 (1878), 114.

53. For the story of the siege see Alexander A. Lawrence, *Storm Over Savannah* (Athens, Georgia, 1951).

Action on land was not the only fighting contribution of Negro Americans. From the birth of the Revolutionary navy they were employed in naval service. Three colored men were aboard the *Cabot* and the *Andrea Doria* when these brigs made their maiden voyages as two of the first four merchantmen purchased and fitted out by the Naval Committee of the Continental Congress. On the *Cabot's* crew were Surriname Wanton and Loushir, and the *Andrea Doria's* crew listed Dragon Wanton, all three bondmen of Esek Hopkins, the naval commander-in-chief. When the *Cabot* captured a British merchant ship, *True Blue*, in June 1776, Hopkins received £120 in prize money "for his Two Negro's share." Hopkins kept a close check on the third of his seafaring slaves, sending word in November 1776 to the *Andrea Doria's* captain Nicholas Biddle, that he could either retain Dragon Wanton as a member of the crew or discharge him.[54]

The use of Negroes in ships of the Continental navy and on other American ships of war—those of the state navies, those operated by the army, as well as the hundreds of privateers commissioned by Congress—was inevitable in view of manpower shortages. Navy recruiting officers were even less in a position to pick and choose men than their counterparts in the army. Thus many navy vessels had to put to sea dangerously shorthanded even after they had signed on green men, foreigners, English prisoners, and boys in their lower teens. Under such circumstances few ship officers were likely to draw the color line.

The use of Negro sailors was easily accepted because there was nothing novel about it. The waterways of the Atlantic coast bred black seafaring men as well as white. From the earliest times Negroes had been signed aboard fishing fleets or employed on coastal vessels that ranged the bays and rivers of the seaboard. Colored seamen were a common sight in colonial America: "Many took service on merchant ships or ships of the royal navy," writes Charles M. Andrews.[55] Some of the Negroes

54. "Commodore of the Fleet, in Acct. Current with Daniel Tillinghast, Continental Agent, Cr." pt. 3, 213, Esek Hopkins Papers, Navy Department Records Division, National Archives, Washington, D. C.; Hopkins to William Ellery, Nov. 28, 1776, Letter Book of Esek Hopkins, *ibid.*

55. Charles M. Andrews, *The Colonial Period of American History*, 4 vols. (New Haven, 1934-38), IV, 83.

who wound up in the royal navy had originally been crew members of ships which British war vessels had seized while enforcing the Navigation Acts. Even in colonial times service at sea opened to many a slave the door to emancipation. Jeremy Belknap held an opinion that in Massachusetts the number of slaves had declined by 1763 "because in the two preceding wars, many of them were enlisted either into the army or on board vessels of war, with a view to procure their freedom."[56]

* * *

With its chronic shortage of sailors, the half a hundred ships of the Continental navy made use of whatever Negroes they could get. Many of these black seamen were free-born inhabitants of New England waterway towns—men such as Cato Carlile and Scipio Africanus who in 1777 were enlisted from a Piscataqua River port for service under Captain John Paul Jones.[57] Many, on the other hand, were slaves. As in the military arm, freedom was not a precondition for enlistment; if one happened to be a slave this in itself did not preclude his enlistment. A bondman might be brought into the service by his naval officer owner; the cabin boys on the twenty-gun sloop *Ranger* were former slaves of Captain Jones.[58]

American naval officers showed no reluctance to make use of Negroes who had previously seen service with the royal navy. In October 1779 Abraham Whipple, commander of the Continental frigate *Providence,* asked the Massachusetts Council to turn over to him Negro John Onion and Indian William Bartlett, both of whom were then on board a prison ship in the Boston harbor, having been captured while crewmen aboard a British vessel. Whipple reasoned that as these men had fought against America they should, "when in our hands," be obliged to fight for her. The Massachusetts Council was in a complaisant mood toward a commander who two months earlier had, in a single haul, brought into the Boston harbor eight East India-men laden with rum and sugar, a capture appraised at

56. "Judge Tucker's Queries Respecting Slavery. . . ," Mass. Hist. Soc., *Coll.,* 5th Ser., 4 (1795), 199.
57. Samuel E. Morison, *John Paul Jones* (Boston, 1959), 114.
58. Augustus C. Buell, *Paul Jones, Founder of the American Navy,* 2 vols. (New York, 1900), II, 341.

over a million dollars. The Council directed the state commissary of prisoners to enlist Onion and Bartlett on the *Providence,* provided that they were willing.[59]

On another occasion the Massachusetts Council declared free a Negro, David Mitchell, who had been captured on a British sloop. Brought a prisoner into Newburyport, he had then taken service on the Continental war vessel, *Alliance.* Originally from Bermuda, Mitchell had enlisted on the *Alliance* because he had decided he would like to stay in the United States. He thereupon petitioned the Council to grant him the status of a prisoner of war and give him his freedom because he had joined the American navy. This the Council did.[60]

The Negro in the Continental navy usually served in the lowliest rank and occupations. Not uncommon was the colored semi-servant, such as Britain, a "captain's boy" on the *Alfred,* first vessel to fly the Continental flag. Some Negroes carried powder to the guns; among such powder boys were Scipio Brown and Caesar Fairweather, who handled the ammunition in the main and fore hatchways of the frigate *Boston* when she pulled out of a Massachusetts port in May 1777 "bound out on a Cruse by God's parmission."[61] The *Boston's* roster shows, however, that the Negro sometimes advanced to higher positions; Cuff Freeman was on the larboard watch and Cato Austin operated the number one gun on the starboard watch. A year later the *Boston* was carrying John Fyds as a "Negro seaman" with wages of £48 a month.[62] Sometimes the records show that Negroes served on a vessel but not in what capacity. Such is the case in an entry in the logbook of the *Ranger* as it lay off the Charleston harbor on February 25, 1780: "at ten this Night a Negro Called Cesar Hodgsdon died."[63]

59. Whipple to Council, and Council to Joseph Anderson, Oct. 14, 1779, Revolutionary Rolls Coll., CLXXV, No. 634, Mass. Arch.

60. Mitchell to the Council, Aug. 13, 1778, *ibid.,* CLXIX, Nos. 77, 79, Mass. Arch.

61. "A Roll of all of the Officers and Men of the *Alfred* until September 5, 1776," R. I. Hist. Soc., Military Papers, V; "A Journal of the Intended Cruse in the Good Ship Boston," in Gardner W. Allen, "Captain Hector McNeill, Continental Navy," Mass. Hist. Soc., *Proc.,* 3rd Ser., 55 (1923), 90.

62. *Ibid.,* 85, 86; John H. Sheppard, *The Life of Samuel Tucker* (Boston, 1868), 346.

63. Logbook of the United States Ship of War *Ranger,* 235, Navy Department, National Archives.

In the competition for the services of seamen the Continental navy was no match for the separate state navies. In the latter the period of enlistment was likely to be shorter, and the range of operations was often limited to the state's own seaports and coast. A state navy, too, was likely to give to a ship's crew a larger share of the prize money from seizures of enemy vessels. The northern states used whatever Negro seamen they could get. Like the Continental Congress, the Massachusetts Council did not scruple to enlist captive Negro sailors. On May 18, 1779, the Council directed the commander of the brig *Active* to sign on five Negroes who had lately been taken from the British. Then held at Plymouth, these Negroes had indicated their willingness to serve on the state's vessels. On the same day the Council directed the commissary of prisoners to release Negro Jack from the guard ship in Boston provided that he was willing to become a sailor for Massachusetts.[64]

Negroes serving in the navies of the Northern states held a variety of jobs. Commonest of these was that of seaman, with no specification as to the kind of seaman. The frigate *Protector,* largest vessel in the Massachusetts navy, carried two colored seamen in March 1780, one of whom died four months later.[65] Pennsylvania and Connecticut also employed Negroes in the rank of seamen, John Pompey serving on the armed boat *Burke* in August 1776, and George serving on Connecticut's brig *Defence* during the same year.[66] Pennsylvania used Negroes as marines,[67] as did Connecticut. When the Connecticut state brigantine *Minerva* was fitted out in August 1775 she took on two Negro marines, Peter and Gist. Five Negro marines were aboard the largest vessel of the state navy, the *Oliver Cromwell,* in 1777 and 1778 when she made her successful cruises off the Lesser Antilles and the Azores in quest of British vessels bound to and from the West Indies. Their presence brought forth a comment from a historian of a later day, Thomas S. Collier: "It thus appears that negroes enlisted and served in consider-

64. Revolutionary Rolls Coll., CLXX, No. 121, Mass. Arch.
65. *Mass. Soldiers and Sailors,* XII, 885.
66. "Officers and Men of the Pennsylvania Navy," *Pa. Arch.,* 2nd Ser., I (1874), 257; James L. Howard, *Seth Harding, Mariner* (New Haven, 1930), 200.
67. "Officers and Men of the Pennsylvania Navy," *Pa. Arch.,* 2nd Ser., I (1874), 296.

able quantities during the Revolution, for five privates in one marine guard is certainly a marked example."[68]

The navies of the Chesapeake Bay states, Maryland and Virginia, frequently used Negroes as pilots. Since the naval vessels of these states operated almost wholly in bay and river waters, they were primarily small craft. Even before the war such inshore boats had often been constructed by Negroes and piloted by them. Hence many Negroes who grew up in the counties lying on the bay or its tributaries had become skillful in the navigation of these waters.

Maryland employed some of these black pilots. In April 1777 the state hired Dick to take the *Lydia* from St. Mary's to Alexandria, paying him £8 for the service.[69] Two months earlier Stephen Steward of West River sent to the Maryland Council two slave-piloted boats to be used as transports. Steward asked the Council to take good care of his "two sailor negroes" since they were "as fine fellows as ever crost the sea." Later another West River master, David Weems, sent to the Council a schooner which had a "Negro Skiper as no whit man would go."[70]

Virginia made the most extensive use of Negro pilots. Her reasons were stated by Thomas Anderson, state commissioner of provisions. Negroes could be hired cheaper than whites; they could be used as substitutes by "those who propose to put in a Negro and get exemption from military duty," and they were "accustomed to the navigation of the River."[71]

Best known by far of the pilots in the Virginia service was Caesar, the slave of Carter Tarrant of Hampton. He entered "very early into the service of his country, and continued to pilot the armed vessels of this state during the . . . war." During the course of his long service, boats he piloted had their share of engagements with the enemy. In one of these encounters

68. Louis F. Middlebrook, *History of Maritime Connecticut during the American Revolution, 1775-1783*, 2 vols. (Salem, Mass., 1925), I, 26; Thomas S. Collier, "The Revolutionary Privateers of Connecticut," New London Historical Society, *Records and Papers*, 1, pt. 4, (New London 1892), 44.

69. "Accounts of Sundry Vessels," Revolutionary Papers, Box 2, fol. 3, Hall of Records, Annapolis, Md.

70. Stephen Steward to Council, Feb. 11, 1777, Mar. 7, 1781, *Arch. of Md.*, XVI, 130, XLVII, 111.

71. Anderson to William Davies, Aug. 26, 1781, *Cal. of Va. State Papers*, II, 362.

Caesar "behaved gallantly" while steering the schooner *Patriot*. On another occasion he was at the wheel when the *Patriot* captured the *Fanny*, a brig carrying stores and supplies for the British troops. For his wartime efforts Caesar was set free in November 1789, the legislature voting to purchase him from his owner. Many years after his death his daughter Nancy received 2,667 acres of land in Ohio for her father's service in the war.[72]

Two of Virginia's Negro pilots lost their lives in naval service. Cuffee, a slave owned by naval lieutenant William Graves, died in 1781 of wounds received while at the wheel of a vessel commanded by Richard Barron. Another slave, Minny, volunteered as a pilot in the spring of 1776 when an enemy supply ship ravaged the Rappahannock. Minny met his death attempting to board the "piratical tender." According to an official statement, Minny "bravely and successfully exerted himself against the enemy, until he was unfortunately killed." The grateful state voted the sum of $100 to his owner.[73]

The Virginia navy had other slaves who, like Minny, were commended for their service. Harry and Cupid were on the schooner *Liberty* during more than twenty sharp actions. Harry was "distinguished for his zeal and daring," and Cupid "discharged all his duties with a fidelity that made him a favorite of all of the officers."[74] So wrote James Barron who during the Revolutionary War was the teen-age midshipman son of a commodore in the Virginia navy, and who later became a commodore in the United States navy and its senior officer. Such devotion to the Virginia navy as that of Harry and Cupid was by no means matched by all its colored seamen. Indeed, some were deserters like Augustine Boyd of Wicomico Parish in Northumberland County who, in the summer of 1779, was advertised as being among the missing.[75]

Numerous blacks of varying skills and capacities performed a range of functions in the Virginia navy. Besides anonymous Negroes whom the state employed as dock laborers and steve-

72. Hening, ed., *Statutes of Va.*, XIII, 102; Jackson, *Va. Negro Soldiers and Sailors*, 22.
73. *Ibid.*, 33-34; *Proceedings of the Convention of Delegates in the Colony of Virginia*, 49, 77.
74. "J. B.," "The Schooner Liberty," *Va. Hist. Reg.*, 1 (1848), 80.
75. Robert A. Stewart, *A History of Virginia's Navy of the Revolution* (Richmond, 1934), 154.

dores, an official return lists them as seamen, ordinary seamen, able seamen, and sailors.[76] The total number serving in the fleet probably reached at least 140, since it is a fair estimate that the state's seventy vessels carried an average of two colored men apiece. The *Dragon,* for example, had at one time or another ten Negroes, one of whom was John De Baptist from Spotsylvania, whose son and grandsons would serve respectively in the War of 1812 and the Civil War.[77] The galley *Hero* had six Negroes serving at the same time. One of the state vessels at Turkey Island in the James on March 22, 1781, had five Negroes aboard. A "Return of Spirit" for the *Tempest,* dated December 7, 1779, indicated that among those receiving the whiskey ration were George Negro, Charles Negro, Emmanuel Negro, and Negro James.[78]

Probably one out of every ten sailors of African descent in the Virginia navy was a free man, enlisting of his own accord. The remainder were slaves, many of whom were enlisted in the guise of free men as substitutes for their masters. Some were runaways; on one occasion the Navy Board ordered the captain of the sloop *Defiance* to release three slaves to their master, Anthony Lawson of Princess Anne County.[79] In her sea forces Virginia also used slaves which had been purchased by the Navy Board or other state agencies.

At war's end practically all the public Negroes were sold, but two of the *Cormorant's* colored sailors remained in service. In the fall of 1783, after Congress had given Virginia permission to retain two of her vessels in service, the state Council directed that William Bush and Jack Knight be employed on these ships. Thus for five years after the war these two state-owned Negroes saw service on one of Virginia's two revenue cutters. They

76. "A List of State Soldiers and Seamen who have received Certificates for the balance of there (*sic*) full pay. Agreeable to act of Assembly passed November Session, 1781," 31, 196, 215, 153, Manuscript, Virginia State Library, Richmond.

77. Jackson gives 68 by name. *Va. Negro Soldiers and Sailors,* 28-46, 34.

78. "Officers, Seamen and Vessels, State Navy, 1776-1779," 10, MS, Va. State Lib., Richmond; *Cal. of Va. State Papers,* I, 588; "Officers, Seamen and Vessels, State Navy, 1776-1779," 15, MS, Va. State Lib., Richmond.

79. Brumbaugh gives the names of the 10 free Negroes who enlisted. Gaius Marcus Brumbaugh, *Revolutionary War Records, Volume I: Virginia* (Washington, 1936), 70; Navy Board to Captain John Calvert, July 11, 1777, Letter Book of Navy Board, July 1776 to October 9, 1777, Va. State Lib., Richmond.

did not go unrewarded; after the two ships had been decommissioned in 1789, the legislature voted to free Bush and Knight as a reward for faithful service.[80]

To the Negroes who saw service in the Virginia fleet should be added those who worked ashore. The Navy Board hired slave sawyers, rope makers, and ship carpenters. Often they were hired by the day; an account of the "Negro hire for heaving down the Schooner Harrison," in July 1783 lists ten laborers as having been employed from one to three days apiece. Some slaves were hired by the month; owner Henry Brown, a well-known Presbyterian layman of Bedford County, received £3 a month for each of his three sawyers. One master, Thomas Newton of Norfolk, let as many as nine slaves out to hire at one time, among them a woman cook.[81]

* * *

The navy of South Carolina, second largest of the state navies in the South did not materially differ from Virginia in its use of Negroes. Black seamen were nothing new in South Carolina, having been employed since early colonial times; hence in time of war there was far less resistance to Negro sailors than to Negro soldiers. In the spring of 1778 the assembly authorized the hiring of men, white or black, to navigate and man the several pilot boats at Charleston, Stono Inlet, Georgetown, and Beaufort. If a Negro was a slave, his owner was to be paid; if a slave was killed or taken by the enemy, his owner would receive the compensation. Slave pilots were in particular demand; for this reason the Council continued to take out insurance on them after voting in July 1777 to stop insuring other slaves aboard state vessels.[82]

As in Virginia, the state's need for seamen cut across color considerations: "Endeavour by Every means in Your Power,"

80. McIlwaine and Hall, eds., *Journals of the Council of State of Virginia*, III, 300; Hening, ed., *Statutes of Va.*, XIII, 103. A pay roll of the state boat *Liberty* for July 15, 1785, lists the amount of pay for 10 members of the crew but it simply has a long line opposite the name of "William Bush, Public Negro." Brumbaugh, *Revolutionary War Records: Virginia*, 22.
81. Navy Account Book, 66, Va. State Lib., Richmond; see "Papers Concerning the State Navy," vols. I and II, *passim, ibid.*
82. A. S. Salley, Jr., ed., *Journal of the Commissioners of Navy of South Carolina, October 9, 1776-March 1, 1779* (Columbia, 1912), 97. Hereafter cited as Salley, ed., *Journ. of Com. of Navy, 1776-1779. Statutes at Large of South Carolina, 1752-1786* (Charleston, 1838), 432.

ran an order from the navy commissioners on September 14, 1779, "to Enlist Seamen and able bodied Negro Men to Serve on board the Rutledge Galley for Six Months." A few months later the lower house voted to employ a thousand Negroes, many of whom were to be oarsmen and mariners in the navy.[83]

For labor on the docks and in the state shipyards, the commissioners of the state navy hired Negroes and purchased slaves. In October 1776 the public boat keeper was ordered to hire Negroes "to cleanse the entrance at the Flood Gate," at Charleston, so that boats could be received there. A month later public boat keeper McCulley Righton was ordered to procure eight good Negro boatmen to be constantly employed under his supervision; he was given £100 a month to pay their wages. In April 1777 the commissioners agreed to use the following form in placing an advertisement in the *Gazette*: "The Commissioners of the Navy are in want of a Number of Negro ship Carpenters or Caulkers; any person having such to hire by the Year, are desired to apply to——."[84] Also, the navy of South Carolina had slaves of its own. In May 1777 the commissioners purchased Titus for £700, and a few weeks later bought Jack and Horace for use at the rope walk. In October 1778 the legislature authorized the commissioners to purchase slaves to work either in the public shipyard or at the rope walk. Navy-owned Negroes made up a portion of the 120 ship carpenters which the commissioners employed in and around Charleston in February 1779. Doubtless the Negro naval laborers were as well treated as any other employees, although in one instance the commissioners ordered that the white workmen on the job were to receive a pint of rum apiece whereas the Negroes were to receive only a gill.[85]

* * *

Just as the Continental navy tended to lose out to the state navies in the struggle for manpower, so the state navies tended to lose out to the privateers and vessels sailing under letters of marque. Service on the privateers had obvious attractions; the financial rewards were greater, the period of enlistment was much shorter, and no strict naval discipline was observed. For

83. Cited from Lawrence, *Storm Over Savannah*, 81; Charles O. Paullin, *The Navy of the American Revolution* (Cleveland, 1906), 432.

84. Salley, Jr., ed., *Journ. of Com. of Navy, 1776-1779*, 9, 28, 41, 59.

85. *Ibid.*, 64, 76, 81, 241; *Statutes of S. C.*, IV, 455.

although privateers were authorized vessels of war operating under commissions from the state authorities acting as agents of Congress, they were privately owned, manned and run. A privateer was a free-lance raider, going where and when it pleased. More often than not, the owners evaded laws requiring payment of a share of prize money to the government and simply divided the loot equally with the crew. Since not much care was taken to screen the crews, privateers were a mecca to runaway slaves.[86] No embarrassing questions were asked, and it was unlikely that a written roster of the crew would be kept on deposit at any place where it might catch the eye of a prying slave-catcher.

A typical New England privateer might carry two or three Negroes. On the roster of the New London privateer *General Putnam* in 1779 were four colored men, one of whom was a cook. On board the *Aurora,* lying at Boston in June 1781, were three Negroes of varying ages and statures, but all bearing the name of Cato.[87]   In nearby Salem the enlisting of Negro seamen brought a good income to slave Titus, a business agent of the privateers. Titus knew that his owner, Mrs. Joseph Cabot, had made a will freeing him and bequeathing him £40 if he remained in her service until she died. For this generosity, however, the well-to-do agent for the privateersmen was unmoved since, as a contemporary put it, he "wears cloth shoes, ruffled shirts, silk breeches and stockings, and dances minuets at Commencement."[88]

Of the Negroes serving on the privateers the best known to history was James Forten who while not yet fifteen enlisted as a powder boy on the *Royal Louis,* commissioned by Pennsylvania in 1781. On her second cruise the *Royal Louis* was captured by the frigate *Amphyon,* assisted by two other British vessels. Young Forten became a playmate of the son of the

86. For the non-selective character of privateer crews, see Sidney G. Morse, New England Privateering in the American Revolution (unpubl. Ph.D. diss., Harvard Univ., 1941), 398; also Morse's "The Yankee Privateersman," *New England Quarterly,* 17 (1944), 78.

87. Ernest E. Rogers, *Connecticut's Naval Office at New London During the War of the American Revolution* (New London, 1933), 60; *Mass. Soldiers and Sailors,* III, 212.

88. Fitch Edward Oliver, ed., *The Diary of William Pynchon of Salem* (Boston, 1890), 103. The date of this entry in Pynchon's diary was Aug. 13, 1781.

Amphyon's commander, but the powder boy resisted efforts to persuade him to renounce his American allegiance. As a consequence he was sent to the floating dungeon, the *Jersey*, where he spent seven months before being released in the general exchange of prisoners which took place as the war drew to a close.[89] After the war Forten become a sailmaker in Philadelphia, eventually amassing a fortune of $100,000, a portion of which came from his invention of a device for handling sails. Forten spent some of his money in support of reformist movements, particularly the William Lloyd Garrison wing of the abolitionist crusaders.

* * *

Slave and free, voluntarily or involuntarily, the Negro had joined in America's fighting forces. Arms-bearing, however, was not to be his only role in the war effort.

89. For Forten's war-time experiences see Ray Allen Billington, "James Forten: Forgotten Abolitionist," *Negro Hist. Bull.,* 13 (1949), 31.

CHAPTER VI

BEHIND THE MAN BEHIND THE GUN

> I should be glad that the Sale of the two Negroe women . . . might be suspended. Their services will not only be valuable to me, but will promote the good of the Service as they will supply the Place of Soldiers—who other ways must be necessarily employed in my kitchen.
>
> General William Smallwood to President of the Maryland Council, July 24, 1781.

Although not enrolled as soldiers, thousands of Negroes proved to be of great service to the American land forces. The great majority of them were laborers whose brawn and skill contributed to the shaping of military operations. A few acted as spies, messengers, or guides.

Best known of the Negro spies was James, a slave of William Armistead of New Kent County, Virginia. With his master's permission, James took service with Lafayette when the young Major General came to Williamsburg in mid-March 1781, bent on relieving Virginians from harassment by the British under Benedict Arnold. To ascertain the enemy's movements, Lafayette sent numerous spies to Arnold's base at Portsmouth.

Operating in a region for which he needed no road map, James made a number of trips to Portsmouth, where he delivered letters to other American spies and then hovered around the British camp. James won the praise of Lafayette. The marquis wrote that his Negro spy "properly acquitted himself with some important communication I gave him . . . his intelligence from the enemy's camp were industriously collected and more faithfully delivered."[1]

1. Certification of Lafayette, dated Nov. 21, 1784. Reproduced from original in Virginia Historical Society in Jackson, *Va. Negro Soldiers and Sailors,* 9. When the defeated Cornwallis paid Lafayette a courtesy call before leaving Yorktown he was surprised to find at Lafayette's headquarters

Lafayette's appraisal prompted the Virginia assembly to give James his freedom; a law passed in October 1786 ordered the state treasurer to pay to James's master the equivalent of the price the slave would have commanded on the auction block. In 1819, a third of a century later, another legislature voted the former spy a $40.00 a year pension.[2] A final moment of glory in James's life came in October 1824 when he was greeted in Richmond by Lafayette, who was on a return visit to America. Long before James had adopted the surname of his distinguished French idol, proudly subscribing himself "James Lafayette."

Saul Mathews was another slave spy operating in the Portsmouth region during the Cornwallis occupation. Saul's superior, Colonel Josiah Parker, who commanded the militia of four counties, had been ordered by Lafayette and Baron von Steuben to uncover intelligence about the British troops at Portsmouth and their movements up and down the James River. Parker sent Saul into the British lines several times in search of vital information, and Saul appears not to have returned empty-handed. In 1792, nearly ten years after the formal close of the war, he petitioned for his freedom. The legislature granted his request, basing its action on his "many very essential services rendered to the commonwealth, during the late war."[3]

In March 1783 Antigua, a slave, was cited by the South Carolina legislature for his work in "procuring information of the enemy's movements and designs." Going within the British lines, often at the risk of his life, Antigua had "always executed the commissions with which he was entrusted with dilligence and fidelity." Since he had been of some service to the state, it

a Negro who had been in the pay of the British to spy on the Americans but who, as it now became obvious, had really been a counter-spy for the Americans. Louis Gottschalk, *Lafayette and the Close of the American Revolution* (Chicago, 1942), 330. Very likely this was James since he was at Lafayette's Yorktown headquarters two days after Cornwallis's surrender. Jackson, *Va. Negro Soldiers and Sailors*, 11.

2. Hening, ed., *Statutes of Va.*, XII, 380-81 ; Jackson, "Negro Soldiers and Seamen in the American Revolution," *Journal of Negro History*, 27 (1942), 282.

3. Jackson, *Va. Negro Soldiers and Sailors*, 40 ; Lafayette to Parker, May 17, 1781, James F. Crocker, "The Parkers of Macclesfield, Isle of Wight, Va.," *Va. Mag. of Hist. and Biog.*, 6 (1889), 423; Steuben to Parker, Jan. 13, 1781, "Revolutionary Correspondence of Col. Josiah Parker, of Isle of Wight County Va.," *ibid.*, 22 (1914), 259; Hening, ed., *Statutes of Va.*, XIII, 619.

was only reasonable, said the legislature, to reward him. It decreed that he, his wife Hagar, and their child should be freed from the yoke of slavery.[4]

Sometimes Negroes who were not spies supplied information to American officers. In May 1779 it was a Negro who brought valuable intelligence to General William Moultrie concerning the British forces under General Prevost. With 2,400 men Prevost had made a thrust toward Charleston where Moultrie was stationed, withdrawing quietly on the night of May 12. Moultrie did not know where the British were until "a sensible, faithful negro" brought word that they were encamped three miles above the Ashley River Ferry. Moultrie had erroneously supposed that Prevost had moved in another direction.[5]

In the preliminaries leading to the Battle of Green Spring in July 1781, the American command had to weigh two conflicting reports supplied by Negroes. Sent to obtain information on Cornwallis's movements after he withdrew from Williamsburg on July 4, Colonel John F. Mercer and his scouting party met a Negro who told them that Banastre Tarleton was quartered at Green Spring Farm and Cornwallis within a mile from there. His information was in direct contrast to a report brought to the American camp by a Negro and a dragoon who, posing as deserters, bore false news that the British contingent nearby was a rear guard.[6] After evaluating the conflicting reports, the American command decided to order an offensive, thereby playing into the hands of the British. Only the brilliance of General Anthony Wayne prevented the attacking army from becoming encircled.

A Negro who had lived among the Shawanees supplied comprehensive information about operations of the enemy in the Indian country during the spring and summer of 1782. Arriving at the American headquarters at Fort Pitt late in August he was interviewed by General William Irvine, commander of the Western Department. The informant, wrote Irvine, "was minutely examined." With a background that in-

4. *Statutes of S. C.,* 545.

5. Moultrie to Benjamin Lincoln, May 15, 1779, William Moultrie, *Memoirs of the American Revolution,* 2 vols. (New York, 1802), I, 443.

6. Henry Lee, *Memoirs of the War in the Southern Department,* ed. R. E. Lee (New York, 1869), 432-33; Banastre Tarleton, *A History of the Campaigns of 1780 and 1781, in the Southern Provinces of North America* (Dublin, 1787), 363.

cluded two years as steward to the Shawanee chief, Blue Jacket, he told Irvine of the plans and activities of Captain Alexander McKee, an Indian trader with Tory leanings who had fled to the British and their Indian allies in the spring of 1778. The Negro also reported that the Indian tribes—the Shawanees, Delawares, Wyandots, Mongoes, Monseys, Ottawas, and Chippewas—were massing for a showdown battle at Piqua with George Rogers Clark. His recital bore the ring of truth. In a letter to Colonel Edward Cook, General Irvine urged the Lieutenant of Westmoreland County in Pennsylvania to "circulate his intelligence, letting it be as generally known as possible."[7]

Negroes were sometimes employed as messengers. Lachlan McIntosh at Charleston dispatched "his Negro Fellow Weaver" to carry letters to General Robert Howe in the winter of 1776. When Stephen Bull at Savannah sent a letter dated March 13, 1776, to Henry Laurens in Charleston, the bearer was "a negro hired to ride post in the Continental service." During the siege of Charleston a Negro messenger bearing a letter from an officer in General Isaac Huger's camp was captured near Goose Creek. This letter, plus additional information supplied verbally by the bribed messenger, "proved lucky incidents," wrote British officer Banastre Tarleton, adding that his "information relative to the situation of the enemy was now complete."[8] No wonder that on the following day his cavalry surprised and severely routed an American outpost at Moncks Corner.

* * *

In the war's activities military laborers played a major supporting role. An enemy advance could be effectively slowed by laborers who destroyed bridges, felled trees, and erected fortifications at strategic locations. Likewise, in preparing an offensive an army needed artisans to produce munitions, axemen

7. Irvine to Edward Cook, c. Sept. 1, 1782, C. W. Butterfield, *Washington-Irvine Correspondence* (Madison, Wis., 1882), 331. For Irvine's letter see *ibid.*, 332-33. Historian Butterfield, who made it a point to check on the intelligence supplied by the former steward, found it "singularly truthful and clear," noting especially that George Rogers Clark met the enemy at Piqua on Nov. 10, 1782, surprising and routing them, *ibid.*, 333*n*.

8. Lilla M. Hawes, ed., "Letter Book of Lachland McIntosh, 1776," *Georgia Historical Quarterly*, 38 (1954), 261, 263; Stephen Bull to Henry Laurens, Mar. 13, 1776, Gibbes, ed., *Doc. Hist. Amer. Rev.*, I, 267; Tarleton. *Campaigns in the Southern Provinces*, 16.

to march with the soldiers, and laborers to repair the roads. Much of this toil, particularly below the Mason-Dixon line, was performed by Negroes. Perhaps the extent and variety of their employment can be best illustrated by indicating the agencies that recruited blacks and the tasks for which they were recruited.

Negroes were frequently procured by public levy and ordered by civilian authorities to perform certain services. This was not an unfamiliar practice. In colonial America legislative bodies that barred Negroes from the militia had hit upon the device of labor service as a substitute.[9] In the war's early stages New York made use of this technique. Knowing that the British would have designs on New York City after they evacuated Boston, the president of Congress, John Hancock, urged General William Alexander, who was in command of the American troops in New York, to lose no time in fortifying the city. On March 14, 1776, the Provincial Congress empowered the commanding officer of each corps in the city and county of New York to summon all the male Negroes in his district, slaves included, to appear at the Common with "all the shovels, spades, pick-axes and hoes they can provide themselves with." The slaves were to work every day until the defenses were completed; those who were not slaves were to report every other day. The Provincial Congress also directed King's County officials to make available to military commanders one-half of their white male inhabitants and all their male Negroes to work on the Long Island fortifications. Workers were to bring with them their own spades, pick-axes, and hoes, and were to remain in service until "a proper posture of defense" had been effected.[10]

Another labor procurement device was state purchase of slaves, a practice most common in Virginia. Most masters were reluctant to sell their slaves for the depreciated currency offered by the state; hence many of the purchased slaves were runaways who had been recaptured from the British or caught trying to reach them. By purchasing such a slave the state did three things at once: it punished the runaway, recognized the property stake of a loyal master, and gained a badly needed military laborer.

9. Benjamin Quarles, "The Colonial Militia and Negro Manpower," *Miss. Valley Hist. Rev.*, 45 (1959), 646.
10. *Amer. Arch.*, 4th Ser., V, 218, 219.

Late in August 1777 the state employed Duncan Rose to buy slaves to work the lead mines at Chiswells, agreeing to pay him a commission of 5 per cent. Six weeks later Rose had rounded up five slaves. Later that year the state purchased five additional slaves, two of whom had been taken from the British and ordered sold by a decree of the Admiralty Court.[11] These, too, were sent to the lead mines. On April 5, 1780, the Board of Trade purchased twenty-six Negroes, including three women and a boy. Six state-owned Negroes were employed at the Warwick tannery in October 1781; they ranged in age from twenty to thirty-five, and varied in color from "yellow and slim" Charles to "black and well made" Ambrose. Fifteen other Negro men belonging to the public tannery had been taken by the British or had gone over to them.[12] At the state-owned Westham iron works "Negroes were depended upon" in molding and casting cannon. In December 1779, when the commissioners of the Virginia navy asked the Board of War for twelve carpenters and axemen, twelve laborers, ten sawyers, and five blacksmiths, the Board recommended to the governor that slaves be purchased for these jobs. In the spring of 1780 six purchased Negroes were working as armorers under the supervision of the Board of Trade, and in the summer of 1782, ten state-owned slaves were working as wagoners in the quartermaster's department.[13]

The Virginia Board of Trade preferred to buy slaves outright whenever possible, rather than hire them, because it was ultimately less expensive; however, the more common practice was to hire slaves for war service.[14] It required less money at the outset, and   permitted a much greater degree of flexibility in dovetailing supply with demand. As early as January 1778,

11. McIlwaine and Hall, eds., *Journals of the Council of the State of Va.*, II, 3, 16, 22, 43.

12. Boyd, ed., *Papers of Thomas Jefferson*, III, 344; *Cal. of Va. State Papers*, II, 536.

13. Kathleen Bruce, *The Manufacture of Ordnance in Virginia during the Revolution* (Washington, 1927), 391; Entry under date of Dec. 17, 1779, in "Virginia Board of War Book," Clinton Papers, Clements Lib.; H. R. McIlwaine, ed., *Official Letters of the Governors of the State of Virginia*, 3 vols. (Richmond, 1926-29), II, 97; hereafter cited as *Off. Letters of Govs. of Va.; Cal. of Va. State Papers*, III, 231.

14. Purchases had to be suspended in 1780 for lack of money. Board to Jefferson, Feb. 4, 1780, *Off. Letters of Govs. of Va.*, II, 96.

Washington had broached the idea that free Negroes from Maryland, Virginia, and the Carolinas be employed as wagoners.[15]
Relatively few Negroes were available for hire in the North;[16]
the practice was most common in the Southern states. In September and October 1776 five payrolls for the fort at Whetstone
in Maryland listed six slaves, and an advertisement in the *Maryland Gazette* on August 15, 1776, called for "a number of slaves,
or freemen labourers, for the purpose of carrying on a cannon
foundry at Antietam in Frederick County." The wages were unspecified, but prospective workers were told they would be given
"good encouragement." The North Carolina militia stationed at
the Port of Halifax in February 1782 employed six Negroes—two
stockgetters, a carpenter, a sawyer, a fireman, and a hostler.[17]

In Virginia slaves were hired during the first year of the
war, for service with military units such as the Lancaster District Minute Men and the Second Regiment. Late in 1777,
upon the request of the quartermaster of the York garrison,
the state council authorized an agent to obtain eight slaves for
work at the garrison and its hospital. He was instructed to
contract for them by the year "upon the best terms he can."
Hired slaves were employed in 1781 at the Fredericksburg gun
factory, and in 1782 as wagoners in the quartermaster's department.[18] The Hospital Department signed on a Negro woman in July 1780 but six months after the hiring her master
had received not a shilling.[19] In Virginia's domain west of the
Alleghanies, the estate of James Robinson received payment for
945 days of skilled labor performed by Caesar, perhaps a record
in long-term hired service.[20]

15. Headquarters to the Committee of Congress with the Army, Jan.
29, 1778, Fitzpatrick, ed., *Writings of Washington*, X, 401.
16. In 1780 the commissary department of the army stationed at Albany
had three Negroes on the payroll. "United States Army muster rolls, returns, etc., Feb. 20, 1780," Schuyler Papers, N. Y. Pub. Lib.
17. Revolutionary Papers, Box 6, fol. 16, Md. Hall of Records; Revolutionary War Muster Rolls, Pensions, and Inspection Returns (one box),
N. Y. Pub. Lib.
18. "Journal of the Committee of Safety, March 7, June 22, 1776," *Cal.
of Va. State Papers*, VIII, 111, 216; McIlwaine and Hall, eds., *Journals of
the Council of State of Va.*, II, 54; Charles Dick to Jefferson, Feb. 26,
1781, "Return of Staff Departments of the State, July 25, 1782," *Cal. of Va.
State Papers*, I, 542, III, 231.
19. Pope to Jefferson, Jan. 22, 1781, *ibid.*, I, 452.
20. James Alton James, ed., *George Rogers Clark Papers, 1781-1784*
(Illinois State Historical Library, *Collections*, 8, Virginia Ser., 3 [1926]), 333.

When Lafayette was dueling with Cornwallis in Virginia during the summer of 1781, he sent an urgent letter to Governor Jefferson asking for 250 Negro laborers to march with the army, plus a corps of 150 Negro wagoners.[21] Lafayette's request was beyond the Governor's reach. Jefferson had just had a sobering experience in trying to procure Negroes for a fortification requested by Steuben. On February 11, 1781, the Prussian-born General had told Jefferson of the importance of erecting a small work at Hood's, in Prince George County. Anxious to cooperate with a hard working professional soldier of Steuben's rank and reputation, Jefferson immediately directed the state quartermaster, Granville Smith, to "go out yourself" and hire forty slaves. Smith was advised to apply first to those masters who lived in the vicinity of Hood's, inasmuch as they would be more "immediately" interested in its defense. Five days later thirteen Negroes, one of them a bricklayer, had been hired.[22]

The number never went much higher. On March 12 Captain John Allen reported that a total of nineteen Negroes, procured from nine different masters, were working at the garrison; but it was too small a group to do the job. Not a single Negro had been gotten from Dinwiddie or Prince George counties.[23] Ten days later another disappointed agent reported that in Charles City County he had been able to raise only five Negroes, and that he despaired of raising a single additional one, even at a high rate of pay. Early in April, as if to compound the woes of the military officers in charge, the Negroes at Hood's went home "to hold their Holydays." Not enough soldiers were present to prevent this walkout, but by April 19 all but four of the workers had returned.[24]

It was hard to hire able-bodied slaves because so many had joined the British that masters did not care to part with those who remained. This reluctance of the master was an insurmountable barrier to Jefferson, for, as he informed General Steuben,

21. Lafayette to Jefferson, July 1, 1781, "Letters of Lafayette in Virginia State Library," *Va. Mag. of Hist. and Biog.*, 5 (1898), 377.
22. Jefferson to Granville Smith, Feb. 11, 1781, *Off. Letters of Govs. of Va.*, II, 332, 348.
23. Allen to Jefferson, Mar. 12, 1781, *Cal. of Va. State Papers*, I, 569.
24. William G. Mumford to Jefferson, Mar. 22, Sent to Jefferson, Apr. 19, 1781, *ibid.*, I, 587, II, 54.

Virginia officials had no power to call a slave to labor without first obtaining the master's consent.[25]

Finally, with the British in Chesapeake waters, Jefferson made one last desperate appeal. In a message to the legislature on May 10, 1781, he asked whether slaves might not be taken into the army solely for labor service. Such non-arms-bearing slave soldiers would permit Virginia to throw up batteries on every river and thus protect her commerce and property.[26] Nothing came of Jefferson's proposal, and the state authorities, civilian and military, resumed the dreary task of trying to cajole masters to lease out their black retainers.

Equaling Virginia in Negro hire, if not surpassing her, was South Carolina. Hired slaves were extensively employed in the boat yards and military hospitals.[27] Their use in defensive operations was illustrated in the early months of the war when the British in June 1776 launched a sea attack against Charleston. But months before the British arrived, the state capital had set to work erecting fortifications. As early as November 10, 1775, the Provincial Congress had authorized the hiring of "a sufficient number of Negroes to give all possible despatch to the completing of the Redoubt erecting upon James Island, to the westward of Fort Johnson."[28] Five weeks later the city authorities began training hired Negroes to extinguish fires and pull down houses, furnishing them with firehooks, axes, and ropes. The Negroes were then ordered to remove the lead ornaments from public buildings and melt them into bullets. The Council of Safety ordered that colored laborers be employed at all of the town's harbor batteries at the rate of two Negroes to each gun.[29] At Sullivan's Island, key to the city's sea defenses, salaried Negroes did much of the work in putting up the double-walled fort of spongy palmetto logs, with outworks for thirty cannon. As a result of these preparations, one week

25. Jefferson to Steuben, Feb. 12, 1781, *Off. Letters of Govs. of Va.*, II, 333.

26. Jefferson to Speaker of House of Delegates, Benjamin Harrison, May 10, 1781, *ibid.*, II, 512.

27. Wylma A. Wates, ed., *Stub Entries to Indents—Book K* (Columbia, S. C., 1956), 2; Nathanael Greene to Mordecai Gist, Mar. 2, 1783, Gist Papers, Md. Hist. Soc. Also A. S. Salley, ed., *Stub Entries to Indents, Books L—N* (Columbia, 1910), 8.

28. *Amer. Arch.*, 4th Ser., IV, 47.

29. "Journal of the Council of Safety" (Jan. 22, 1776), S. C. Hist. Soc., *Coll.*, 3 (1859), 208; Laura E. Wilkes, *Missing Pages in American History* (Washington, 1919), 52.

before His Majesty's forces sailed into Charleston waters, a hundred large guns were poised to greet them. When, on June 28, the British finally launched their ill-starred naval attack on the harbor batteries, they were scarcely more amazed by the courage of the American defenders than by the manner in which their forts withstood a ten hour cannonade, absorbing the missiles as if harmlessly sucking them in.

As was the case elsewhere, army officers in South Carolina could use more Negroes than were available for hire. Writing from the High Hills of Santee in June 1781, Colonel Peter Horry explained to General Greene that lack of Negro laborers handicapped military operations. He would try to hire them, but he feared that masters would not be responsive. General Marion had agreed to supply him with the necessary Continental currency for hiring the slaves, although, as Horry ruefully added, Marion would "not suffer Negroes to be seized on or taken out of his Brigade."[30]

Georgia, too, made use of leased blacks. In June 1776 her Council of Safety authorized the military to hire enough Negroes to complete the entrenchments around Sunbury. In June 1778 the Executive Council empowered Colonel Andrew Williamson to hire Negroes to repair the roads between Ogeechee and Alatamaha. To this ruling the Executive Council added a significant stipulation: if owners refused to hire out their slaves, Colonel Williamson would be permitted to impress them. Such impressed slaves could not be taken out of their home district, however, nor detained for more than ten days.[31]

Like all civilian authorities in the South, the Georgia Council disliked to resort to impressment. Nothing so aroused the condemnation of the master class. To take his slave even temporarily was to tamper with his labor supply. More important, it jeopardized his property rights, for an impressed slave might make his escape or die. Owners were told that if an impressed laborer took ill or was wounded, he would be "conveyed to a proper Hospital, and there supplied with necessary sustenance, medicines, and attendance," and that if he were maimed or

30. Horry to Nathanael Greene, June 28, 1781, Greene MSS, Clements Lib.
31. "Proceedings of the Georgia Council of Safety, 1775 to 1777," Ga. Hist. Soc., *Coll.*, 5, pt. 1 (1901), 60; Allen D. Candler, ed., *The Revolutionary Records of the State of Georgia*, 3 vols. (Atlanta, 1908), II, 78. Hereafter cited as Candler, ed., *Rev. Rec. of Ga.*

killed his owner would be indemnified.[32]   But to masters who refused even to hire out their slaves, no guarantees were acceptable.
Despite all objections to impressment, the civilian authorities
in the lower South felt they had no other recourse. Georgia
took the step early. On November 4, 1775, the Council of Safety,
having been requested by General Charles Lee to enclose the
military storehouse at Savannah, ordered that 100 Negroes be
impressed to do it.[33]   In September 1777 a comprehensive act
was passed obliging slaves to work on the several forts, batteries,
and public works for the "better security" of the state.   Masters
were ordered to furnish lists of their male slaves between the ages
of sixteen and sixty, one-tenth of whom would be subject to a
draft for twenty-one days at three shillings a day.   As was
customary in impressment legislation, a slave who was selected
would first be carefully appraised, in this case by four freeholders and one of the commissioners executing the act.   If
injury or death befell him the master would be paid from public
funds. The act was to remain in effect until February 1, 1778,[34]
and it was to be enforced by levying fines upon masters who
refused to furnish lists of their slaves.   As the state authorities
discovered, the penalty was not always effective; owners supplied lists but were skillful in resisting induction of their slaves.

In South Carolina, with a high percentage of Negroes in
its population, slave impressment was more common than in
any other state. As early as November 20, 1775, the Provincial
Congress gave military officers the right to enroll able-bodied
male slaves as pioneers and laborers. A year later the state's
president and commander-in-chief was empowered to take the
same step, paying masters 10s. a day for the impressed slave.[35]
In some parishes the owners were unresponsive, and in February 1777 the state's chief executive was authorized to appoint
persons to help him enforce the impressment ordinance. When
the British threatened Charleston in the spring of 1780, troop
detachments were sent out on February 27 to round up every
slave in the city and put him to work on the fortifications. Soldiers in the impressment detail were told to excuse no slave

32. Act of South Carolina Assembly, Oct. 15, 1776, *Amer. Arch.*, 5th
Ser., III, 68.
33. Candler, ed., *Rev. Rec. of Ga.*, I, 199.
34. Allen D. Candler, ed., *The Colonial Records of the State of Georgia*,
26 vols. (Atlanta, 1904-16), XIX, pt. 2, 80-86.
35. *Amer. Arch.*, 4th Ser., IV, 61; *Statutes of S. C.*, VII, 428-29.

unless he bore a written pass from the governor. In the summer of 1781 General Sumter ordered Captain W. R. Davis to impress Negroes, as well as wagons and oxen in order to seize goods and property of the enemy at Georgetown.[36]

On March 12, 1782, from his shifting headquarters along the Santee River, General Francis Marion ordered Colonel Peter Horry to build a circular redoubt with Negro labor. Marion advised Horry to lay a requisition upon each owner in proportion to the number of his slaves; if a master refused to furnish information as to their number, the requisitioning officers would make their own estimate. After a master's holdings in blacks had been established, he was to be issued a certificate informing him of the number of slaves he would be required to provide and the conditions of their service. If a master refused to cooperate, a detail would be sent to take his slaves.[37]

A final source of black military labor in the South was captured or recaptured slaves. If their owners were patriots, the property right of their masters was respected. In Virginia Governor Nelson ordered in September 1781 that all captured slaves be returned to their former proprietors. Americans were fighting, he stated, not to procure plunder, but to safeguard the liberty and property of their fellow citizens as well as their own. In South Carolina two runaways who were captured trying to reach a British ship were restored to their owner upon payment of a fee. In the spring of 1782 Governor Mathews informed General Marion that captured slaves of patriot masters should be delivered to their masters, "they paying the charges for recovering them."[38]

Congress was late in formulating a policy on recaptured slaves, although as early as October 14, 1776, a committee of three had been appointed to consider what was to be done with Negroes taken by American ships of war. Since, under the Articles of Confederation, the central government was given the

36. "Regimental Book of Captain James Bentham, 1778-1800," *S. C. Hist. Mag.*, 54 (1953), 41, 44; Sumter to Davis, July 25, 1781, Edward McCrady, *The History of South Carolina in the Revolution, 1780-1783* (New York, 1902), 429.

37. Marion to Horry, Mar. 13 and 29, 1782, Gibbes, ed., *Doc. Hist. Amer. Rev.*, III, 271, 280.

38. Robert Andrews to George Weedon, Sept. 26, 1781, *Off. Letters of Govs. of Va.*, III, 68; "Journal of the Council of Safety, Dec. 20, 1775," *S. C. Hist. Soc., Coll.*, 3 (1859), 141; Gibbes, ed., *Doc. Hist. Amer. Rev.*, III, 274.

power to decide on captures, Congress finally ruled on December 4, 1781, that a recaptured person "from whom labor or service is lawfully claimed" should be restored to his master, who would pay a salvage fee to the recaptor. If such persons, which included slaves, should be captured below the high water mark and not claimed within a year and a day, they were to be set free.[39]

The Continental army usually returned slaves of patriot masters. Writing from Washington's headquarters at Morristown in July 1777, Alexander Hamilton informed an officer that slaves captured by the Continental forces were to be returned to patriot owners. But if a slave were taken by the state forces, continued Hamilton, the matter was out of General Washington's hands. In such a case a Continental officer would refer the master to the governor of the state.[40]

Slaves of loyalist or British masters, on the other hand, were regarded as the spoil of war. From the days of Dunmore, Virginians had appropriated slaves of "those unfriendly to the American cause" and put them to work mining lead and the always scarce salt. In Georgia in 1776 the Council of Safety ordered that twenty Negro axemen taken from the plantations of two Tory masters be employed in building a battery at Typee. The Executive Council in June 1778 authorized militia captains in whose districts confiscated estates were located to take slaves for service as pioneers in a proposed expedition against East Florida.[41]

South Carolina, with its many wealthy British-minded masters offered a fruitful yield of confiscated slaves, many of whom were used as military laborers. General Marion in January 1781 directed a subordinate to collect fifty Negroes for use by General Greene; these were to be taken from the Tory estates. On February 19, 1782, when the legislature voted to furnish Greene with 440 Negroes as wagoners, artificers, and servants, it was with the stipulation that these would come from the confiscated estates. Whenever confiscated slaves were not needed by the army, they were to be turned over to the Committee for

39. Ford, ed., *Journ. of Cont. Cong.,* VI, 874, XXI, 1155-56.

40. Hamilton to Elias Dayton, July 7, 1777, Revolutionary Papers, I, 457-59, N. Y. Pub. Lib.

41. Ga. Hist. Soc., *Coll.,* 5 (1901), 116; Candler, ed., *Rev. Rec. of Ga.* II, 77-78.

the Improvement of Inland Navigation to be employed in clearing the Edisto and Catawba Rivers.[42]

Captured slaves of the enemy did not always become public property; they were often taken as private booty. "My men seem to expect something to fall to them out of the value of the *Ethiopian*," wrote Colonel William Malcolm to General Heath, after a scouting party from Niack had seized a slave belonging to a British sympathizer.[43] A slave captured by Connecticut soldiers during a raid upon Morrisania early in 1781 was sold "for the benefit of the regiment." In Maryland the state Court of Admiralty ruled that three Negroes seized on a British privateer be sold, the proceeds to go to the captors. In Georgia the Executive Council, on February 8, 1780, ordered that Negroes taken at the siege of Savannah and belonging to persons in arms against the United States were to be sold; the proceeds were to be divided among the soldiers who took part in the campaign.[44] One military commander, however, did not view captured Negroes as spoils of war. Anthony Wayne and his officers wished to set free three Negro prisoners taken at the successful assault on Stony Point.[45]

In South Carolina some military officers looked upon slaves as part of the plunder of war, promising their men they could have all the Negroes they could seize. On his expedition to the Cherokee country in September 1781, General Pickens told his troops that they could divide the property they captured, including slaves.[46] Carrying off enemy-held Negroes was standard practice for Americans, and sometimes upwards of a hundred slaves were plucked from the British and their loyalist supporters in a single raid. A few officers like Pickens would not scruple to distribute these slaves within the corps, other officers would put them to work as military laborers, and still others would

42. William D. James, *A Sketch of the Life of Brigadier General Francis Marion*, ed. A. S. Salley, Jr. (Marietta, Ga., 1948), appendix, xiv; Salley, Jr., ed., *Journal of S. C. House of Representatives*, 101; W. T. R. Saffell, *Records of the Revolution* (New York, 1858), 77.

43. Malcolm to William Heath, Dec. 9, 1776, *Amer. Arch.*, 5th Ser., III, 1139.

44. Samuel H. Parsons to William Heath, Feb. 7, 1781, Heath Papers, Mass. Hist. Soc., *Coll.*, 7th Ser., 5 (1905), 173; *Arch. of Md.*, XLV, 490, 634; Candler, ed., *Rev. Rec. of Ga.*, II, 215.

45. Wayne to Return J. Meigs, July 25, 1779, Henry B. Dawson, *The Assault on Stony Point* (Morrisania, N. Y., 1863), 118.

46. *Statutes at Large of S. C., 1752-1786*, 599.

turn them over to the state commissioners of confiscated estates. These commissioners generally sold them, duly noting the state law which forbade the separation of families in such sales.

Another use for slaves was as enlistment bounty to supplement land grants. The awarding of unoccupied land to those who bore arms was a familiar practice in colonial America; it was natural that during the Revolutionary War such a policy would be adopted by the central government and more than half the states.[47] But in the South, slaves were an acceptable form of currency and superior in many respects to land as a bounty because slaves were deliverable, whereas a land bounty required the recipient to go where the plot was located, sometimes many miles distant, or sell it for a fraction of its worth. Both slaves and land, however, were preferred to paper money with its rapid depreciation.

Some Virginians regarded the use of slave bounties as a cruel and oppressive practice. James Madison commented that it would better accord with the principles of liberty to make soldiers of the Negroes than to use them as a means of inducing whites to enlist.[48] But to most Virginians the slave as soldier was even more painful to contemplate than the slave as bounty. Faced with British invasion, the legislature voted at its October 1780 session to give every recruit who would serve until war's end 300 acres of land plus a choice between a healthy, sound Negro between ten and thirty years of age or £60 in gold or silver. These slaves were to come from "Negro holders" of twenty or more, who would be paid within an eight year span.[49]

South Carolina had fewer qualms than Virginia over using slaves as bounty. In April 1781 General Sumter offered a slave bonus in attempting to recruit six regiments for an enlistment of ten months. The bonus varied according to rank; a private was to receive one grown Negro, whereas a colonel was to receive three grown Negroes and a small one.[50] The only hitch in Sumter's scheme was that he had no Negroes to begin with;

47. On this point see Benjamin H. Hibbard, *A History of the Public Land Policies* (New York, 1924), 116-18.

48. Henry D. Gilpin, ed., *The Papers of James Madison*, 3 vols. (Washington, 1840), I, 68.

49. Hening, ed., *Statutes of Va.*, X, 331; Ford, ed., *Letters of Joseph Jones*, 47.

50. Richard Hampton to John Hampton, Apr. 2, 1781, Gibbes, ed., *Doc. Hist. Amer. Rev.*, III, 48.

he was hoping to get them from the enemy. Essentially Sumter was dealing in slave futures. General Greene supported Sumter, permitting him to use Negroes taken at Ancrams Plantation on the Congaree as a down-payment on the contract with his men.[51] Andrew Pickens, too, organized troops on the basis of enemy slaves-to-come, a plan which came to be known as "Sumter's law," in deference to its originator.

The civilian authorities soon followed suit. Needing 1,300 soldiers for the Continental service, the legislature in February 1782 promised to each enlistee a Negro between the ages of ten and forty. A slave would be given to anyone who recruited twenty-five men in two months. As was customary, these slaves were to come from the confiscated estates.[52]

It soon developed that there were not enough slaves for all these purposes. Loyalist masters were likely to have carried away their choice slaves, leaving behind only the aged and the ill. Indeed, in February 1782 when the legislature passed the slave-bonus bill, it also authorized the governor to deliver 400 Negroes to Sumter and 60 to Pickens in order to help them meet their back-pay obligations.[53] Inevitably every regiment organized on the enemy-slave-bounty basis suffered from arrears in pay. By late April 1782 Henry Hampton's regiment had received only 46 out of 120 slaves due; William Hill's regiment was due 73 large and 3½ small Negroes, and the payroll of Wade Hampton's regiment revealed a balance due of 93¾ grown Negroes and "Three Quarters of a Small Negro."[54]

Behind in pay, the regiments operating under Sumter's law did not always stop to make sure that the slaves they seized belonged to Tory masters. Indeed, so many court suits were brought by irate patriot masters whose slaves had been spirited away that South Carolina had to give legal protection to Pickens and his officers. In 1784 the legislature voided such personal suits.[55] But South Carolina masters continued to bring suit against North Carolina soldiers who had signed up with the

51. Greene to Sumter, May 17, 1781, *Year Book of the City of Charleston* (Charleston, 1899), 101-2.

52. *Statutes of S. C.,* 513-14.

53. Salley, Jr., ed., *Journ. of House of Representatives,* 80.

54. A. S. Salley, Jr., ed., *Documents relating to the History of South Carolina during the War* (Columbia, 1908), 51, 65, 55.

55. *Statutes of S. C.,* 514. But such cases did reach the courts until 1792. McCrady, *South Carolina in the Revolution,* 145-47n.

Sumter-Pickens regiments, attracted by the promise of a slave. Cases against North Carolina soldiers for recovery of slaves ceased only in 1788, when a law of that state made it mandatory that the verdict and judgment had to be for the defendant.[56]

Perhaps no state surpassed Georgia in the variety of ways in which enemy slaves were used as wartime money. On one occasion the state donated a slave to every soldier who had taken part in a successful campaign; in another instance the state exchanged slaves for provisions for the troops. Enemy slaves were transmitted to public officials in payment of salaries; in the fall of 1782 the legislature ordered the commissioners of confiscated estates to send ten slaves to Governor Martin for the support of his family. A month earlier the legislature had voted slave deliveries to the members of the Executive Council, "as otherways there is just reason to fear the public business must inevitably be protracted."[57]

* * *

The use of Negroes was not limited to the American side; thousands of colored persons cast their fortunes with His Majesty's forces. This game was more perilous, but the chances of freedom were greater. In the end, the lot of those who took this choice was determined by circumstances over which they had little control.

56. *The Public Acts of the General Assembly of North-Carolina* (Newbern, 1804), 447.
57. Candler, ed., *Rev. Rec. of Ga.*, I, 607, II, 364, 424, III, 70.

CHAPTER VII

THE BRITISH AND THE BLACKS

"Our non-emancipated soldiers are almost irresistibly tempted to desert to our foes, who never fail to employ them against us."

Antibiastes (pseudonym), *Observations on the Slaves, and Indented Servants in the Army, and in the Navy of the United States,* Philadelphia, 1777 (broadside).

"Man is a want of the most serious nature," wrote a British lieutenant commander in April 1780 from Wappoo Creek,[1] a strait to the west of James Island and facing Charleston across the Ashley River. England's need for men, apparent as early as Dunmore's abortive campaign, worsened as the war dragged on. At home His Majesty's government at first tried to raise troops by voluntary enlistment, going so far as to pardon criminals who would consent to serve in the army. But the pay of a soldier was poor, the army had a reputation for harsh discipline, and the war was not popular with the humble class of Englishmen from which enlistments came. German mercenaries totaling some thirty thousand, and Indian allies on the frontier by no means filled England's manpower needs.

The use of Negroes had been contemplated from the first threat of trouble. Five months before Dunmore issued his call to the slaves, General Gage had considered raising the Negroes in the British cause. He took no action on this score, heeding the admonition of Lord William Campbell who advised him not to "fall a prey to the Negroes."[2] His hesitation arose from the fact that the military employment of Negroes was no more

1. James Duncan to George K. Elphinstone, Apr. 9, 1780, W. G. Perrin and Christopher Lloyd, eds., *The Keith Papers,* 3 vols. (London, 1926-55), I, 163.

2. Gage to Viscount Barrington, June 12, 1775, Carter, ed., *Correspondence of General Thomas Gage,* II, 684; Campbell to Gage, Aug. 9, 1775, Gage MSS, Amer. Ser., Clements Lib.

popular in England than the later use of Hessian troops. In London in October 1775, at a meeting called by public advertisement, a group of "Gentlemen, Merchants and Traders" addressed a petition to King George informing him that they viewed with indignation and horror all reports about slaves being incited to insurrection against "our American brethren."[3] As it turned out, however, the attitudes of the British public merely obliged commanders in America to do what necessity required without saying anything about it. For use Negroes they must; the war brought realities of its own. Slaves represented a badly needed labor supply, and recruiting them to the British side would deprive the Americans of much of their strength, particularly in the South.

These elemental facts were quite visible to American loyalists and British informants on the scene. "Their property (slaves) we need not seek," wrote youthful spy John André, "it flys to us and famine follows."[4] "The Negroes may be all deemed so many Intestine Enemies, being all slaves and desirous of Freedom," wrote Joseph Galloway to the Earl of Dartmouth in January 1778. Five months later Galloway sent Dartmouth a statistical analysis of America's manpower resources, pointedly adding "that in the class of fighting men among the Negroes, there are no men of Property, none whose attachments would render them averse to the bearing of Arms against the Rebellion."[5]

Loyalists continued to emphasize that with its numerous Negroes, the Southern states were especially vulnerable. The two Carolinas, Virginia, and Maryland, could be kept in a state of apprehension over having their slaves armed against them, wrote Jonathan Boucher in November 1775 to the secretary of state for the Colonies.[6] In similar vein Moses Kirkland pointed out that in the Southern states "the principal resources for the Rebellion are drawn from the labour of an in-

3. *Amer. Arch.*, 4th Ser., III, 1011.

4. John André, "Suggestions for regaining dominion over the American colonies," undated, but in 1780 shortly after May 12, Clinton Papers, Clements Lib.

5. Galloway to Dartmouth, Jan. 23, 1778, Stevens, ed., *Facsimiles*, XXIV, Nos. 2079, 2098.

6. Boucher to Germain, Nov. 27, 1775, Historical Manuscripts Commission, *Report of the Manuscripts of Mrs. Stopford-Sackville*, 2 vols. (London, 1904-10), II, 19.

credible multitude of Negroes." He predicted that the instant the King's troops set foot in these colonies the slaves would be ready to rise against their masters, and compel them to flee to the interior.[7]

This point of view won some official support in England. As early as October 1775 Lord North informed King George that three of the American provinces were in a "perilous situation" because of the great number of slaves in proportion to whites.[8] In 1778 when the British shifted the brunt of the war to the Southern theatre, the presence of Negroes was a factor in determining their strategy. In March 1778 Germain advised Henry Clinton to split South Carolina in two, separating the back region from the seacoast. This would isolate the low country planters, he said, forcing them either to lay down their arms or face the equally grim prospect of abandoning, or being abandoned by, their slaves.[9]

With the southward shift of military operations, the British no longer tried to conceal their intention to make the utmost use of Negroes. Commander-in-Chief Clinton on June 30, 1779, issued a policy statement from his headquarters at Philipsburg in upper Westchester County, New York. He began by placing the onus for the proclamation on the Americans. Inasmuch, he said, as they had adopted the practice of enrolling Negroes among their troops, he ordered that whenever captured by the British, Negro soldiers or auxiliaries be purchased for the public service. The Philipsburg announcement then proceeded to forbid any person from selling or claiming any enemy-owned slave who had taken refuge in the British lines. And, finally, the proclamation promised every Negro who deserted from an enemy master full security to follow any occupation he wished while in the British lines.[10]

Unlike the similar announcement by Lord Dunmore some

7. "Moses Kirkland to His Majesty's Commissioners, Oct. 21, 1778," Clinton Papers, Clements Lib.
8. North to King George, Oct. 15, 1775, John W. Fortescue, ed., *The Correspondence of King George the Third from 1760 to December 1783*, 6 vols. (London, 1927-28), III, 266.
9. Germain to Clinton, Mar. 8, 1778, Stevens, ed., *Facsimiles*, XI, No. 1062.
10. The original proclamation may be found in the Clinton Papers. Rivington's *Royal Gazette* carried the proclamation in every issue from July 3, 1779, through Sept. 25, 1779; from the latter date to Dec. 1. 1779 it ran the proclamation sporadically.

three years previously, the Philipsburg proclamation attracted little notice. True, the *Boston Evening Post* informed Clinton that in publishing Negro recruiting proclamations he had exceeded even his former disgrace; a New York newspaper accused him of scheming to use the refugee Negroes to increase his personal fortune,[11] and the *New Jersey Journal* carried a sonnet with the concluding lines:

> A proclamation oft of late he sends
> To thieves and rogues, who only are his friends;
> Those he invites; all colours he attacks,
> But deference pays to *Ethiopian blacks*.[12]

But Clinton's proclamation aroused no general outcry in America. "I have long expected some notice from authority would have been taken of that insulting and villanious proclamation," wrote a soldier correspondent to a New York weekly.[13] But the indignant private need not have been surprised. By the summer of 1779 American commanders themselves were using Negroes on a considerable scale, and the open disclosure that the enemy was attempting the same thing was not shocking nor even new—the British had been employing Negroes since the outbreak of hostilities. Hence, the proclamation had no propaganda value for home-front consumption, nor could it be exploited for any effect upon public opinion in the capital cities of continental Europe. Silas Deane and Franklin had seized upon Dunmore's earlier proclamation in an effort to influence France to assist the Americans.[14] But a Franco-American alliance had been signed early in 1778, and after that it was a pointless exercise in diplomacy to charge England with inciting slaves to rise against their masters.

Many slaves who came into British hands were merely victims of military force. By seizing slaves the British army in-

11. *Boston Evening Post*, Nov. 13, 1779; *New York Packet*, Nov. 18, 1779, quoted in Frank Moore, *Diary of the American Revolution*, 2 vols. (New York, 1866), II, 176.

12. *New Jersey Journal*, July 20, 1779, quoted in "Poems of the American Revolution, 1779-1782," undated and unbound collection in N.-Y. Hist. Soc.

13. *New York Packet*, Nov. 18, 1779, Moore, *Diary of Amer. Rev.*, II, 176.

14. Silas Deane, "Memoir to induce France to Engage in a War with Great Britain, December 31, 1776," Stevens, ed., *Facsimiles*, VI, No. 607; American Commissioners to the Count de Vergennes, Jan. 5, 1777, "Memoir concerning the present State of the late British Colonies in North America," *ibid.*, No. 614.

creased its resources and depleted those of the enemy. When major campaigns shifted to the South after 1778, the loss of slaves in Virginia and South Carolina was severe. British depredations in Virginia, which had begun with the Lord Dunmore incident, were resumed on a larger scale. In the late spring of 1779, the British took 500 Negroes in Norfolk County alone.[15] Shortly afterwards, General Edwards left Virginia to rejoin Clinton in New York, taking with him 518 Negroes, comprised of 256 men, 135 women, and 127 children.[16] South Carolina had suffered losses since the beginning of the war. By August 1776 the British had taken "many hundreds" of Negroes.[17] In 1781 General Sumter reported that the country around the Broad River had been stripped of Negroes and horses.[18] Georgia also was plundered of slaves. A Savannah merchant and planter complained bitterly about the raids of British "banditti" who crossed the border from East Florida to steal horses and Negroes.[19] In 1779 an English officer returning to General Prevost's headquarters at Ebenezer brought with him 300 Negroes whom he had "carried off."[20]

Many more slaves, however, voluntarily deserted to the British. They had no particular love for England, but they believed that the English officers would give them their freedom. Like a lamp unto his feet, the lure of freedom led the slave to the camps of Clinton and Cornwallis. According to the Lutheran clergyman Henry Melchior Muhlenberg, the belief that a British victory would bring freedom was said to be almost universal in slave society.[21]

Slaves had been running away a century and a half before the Revolution, but what in peacetime was a rivulet became in wartime a flood. Above the Mason-Dixon line most of the

15. John Tazewell to Thomas Burke, June 4, 1779, *ibid.,* XIV, 308.

16. Return of persons who came off from Virginia with General Edward Mathew in the Fleet, Aug. 24, 1779, Guy Carleton Papers (photostats), N. Y. Pub. Lib. Hereafter cited as Carleton photostats.

17. Henry Laurens to John Laurens, Aug. 14, 1776, Wallace, *Life of Henry Laurens,* 446.

18. Sumter to Greene, Apr. 25, 1781, *Charleston Year Book,* 1899, II.

19. Joseph Clay to Henry Laurens, Sept. 9, 1778, "Letters of Joseph Henry, 1776-1793," Ga. Hist. Soc., *Coll.,* 8 (1913), 106.

20. "Miscellaneous Collection," Box 1779-1780, Clinton Papers, Clements Lib.

21. Theodore G. Tappert and John W. Doberstein, trans., *The Journals of Henry Melchior Muhlenberg,* 3 vols. (Phila., 1942-58), III, 78.

runaway slave advertisements pointed out that the absconding blacks would in all likelihood try to reach the British. A Massachusetts master, offering a $50.00 reward for his slave, Diamond, mentioned that the latter had been heard to say that he was going to Newport, then held by His Majesty's warships. Diamond took with him a violin of which he was fond, although he was "a miserable performer." A Trenton runaway, Jack, "who has a down look and is a great liar," was bent on joining the enemy, reported a New Jersey journal. Advertising for his slave, Moses, a Burlington master expressed the hope that every American would be on the lookout for the runaway because he had been trying to induce other Negroes to join him in fleeing to the British army. A New York newspaper notice about Pomp, an escaped slave of Comfort Sands of Poughkeepsie, stated that it was to be expected that he was on his way to the enemy.[22]

The South, however, was naturally the scene of the great majority of runaway attempts. "A great many Negroes goes to the Enemy," wrote a military officer at Murfree's Landing in North Carolina.[23] Such a dispatch was common below the Potomac, for in this section slaves were numerous and they had two avenues of escape: by land and by sea.

Perhaps nearly three-quarters of the slaves who escaped to the British made their way on foot, but others took advantage of the numerous waterways that criss-crossed the low county regions. The Chesapeake Bay tributaries were particularly inviting to slaves who plotted escape. Seacoast Maryland masters wrote doleful letters to Annapolis. On September 29, 1780, a Saulsbury resident informed Governor Thomas Sim Lee that a number of Negroes had gone on board the enemy boats which had penetrated some twenty miles up the river. On the next day the correspondent penned another warning: "If a stop is not put to these Crusers I am Convinced all our most Valuable Negroes will run away."[24] A few months later another citizen

22. Boston Gazette, Oct. 27, 1777; New Jersey Gazette (Trenton), July 11, 1781; Pennsylvania Gazette, Sept. 25, 1776, in Kull, New Jersey in the Revolution, I, 196; New York Packet and American Advertiser (New York), Sept. 2, 1779, in Helen W. Reynolds, "The Negro in Dutchess County in the Eighteenth Century," Dutchess County Historical Society, Yearbook, 26 (Poughkeepsie, 1941), 94.

23. Hardy Murfree to Abner Nash, Nov. 1, 1780, Clark, ed., State Rec. of N. C., XV, 138.

24. Arch. of Md., XLV, 125, 129.

had similar distressing news for the Governor: since the time the British ships anchored off St. Mary's, wrote Robert Armstrong, many Negroes had fled from that neighborhood. The conduct of the slaves on the night the British were at St. Mary's convinced Colonel Richard Barnes that the "greatest part of them" would take flight if given the chance.[25] Moved by these warnings, the Council of Maryland on June 12 advised the lower house to pass special legislation to protect the legal title and property rights of proprietors whose slaves had run away, such legislation being necessary because of "the Facility with which they abandon the Service of their Masters who live on the Waters."[26]

Along the lower Chesapeake the story was the same, as a few typical instances may indicate. In February 1777 British ships in the Bay had taken on board "about 300" Negroes from Gloucester, Lancaster and Northumberland.[27] A master on the Potomac River had taken the precaution of locking his boat in a barn, but it availed him little. A group of Negroes forced open the door, carried the boat to the water, and twenty-one of them sailed away—fifteen men, two women, and four children.[28]

Not always were the attempts so successful. Of four Hampton slaves who tried to reach the British man of war *St. Albans* in December 1777, two never made it; theirs was a James River grave. Three Norfolk slaves took refuge on a British vessel only to have it soon fall into American hands.[29] On a midnight in the spring of 1776 four Negroes in Stafford County, South Carolina, surprised John and Ralph Grissell as they lay drowsing in a small schooner. Hearing noises the Grissells shouted, "Who's there?" The answer came: "Don't speak or the worse shall come to you." The Grissells were kept in the hatch until the boat reached the Potomac. Here they were summoned on deck and ordered to chart the course, the slaves not being familiar with the waters of the Chesapeake. The tables

25. Robert Armstrong to Lee, Jan. 26, Barnes to Thomas Sim Lee, Mar. 25, 1781, *ibid.*, XLVII, 39, 148.
26. *Ibid.*, XLV, 473.
27. Richard Graham to Leven Powell, Feb. 20, 1777, "The Leven Powell Correspondence," *John P. Branch Historical Papers of Randolph-Macon College*, 1 (1902), 123.
28. Dunlap's *Maryland Gazette* (Baltimore), Dec. 30, 1777.
29. *Ibid.;* James Madison and Theodorick Bland to Thomas Jefferson, Jan. 25, 1781, *Cal. of Va. State Papers*, I, 455.

were soon turned. The Grissells steered the schooner into a Maryland port where the Negroes were taken into custody.[30] Hardly less vulnerable than the Chesapeake Bay region was coastal Georgia, with its nearness to British-held East Florida. Half a year before the Declaration of Independence, the officers of the British men-of-war at Tybee Island off Savannah were encouraging slaves to come aboard, and by the middle of March 1776, between 190 and 200 slaves had responded to the invitation.[31] Four months later the Council of Safety spoke feelingly of the losses to East Georgia inhabitants from the "ravages of British cruisers" which daily inveigled and carried away their black servitors.[32] So great was the flood of Negroes into East Florida that Governor Patrick Tonyn had some misgivings; to his superiors in London he sent word that he had formed militia companies to be used to check any American invasion and "in keeping in awe the Negroes who multiply amazingly."[33]

Some individuals lost heavily by the capture or desertion of their slaves. In Virginia John Bannister of Holt's Forge was plundered of eighty-two of his best Negroes, including all the skilled laborers. Governor Benjamin Harrison, a signer of the Declaration of Independence, lost thirty of "my finest slaves."[34] In the spring of 1781 British privateers took thirty Negroes from Charles Carter's plantation at Cole Point in Westmoreland. Two months later William Lee was deprived of sixty-five slaves, of whom forty-five were skilled laborers. Two of Lee's Chantilly neighbors "lost every slave they had in the world."[35] A professor of medicine at William and Mary was in nearly the same condition: "he has no small servants left, and but two girls," wrote St. George Tucker to his wife. Tucker's letter contained other distressing news about Williamsburg

30. "Virginia Legislative Papers," *Va. Mag. of Hist. and Biog.,* 15 (1908), 296.

31. Lachlan McIntosh to George Washington, Mar. 8, 1776, Sparks, ed., *Letters to Washington,* I, 167; Gibbes, ed., *Doc. Hist. Amer. Rev.,* I, 266.

32. *Amer. Arch.,* 5th Ser., I, 7.

33. Tonyn to Germain, Oct. 30, 1776, Edgar L. Pennington, "East Florida in the American Revolution, 1775-1778," *Florida Historical Quarterly,* 9 (1930), 30.

34. Campbell, ed., *Bland Papers,* II, 74; Harrison to George Clinton, Dec. 19, 1783, Boyd, ed., *Papers of Thomas Jefferson,* VI, 431n.

35. Henry Lee, Sr., to Thomas Jefferson, Apr. 9, 1781, *ibid.,* V, 392; Richard H. Lee to Washington, Sept. 17, 1781, Sparks, ed., *Letters to Washington,* III, 410; Richard H. Lee to William Lee, July 15, 1781, Ballagh, ed., *Letters of Richard Henry Lee,* II, 242.

residents: "Poor Mr. Cocke was deserted by his favorite man Clem; and Mrs. Cocke, by the loss of her cook, and is obliged to have resource to her neighbors to dress her dinner for her. They have but one little boy—who is smaller than Tom—left to wait on them within doors."[36] Among the South Carolina masters who suffered sizeable losses was Arthur Middleton of Charleston, a signer of the Declaration of Independence. Four months before he wrote his name on the document, some fifty of his Negroes had deserted him. William Hazzard Wigg in 1780 lost eighty-eight "prime" Negroes and eight "inferior" ones. In the same year Rawlins Lowndes complained that when Charleston fell, seventy-five of his best Negroes disappeared. Lowndes explained his plight to James Simpson, the British Attorney General of South Carolina: "Consider one moment, Sir, the feelings of a man in this condition, used hitherto to all the Comforts and Conveniences of Life, and now divested in the most pressing Exigency even of the use of a Horse."[37]

* * *

The number of Negroes who fled to the British ran into the tens of thousands. The figure was high, but not nearly as high as it might have been. Why individual Negroes who had the opportunity to flee did not take it can only be conjectured, but whatever their reasons, some showed an undeniable reluctance to enter the royal forces. When the British evacuated Boston in March 1776 they tried to persuade Scipio Fayerweather to join them, and when he refused, they pulled down his Belknap Street house and destroyed £30 worth of furniture.[38] A British officer in Rhode Island expressed surprise in 1778 that relatively few Negroes had joined the king's troops, although they had been promised pay and provisions.[39] There may have been many, like Scipio, who were free Negroes and had something to lose.

36. St. George Tucker to Fanny Tucker, July 11, 1781, Charles W. Coleman, "The Southern Campaign, 1781," *Mag. of Amer. Hist.*, 7 (1881), 207.
37. Gibbes, ed., *Doc. Hist. Amer. Rev.*, I, 266; "Wm. Hazzard Wigg—Claim for Slaves taken by the British in the Revolutionary War," House of Representatives, *Reports of Committees*: 36th Congress, 1st session (1860), report No. 471, Apr. 20, 1860, 96; Rawlins Lowndes to James Simpson, May 20, 1780, Clinton Papers, Clements Lib.
38. Revolutionary Rolls Coll., CLXXX, 416-17, Mass. Arch.
39. *Diary of Frederick Mackenzie*, 2 vols. (Cambridge, 1930), II, 326.

Some slaves who did not go over to the British doubtless thought a change might not improve their lot, reasoning that it was better to trust the devil they knew. Negroes could not fail to note one obvious fact: many confirmed Tories as well as British sympathizers were slaveholders. Numbered among the king's friends in New York, South Carolina and Georgia were owners of large, slave-worked estates and plantations. To the most unobservant field hand it must have been plain that England had not the remotest idea of making the war a general crusade against slavery, especially since so many of her loyalist supporters would have protested bitterly.[40] Indeed some of the Negroes who found themselves under the British flag were slaves of Tory masters who had fled their landed estates but who had no intention of relinquishing their black hands.[41]

When, in such cases, Negroes questioned the advantage of changing masters, they were governed by lack of confidence in the British rather than hostility to them. Few Negroes based their actions on personal animus toward the rulers and people of England. Almost in a class by itself is the case of a Negro trader, Jean Baptiste Point Sable, the first permanent settler on the present site of Chicago, whom the British arrested in 1779 at the site of Michigan City. Charged with being anti-British, Sable had his trading stations on the Lake Michigan shore raided and his goods confiscated.[42] Possibly Sable had been personally cool toward the British—his father was French.

Perhaps some Negroes chose not to go with the British because of a passionate belief in the American cause. Although a slave and born in Africa, Mark Starlins (self-styled "Captain"), a James River pilot, appears to have been deeply inspired by patriotic feeling.[43] Less lofty was the patriotism of a Negro like Pompey who challenged to mortal combat one Jem, who had charged that Pompey's fiancée, Phillis, had been overly friendly

40. On England's sensitivity to the slaveholding interests of her supporters in the United States and in the West Indies, see Herbert Aptheker, *The Negro in the American Revolution* (New York, 1940), 20-21.

41. For example of Tories fleeing to West Florida in 1776 with the number of slaves held by each, see Cecil Johnson, "Expansion in West Florida, 1770-1779," *Miss. Valley Hist. Rev.*, 20 (1934), 494.

42. Thomas Bennett to A. S. DePeyster, Aug. 9 and Sept. 1, 1779, Reuben Gold Thwaites, "The British Regime in Wisconsin, 1760-1800," State Historical Society of Wisconsin, *Collections*, 18 (1908), 395, 399.

43. "The Schooner Patriot," *Va. Hist. Reg.*, 1 (1848), 129-31.

with British officers during the occupation of Philadelphia. Pompey and Jem met on the field of honor, exchanging a brace of balls before their seconds interposed.[44] Some slaves may have been deterred from flight by ties of sentiment, having formed an attachment to the people and places of long familiarity. Such a sentiment may account for the action of field hand Nicholas of Kent County, Delaware. When his master's plantation was raided in August 1781, Nicholas rode rapidly to Dover to give the alarm whereas he might easily have gone off with the enemy, as had Isaac, valet to their master.[45]

A few proprietors could speak proudly of the devotion of their black retainers. As of August 14, 1776, not a single one of Henry Laurens's slaves had tried to desert him. They loved him "to a man," holding themselves in readiness to flee from the British if they appeared.[46] A Chesapeake Bay master had a similar experience: "I think our negroes on the island have given proof of their attachment," wrote Charles Carroll from Annapolis to his father. "They might have gone off if they had been so disposed."[47] In the summer of 1781 Fanny Tucker at her plantation near Farmville, Virginia, was much gratified to find out that despite the presence of some nine hundred British light horse in the neighborhood, her servants were every bit as faithful as she could have wished.[48] When General William Moultrie returned to his South Carolina plantation in September 1782 he was deeply moved by his reception as he stood on the piazza to greet his slaves: "Every one came an took me by the hand, saying, God Bless you, massa! we glad for see you, massa! and every now and then some one would come out with a "ky!" . . . The tears stole from my eyes and ran down my checks. . . . I then possessed about 200 slaves, and not one of them left me during the war, although they had great offers."[49]

* * *

44. *Pa. Packet*, in *Boston Evening Post*, Feb. 20, 1779.

45. J. H. Powell, "John Dickinson, President of the Delaware State 1781-1782," *Delaware History*, 1 (1946), 3.

46. Laurens to John Laurens, Aug. 14, 1776, Frank Moore, *Materials for History Printed from Original Manuscripts* (New York, 1861), 19.

47. Charles Carroll of Carrollton to Charles Carroll, Apr. 11, 1781. Carrollton MSS, Md. Hist. Soc., Baltimore.

48. Fanny Tucker to St. George Tucker, July 15, 1781, Mary H. Coleman, *St. George Tucker: Citizen of No Mean City* (Richmond, 1938), 65.

49. Moultrie, *Memoirs of the American Revolution*, II, 355-56.

Although masters may have been touched by the loyalty of slaves who stayed in their places, the Americans who fought England were not disposed to sit with folded hands and depend upon the faithfulness or inertia of the slaves. From the time of the Dunmore scare, the Americans had taken steps to prevent slave flights to the enemy. Military commanders were anxious to thwart the British aim of building up a valuable black labor supply; civilian officials in the South were equally anxious to prevent the loss of a property which formed the base of individual wealth and regional prosperity. On the plantation the slave was not only the field hand working the crops; he was also the skilled laborer—the carpenter, blacksmith, shoemaker, weaver, spinner, and even the distiller.[50] Hence both military and civilian authorities sought to prevent loss of Negroes to the British either by desertion or capture.

Army commanders sensed the importance of American military prestige as factors in keeping the slaves in line. "Your dominion over the black is founded on opinion," wrote General Charles Lee to Richard Henry Lee in early April 1776, "if this opinion fails your authority is lost." Therefore, continued Lee, he was hopeful of "Drawing down some battalions" for the defense of Williamsburg and York. A week later, in giving instructions to an officer going to South Carolina, Lee made the point that Charleston was to be defended to the hilt because "in Slave Counties so much depends on opinion, and the opinion which the slave will entertain of our superiority or inferiority will naturally keep pace with our maintaining or giving ground."[51]

Lee soon furnished concrete evidence of his determination to give no ground, ordering on April 23 that all Negroes capable of bearing arms be "secured immediately and sent up to Norfolk."[52] At Suffolk one of Lee's subordinates took forthright action of another kind. To prevent slave flights Colonel Isaac Read detached twenty-five men to examine the coves of the Nansemond and Chuckatuck rivers, removing all the small craft. The detail was instructed to destroy any boat whose owner re-

50. On this whole point see Leonard Price Stravisky, "Negro Craftsmanship in Early America," *Amer. Hist. Rev.*, 54 (1948-49), 315-25.

51. Lee to Richard H. Lee, Apr. 5, 1776, "Instructions to Brigadier General Armstrong," Apr. 10, 1776, Lee Papers, I, 379, 410, Houghton Lib., Harvard Univ.

52. Lee to John P. G. Muhlenberg, Apr. 23, 1776, *ibid.*, 445.

fused to yield it up for removal—a painful duty but one which the detail did not shirk.[53]

Virginia's Navy Board lent its assistance. In February 1777 the Board ordered the commanders of four of the state galleys to cruise in the Wicomico, Potomac and Rappahannock rivers to prevent Negroes from going on board British ships. Similar measures were taken in the upper Chesapeake Bay: "I have posted guards at the most Convenient places to prevent the Negroes from going to the Enemy & Secur'd all Boats & Canoes," wrote the ranking officer of the Anne Arundel County militia.[54]

Commanders below Virginia took equal precautions. In South Carolina General Marion ordered his subordinates to see to it that no Negroes traveled anywhere without a pass signed by him or some other officer commanding a detachment in the Continental service.[55] Some generals made it clear that a close check was to be kept on impressed or hired bondmen. In South Carolina late in 1781, General Otho H. Williams ordered that the road between Ferguson's Mills and Orangeburgh be repaired as quickly as possible in order that the slaves who were working on it have fewer days in which to attempt an escape. Just as soon as the road was repaired the laborers were to be marched back to their masters under military guard.[56] At Camp Howe, Georgia, where two companies of Negroes were employed in May 1778, the roll had to be called morning, noon and night, and an immediate report filed if anyone were missing. Overseers were required to encamp near enough to the slaves to discourage their desertion at night.[57]

Civilian authorities, alone or in concert with military officers, took various steps to keep Negroes from swelling the enemy ranks. The Boston Committee of Correspondence Inspection and Safety in March 1778 committed to jail a slave, Middleton, who was suspected of planning to run off to the

53. Read to Lee, Apr. 7, 1776, ibid., 390.
54. Navy Board to John Calvert, Feb. 8; Navy Board to James Markham and William Saunders, Feb. 12, 1777, "Excerpts from the Letter Book of the Navy Board," The Researcher, 1 (Richmond, 1927), 207, 2 (1927), 15; John Weems to James Brice, Mar. 21, 1781, Arch. of Md., XLVII, 140.
55. Marion to Horry, Mar. 10, 1782, Gibbes, ed., Doc. Hist. Amer. Rev., III, 267.
56. Williams to Capt. Linde, Dec. 7, 1781, Williams Papers, Md. Hist. Soc.
57. "Order Book of Samuel Elbert, Colonial and Brigadier General in the Continental Army, October 1776 to November 1778," Ga. Hist. Soc.. Coll. 5, pt. 2 (1901), 154.

British.[58] New York state had its Commission for Detecting and Defeating Conspiracies, which made it a business to apprehend Negroes who tried to reach the British, often giving a cash reward to their captors. On one occasion the Commission took into custody six slaves who confessed they had plotted to go to Canada.[59] In Maryland the Council of Safety ordered militia companies to keep guard "in the most proper places" to prevent slaves or servants from boarding the British ships of war.[60] In August 1777 the Virginia Council decreed that in every county which had navigable waters the county lieutenant collect and put under guard all boats which Negroes might use to escape. Officers of the state army and navy were ordered to assist in carrying out the measure.[61]

North Carolina, with fewer good waterways than her neighbors, resorted mainly to patrols. In June 1775 the Safety Committee of New Hanover County appointed guards to search for and seize "all kinds of arms whatsoever" which Negroes might possess. In 1779 the assembly strengthened its Negro patrol law of 1753 by giving rewards to those who served as searchers. Those who took the job of making a monthly descent upon the Negro quarters in search of guns and other weapons would receive a tax cut and be exempt from road work, militia duty, and jury service.[62]

South Carolina's approach to the problem of the blacks who might succumb to the blandishments of the British was many-sided. In the early months of the Revolution when trouble was brewing but the open break had not come, the Council of Safety took steps to cut off the food supply to British ships which harbored runaways. After an angry exchange of letters with Ed-

58. Robert Templeton to Committee, Mar. 6, 1778, Mass. Arch., CLXVIII, 195.

59. V. H. Paltsits, ed., *Minutes of the Commissioner for Detecting and Defeating Conspiracies in the State of New York: Albany County Sessions, 1778-1781*, 2 vols. (Albany, 1909), II, 704. For instances of slaves seized while en route to the British see *Minutes of the Committee and of the First Commission for Detecting and Defeating Conspiracies in the State of New York, December 11, 1776-September 23, 1778*, 2 vols., N.-Y. Hist. Soc., *Coll.*, 57 (1924), I, 70, 178, 202, 279.

60. Journal of the Council of Safety, June 23, 25, 1776, *Arch. of Md.*, XI, 511, 517.

61. *Off. Letters of Govs. of Va.*, I, 177.

62. Clark, ed., *State Rec. of N. C.*, X, 25. *Public Acts of General Assembly of North-Carolina*, 281.

ward Thornborough, captain of the sloop of war, *Tamar,* the Council voted in December 1775 to stop provisioning vessels which gave asylum to Negroes fleeing from their masters. "We have daily complaints," wrote Council President Henry Laurens, "from inhabitants on the sea-coast of robberies and depredations committed on them by white and black armed men from on board some of the ships under your command." A month later when the British men of war left Charleston waters they carried with them "a very considerable number" of Negroes.[63]

Checking on the crews of out-going vessels was another tactic employed by South Carolinians. Early in 1776 the Council learned that five Negroes had been secreted aboard a Spanish snow docked at Charleston. The Council ordered that the ship's clearance papers be withheld until the fugitives were delivered up. A crew from the schooner *Defence* boarded and searched the Spanish boat and found the Negroes, one of whom had been "very artfully concealed." Upon examination the colored men declared that they had been induced to join the ship's crew by a promise of £100 a month wages, plus clothing, "good usage" while aboard ship, and freedom when they arrived in Spain.[64]

Late in February 1776 the Council ordered a militia captain to take thirty-four Catawba Indians and make a scouting expedition to catch runaway Negroes in the parishes of St. George, Dorchester, St. Paul, and St. Bartholemew.[65] A few weeks earlier the Council advised the authorities in Christ Church Parish to arrest a Negro, Tom, for attempting to influence other slaves to desert to the British.[66] What South Carolinians expected of their slaves was expressed by General Robert Howe who, in February 1777, suggested to the president of Congress the advisability of keeping seven to eight thousand regular troops stationed in the state to control the "numerous black domestics who would undoubtedly flock in multitudes to the Banners of the enemy whenever an opportunity arrived."[67] Striving for maximum security, the state legislature early in 1782 required each militia company to furnish a six-man patrol whose "con-

63. Dunlap's *Md. Gazette,* Jan. 9, 1776; Minutes of South Carolina Council of Safety, Dec. 18, 1775, Laurens to Archibald Bulloch, Jan. 20, 1776, S. C. Hist. Soc., *Coll.,* 3 (1859), 94-95, 202.
64. Journal of the Council of Safety, Jan. 18, 1776, *ibid.,* 190-96.
65. Journal of the Council of Safety, Feb. 21, 1776, *ibid.,* 265.
66. Journal of the Council of Safety, Jan. 30, 1776, *ibid.,* 233.
67. Clark, ed., *State Rec. of N. C.,* XI, 708.

stant duty" would be to police the plantations, keeping the slaves in peace and good order.[68]

Georgia shared fully in this apprehension. In April 1776 when she sent her delegates to the Continental Congress at Philadelphia she gave them instructions on one point only: they were always to bear in mind that Georgia was exposed to the Indians on one border and the British on another, and endangered internally by the presence of Tories and Negroes. In 1778 when the war shifted to the South, the Georgia assembly, fearful that "grave danger might arise from insurrections, or other wicked attempts of slaves," took the precautionary step of requiring one-third of the troops in every county to remain where they were as a permanent local patrol.[69]

Individual masters themselves took steps to prevent the flight of slaves to the British forces. In April 1781 a group of Baltimoreans purchased two look-out boats at their own expense. Down along the Santee River in South Carolina, one slave proprietor tried psychology; he advised his overseer to keep his mouth shut in handling Negroes, singling out one of the black women as an example: "If you say the least about Ruth, she will run off, for she is an arch bitch."[70] A more direct procedure was simply to remove slaves from the vicinity of the British forces. Known in the Civil War as "running the Negroes," this practice had the backing of the Virginia lawmakers. In April 1776 the Convention passed a resolution requiring the removal of all slaves in Norfolk and Princess Anne counties, an order that had to be modified five weeks later so that male slaves not capable of bearing arms might remain to tend and gather the corn crop. A year later Governor Henry asked the Council to advise him on how to check the flight of the Negroes from Northampton and Accomac counties. The Council recommended that slaves on the Eastern shore be sent to the interior of the state and confined to a safety zone determined by the Governor.[71]

68. Salley, Jr., ed., *Journ. of the Senate of S. C., Jan. 8, 1782-Feb. 26, 1782,* 67.

69. Archibald Bulloch to Delegates, Apr. 5, 1776, Charles C. Jones, *The History of Georgia,* 2 vols. (Boston, 1883), II, 215; Candler, ed., *Col. Rec. of Ga.,* XIX, pt. 2, 118.

70. James McHenry to Thomas Sim Lee, Apr. 7, 1781, *Arch. of Md.,* XLII, 167; William Snow to Mr. Rhodes, Sept. 9, 1781, Gibbes, ed., *Doc. Hist. Amer. Rev.,* III, 140-41.

71. John Burk, *The History of Virginia,* 4 vols. (Petersburg, 1805-16), IV, 147; *Off. Letters of Govs. of Va.,* I, 184-85.

In the autumn of 1780 John Banister informed a friend that in the event the enemy approached Petersburg, he would "send off his Negroes." Many slave masters in the lower South took the same step. When the British came to Georgia "the Negroes in General," wrote loyalist Josiah Wright, were carried into South Carolina. In a reversal of direction one master, Edward Fenwicke of Berkeley County, South Carolina, transported "upwards of 100 Negroes" to Georgia.[72] From British headquarters at Charleston in March 1782, General Alexander Leslie ordered a cavalry detail to proceed to Daniel's Island to collect slaves, making it known to them that if they behaved with fidelity they might depend upon the generosity of the English. A week later the officer in charge of the expedition reported that although he had induced 100 blacks to join him, the number was less than expected because the American masters had "taken the precaution of sending their most valuable slaves across the River."[73]

To masters in the lower South who wished to run their Negroes, Virginia, in May 1780, opened her doors. Two years earlier her legislature had prohibited the further importation of slaves, but the Virginians were eager to help their neighbors, even if it meant a temporary increase in out-of-state blacks. An act of the assembly, passed on May 4, permitted masters from South Carolina and Georgia to bring their slaves into the state and keep them there until one year after the expulsion of the British from their soil.[74] Possibly some twenty-five masters found it expedient to accept Virginia's proposal.[75] Pennsylvania

72. Banister to Theodorick Bland, Oct. 1780, Campbell, ed., Bland Papers II, 36; Wright to Lord Germain, Feb. 10, 1780, "Letters from Governor Sir James Wright to the Earl of Dartmouth and Lord George Germain," Ga. Hist. Soc., *Coll.*, 3 (1859), 274; "Historical Notes," *S. C. Hist. Mag.*, 8 (1907), 22.

73. Leslie to Thomas Fraser, Mar. 27, 1782, Alexander Leslie Letterbooks, N. Y. Pub. Lib.; "Miscellaneous Manuscripts," EM, F. Emmett Collection, N. Y. Pub. Lib.

74. Hening, ed., *Statutes of Va.*, X, 307. While in Virginia, however, these slaves could be sold only with the permission of the governor acting upon the advice of the Council.

75. From Georgia George Haverick brought his 60 slaves to Henry County, McIlwaine and Hall, eds., *Journals of the Council of Va.*, III, 91-92; Joseph Clay registered 33 at Amherst County, and for this list, with names, ages and sex, see *Cal. of Va. State Papers*, I, 491; Joseph and John Habersham brought 22 to the same county (*ibid.*), and South Carolinian Charles Sims deposited 20 slaves in Halifax County (*ibid.*, 613).

likewise offered asylum to enemy-harassed masters of other
states, exempting them from the requirements of the emancipation act of March 1, 1780, on condition that they neither sold
their slaves nor kept them in the state longer than one year
after the war.[76]

Meting out punishment to slaves attempting to make their
way to the British was widely used as a deterrent to other slaves
who might harbor the idea. In the South, where control of the
Negro was deemed of paramount importance, the death penalty
was sometimes invoked. One of the first and most notable instances was that of Jerry, a free, well-to-do South Carolina pilot,
who himself owned several slave fishermen. In August 1775
Jerry was sentenced to be hanged and then burned, being found
guilty of supplying slaves with arms and advising them to take
flight to the British. When the loyalist Governor William Campbell protested, he was warned that unless he kept quiet the hanging would take place at the door of his mansion. On August
18 the sentence was carried out despite Campbell's remonstrances.
"The very reflection Harrows my soul," he wrote to the Earl
of Dartmouth.[77]

When South Carolina was threatened with invasion in the
spring of 1776, she passed a law stipulating death for any slave
who joined any British land or naval forces. On April 27, in
accordance with this law, a three man court decreed that two
Negroes, Charles and Kitt, be hanged by the neck until dead
for their role in making off with a schooner. Negroes who
supplied provisions to the British or carried intelligence to them
were to "suffer death," wrote Governor John Rutledge to General Marion in September 1781. A year later Governor Mathews
informed Marion that Negroes taken in arms were to be tried
"by the negro law," and if found guilty were to be executed,
unless there were factors justifying an executive pardon.[78]

Virginia invoked the death penalty from the early days of

76. The act was passed on Oct. 1, 1781, Mitchell and Flanders, eds.,
Statutes at Large of Pa., X, 367-68.

77. David D. Wallace, *South Carolina: A Short History* (Chapel Hill,
1951), 262; Campbell to Dartmouth, Aug. 19, 1775, Hist. MSS Comm., *The
Manuscripts of the Earl of Dartmouth: American Papers,* 3 vols. (London,
1887-96), II, 354.

78. John F. Grimké, ed., *The Public Laws of South Carolina down to
1790* (Phila., 1790), 284; *Va. Mag. of Hist. and Biog.,* 15 (1908), 296;
Rutledge to Marion, Sept. 2, 1781, John Mathews to Marion, Oct. 6, 1782,
Gibbes, ed., *Doc. Hist. Amer. Rev.,* II, 131, III, 232.

the Dunmore scare, but less frequently than South Carolina. In January 1781 Negro Jack of Botetourt County was condemned to die for assorted crimes—robberies, attempted poisoning, and enlisting slaves to join Lord Cornwallis. Jack's master succeeded in having the execution suspended, much to the indignation of the inhabitants of the county. A few months later, Billy, belonging to John Tayloe of Richmond County, was found guilty of treason for waging war while on an armed British vessel. Sentenced by a six man court to be hanged at the common gallows, Billy was spared when his master's lawyers argued that a slave could not be charged with treason since he owed the state no allegiance, not being entitled to the privileges of a citizen.[79] In "giving aid and comfort to the enemy," Billy had doubtless not reflected upon the constitutional ramifications of his conduct, simply having acted on the notion, sensed if not stated, that if this were treason he would make the most of it—a premise of good antecedents in Revolutionary Virginia.

More common than death as a punishment for attempted flight was the familiar practice of selling an offending slave. In Virginia, particularly during the first year of the war, some Negroes were sold to the non-British West Indies. Four slaves taken at the Battle of Great Bridge in December 1775 were sold out of mainland America. Virginia Congressman Joseph Jones vowed that if he recovered his man Cyrus he would ship him to the West Indies. William Nimmo of Princess Anne County stipulated in his will that if any of his sixteen Negroes who went off to the British were recovered they were to be sold. A Maryland master advertised for sale a healthy young Negro who had worked for twelve years in a "merchant mill" and was "complete in that business," explaining that "no other motive than his having attempted to escape to the enemy induces the proprietor to dispose of him."[80]

In a few instances would-be deserters to the British got off lightly. At Charleston in December 1775 mistress Sarah

79. Letter from inhabitants of Botetourt County, bearing 25 signatures, to Governor and Council, January 1781, Cal. of Va. State Papers, I, 477-78. For this whole case with copies of the court judgments, see Boyd, ed., Papers of Thomas Jefferson, V, 640-43.

80. Journals of the House of Delegates of Virginia (Richmond, 1828), 37; Jones to Madison, July 22, 1782, Ford, ed., Letters of Joseph Jones, 96; Edward W. James, The Lower Norfolk County Virginia Antiquary (New York, 1951), 95; Md. Gaz., Nov. 10, 1780.

Mitchell paid a small fee and took back her two slaves who had been intercepted in their attempt to reach the armed ship *Cherokee*. Even more fortunate was Billy, the recaptured valet of James Madison. Not wanting to punish his slave "merely for coveting that liberty for which we had paid the price of so much blood, and have proclaimed so often to be the right, & worthy pursuit of every human being," the future president disposed of Billy as an indentured servant in Pennsylvania, where in seven years he would become a free man.[81]

* * *

A few slave-bereft masters sought to obtain flags of truce to go into the British lines where they hoped to recover their runaways. In Maryland it was the Council which was vested with the power to grant flags of truce and in March it gave Ann Tilley permission to attempt the recovery of a slave woman and her three children, who had been taken off to the British by the woman's mulatto husband. This Council action was almost unprecedented. Writing to a Somerset County master in April 1778, the Council expressed its regret over "the loss the gentlemen of your county have sustained by their Negroes going away," but pointed out that every previous request for a flag of truce had been rejected. The British would not restore the slaves, said the Council, unless the masters made the sort of concessions "which no American ought to do."[82]

Virginia's Council was less unyielding. In February 1778 it gave permission to Major Thomas Smith of Gloucester and Colonel Littleton Savage of Northampton County to go on board the British ships at York and Hampton to make application for their runaways. A week later the Council granted John Morgan's petition to try to reclaim from the British naval commanders "sundry Slaves" belonging to William S. Benjamin and William Churchill.[83]

High ranking officers were sometimes asked to intercede on behalf of slave masters. In the summer of 1782 when a

81. Journal of the Council of Safety, Dec. 20, 1775, S. C. Hist. Soc., *Coll.*, 3 (1859), 103; Madison to James Madison, Sept. 8, 1783, Hunt, ed., *Writings of Madison*, II, 15.

82. *Arch. of Md.*, XLV, 359; Council to George Dashiell, Apr. 6, 1778, *ibid.*, XXI, 11-12.

83. McIlwaine and Hall, eds., *Journals of the Council of State of Va.*, II, 82, 86.

British raiding party in Georgia took thirty-seven Negroes, Lachlan McIntosh asked General Greene to seek their recovery by appealing to Alexander Leslie, His Majesty's commandant. McIntosh's own brother had lost seven Negroes and some household furnishings in the raid.[84]

The flag of truce as a means of recovering slaves never had a wide use. American authorities—civilian and military—felt that a flag might be used to cover trading with the enemy. Moreover, a flag to recover slaves was, as the Maryland Council contended, a humiliation. Both Lafayette and George Washington expressed their displeasure when the latter's brother Lund went aboard a British sloop in the Potomac and brought food to the naval officers in the hope of persuading them to return the Washington slaves.[85]

The use of flags was made all the more distasteful by the attitude of British officers, particularly naval officers, who assumed an air of righteousness not untinged with the supercilious. George Montagu, commanding the *Fowey* off Annapolis in the summer of 1776, brusquely informed Charles Carroll that his instructions were not to deliver up any subjects of His Majesty, but to receive "all persons well affected," giving them every protection.[86] A similar stand was taken by Sir George Collier, commander of the British fleet in America, when Governor Patrick Henry sent a flag-bearing delegation to the ships in Hampton Roads in May 1779. Collier sent word that although his sovereign's ships had not come to Virginia waters to entice Negroes on board, the British flag, nevertheless, afforded asylum to the distressed wherever they might be found.[87]

British army officers were somewhat more conciliatory. Turncoat Benedict Arnold's policy was to return no Negroes belonging to any American who was in government or army service, or liable to militia duty; however, widows and orphans owning British-held slaves might recover them by following a prescribed procedure. Lord Cornwallis saw fit to add a trouble-

84. Joseph W. Barnwell, ed., "Letters to General Greene and Others," *S. C. Hist. and Gen. Mag.*, 16 (1915), 149.

85. For this episode see Douglass S. Freeman, *George Washington; A Biography*, 6 vols. (New York, 1948-54), V, 282-83.

86. Montagu to Carroll, June 24, 1776, *Arch. of Md.*, XI, 515.

87. "Collier's and Mathew's Invasion of Virginia in 1779," *Va. Hist. Reg.*, 4 (1851), 191-92.

some detail: he would permit masters who were not anti-British to search his camp and take their slaves, provided that the slaves would consent to go.[88] This reluctance to return Negroes foreshadowed the difficulties that would come with the departure of the British when the war ended.

* * *

To recover slaves by a flag of truce was emotionally less satisfying to patriotic Americans than retaliation, and to entice or seize enemy-held Negroes was an effective way to strike back. One of the earliest instances of counterpersuasion occurred in 1775 in southern Maryland. Here loyalist John F. D. Smyth lost five of his bondmen, two of whom were carried away to act as drummers in the militia, and three others who, as Smyth put it, were "inveigled" from him. One of the most prominent and hardest hit of the loyalist losers was South Carolinian William Bull, physician and former colonial governor as well as planter, who was stripped of 160 of his 180 slaves.[89]

Georgia was the scene of the most widespread seizure of British-held blacks. Former Governor Wright reported in 1780 that the main object of the American commanders, besides destroying British provisions, was to seize Negroes. The "Rebel Horse" descended on Sir James's own plantation at Ogeechee in March 1780 and carried away many slaves.[90] The state's island-fringed coast beckoned invitingly to American boats bent on taking Negroes. A loyalist residing along the Little Satilla River lost eight slaves to a privateer, and another British sympathizer residing along the Savannah was deprived of fifteen "working" Negroes and seven children. In a raid at White Bluff in February 1780 four American vessels carried off nearly

88. Arnold to Peter Muhlenberg, Feb. 23, 1781, Henry A. Muhlenberg, *The Life of Major-General Peter Muhlenberg* (Phila., 1849), 387-88; Cornwallis to Thomas Nelson, Jr., Aug. 5, 1781, *American Historical Record,* 1 (1872), 180.

89. "Journals of Capt. John Ferdinand Dalziel Smyth, of the Queen's Rangers," *Pa. Mag. of Hist. and Biog.,* 39 (1915), 151; Bull to Germain, June 28, 1781, Colonial Office Papers, Ser. 5, CLXXVI, 112, Public Record Office, London, Library of Congress transcripts. Hereafter cited as C. O. 5/.

90. Wright to John Graham, Apr. 20, 1780, Hist. MSS Comm.: *Report of American Manuscripts in the Royal Institution of Great Britain,* 4 vols. (London, Dublin, Hereford, 1904-09), II, 114. Hereafter cited a *Amer. MSS in Royal Inst. of G. B.* Wright to Germain, Apr. 4, 1780, Ga. Hist. Soc., *Coll.,* 3 (1873), 281.

140 Negroes. In the following months "rebel" galleys frequently penetrated the coastal inlets, sailing away with their slave loot.[91]

* * *

What happened to the thousands of Negroes who remained with the British is a story in itself.

91. "Papers of Lachlan McIntosh," *ibid.*, 12 (1957), 100; United Empire Loyalists, *Second Report of the Bureau of Archives for the Province of Ontario,* 2 vols. (Toronto, 1905), 793; Augustine Prevost to Henry Clinton, Feb. 11, 1780, *Amer. MSS in Royal Inst. of G. B.,* II, 88; Wright to Germain, Dec. 20, 1780, Ga. Hist. Soc., *Coll.,* 3 (1873), 327.

CHAPTER VIII

IN THE KING'S SERVICE

"These Negroes have undoubtedly been of greatest service"
General William Phillips to Henry Clinton
Portsmouth, Virginia, April 3, 1781

Seven days after Bunker Hill the commander-in-chief of His Majesty's forces in North America ordered the town major of Boston to furnish headquarters with a population report. Soon forthcoming, the officer's report listed the city's civilian inhabitants as numbering 6,247, of which 561 were Negroes. To this figure on the number of colored Bostonians the town major appended an explanatory line: "The Negroes [sic] employed in the King's Service are not included in the above."[1] Early the next year when the British left Boston for Halifax they took with them their "Company of Negroes." Thus the wartime pattern was set: wherever the British were, there also were their black auxiliaries. This use of the colored man may be illustrated by briefly noting the major urban areas occupied by the British at one time or another.

New York was early occupied by the British and here their employment of Negroes extended to some seven years. Most often Negroes worked as teamsters; at one time most of the drivers in the city's quartermaster department were runaway slaves, working for wages and housed in separate barracks. Seeking additional drivers in October 1779 for use in Brooklyn, the British command ordered the captains of the Queen's County militia to compile lists of refugee Negroes in their districts. Negroes, however, were employed in other capacities. In 1781 the British Commissary department in New York counted 10 Negroes among its total personnel of 102. On Long Island—

1. An Account of the Number of Inhabitants in the Town of Boston Agreeable to returns given into the Town Major by Order of His Excellency General Gage, as of June 24, 1775, Gage MSS, Amer. Ser., Clements Lib.

at Flushing and Jamaica—the British employed Negroes in the forage service, the names of all of the eight workers at Jamaica being preceded by the word, "black." At Fort Meadows there were sixty-three Negroes on the payroll of the Seventeenth Regiment of Light Dragoons.[2]

In Philadelphia the British had a "Company of Black Pioneers," consisting of some seventy-two "privates," fifteen women and eight children. Under the command of Captain Allen Stewart this contingent was clothed by the army, each man receiving in September 1778 a great coat, hat, sailor jacket, white shirt and winter trousers. The corps performed whatever task was assigned to them: on one occasion it was "to attend the Scavengers,—assist in Cleaning the Streets and Removing all Newsiances being thrown into the Streets."[3]

Naturally it was in the South that the British found the greatest opportunity to exploit America's Negro population. Their first capture of a major Southern metropolis was Savannah in the early winter of 1778. There they initiated an extensive use of black manpower. Late in the spring of 1779 General Prevost appointed an agent for the army, whose function was to round up captured slaves and place them at the disposal of the military. Prevost spent the summer months in getting ready for the assault he knew was coming from the Americans and their French allies, led by the Count d'Estaing. In Savannah civilian and military authorities put Negroes to work in fortifying the city, building redoubts and raising batteries between them, using materials which they had dismantled from plantation machinery and public buildings.[4] Savannah

2. Thomas Jones, *History of New York During the Revolutionary War,* 2 vols. (New York, 1879), I, 334. Samuel Treadwell to John Kissam, Oct. 15, 1779, Letters of John Kissam of Queen's County (transcripts), N. Y. Pub. Lib.; "Proceedings of a Board of General Officers of the British Army at New York, 1781," N. Y. Hist. Soc., *Coll.,* 49 (1916), 122-26, 139, 141-42. These laborers are listed by name.

3. State of the Black Company of Pioneers Given up by Capt. Martin to Capt. Stewart, July 13, 1777, A Return of Capt. Allen Stewart's Company of Black Pioneers, Sept. 17, 1778, *Howe Orderly Book,* Mar. 22, 1778, Clinton Papers, Clements Lib.

4. *Rivington's Royal Gazette,* July 14, 1779, in F. B. Hough, *The Siege of Savannah* (Albany, 1866), 28. The same source put the number of Negro laborers employed by the British during the siege at 200 to 300. However, the number was 1,000, according to a "List of English in Town on October 9th, 1779, according to statements of Deserters," Stevens, ed., *Facsimiles,* XXIII, No. 2016; it was 2,000, according to the *Maryland Gazette,* Nov. 26,

successfully withstood the siege, eliciting the praise of Sir Henry Clinton as an example of "what perseverance and resolution are capable of effecting behind works."[5]

To the British in Savannah the lifting of the siege was no signal to relax vigilance and dispense with Negro laborers. Within two months Governor Wright had organized 250 of the captured and runaway Negroes into a labor corps. In early December, Wright and the Council issued an order calling for delivery of slaves to British service from all plantations which had not yet furnished them. The slaves were to report to His Majesty's chief engineer, bringing with them hoes, axes, spades, and cooking utensils. They would be supplied with provisions during their six-day work stint. To take charge of them the Council appointed three Commissioners of Claims, who were authorized to appoint overseers to supervise the labor of the slaves on plantations. The commissioners could also hire out able-bodied Negroes, charging £5 a year for them, subject to deductions for clothing and time lost in smallpox.[6]

The commissioners discovered they had very little business, simply because other agencies had already pre-empted the supply of slaves. Negroes were not only being employed "in publick Works," the commissioners complained in April 1780, but they were also being used by the various branches of the army—the engineer, commissary, and quartermaster departments—and by "their Deputies and other Military Departments as also many Officers and even Soldiers of the Army."[7] Indeed, so few slaves did the commissioners have at their disposal that the quartermaster department did not bother to seek their assistance, finding it more fruitful to deal with masters who had black teamsters for hire.

Slave impressment was no more popular in Tory Georgia than elsewhere, but with the threat to Augusta in the late

---

1779; another source placed it at 4,000. Roberta Leighton, "Meyronnet de Saint Marc's Journal," N. Y. Hist. Soc., *Qtly.*, 36 (1952), 272. A modern estimate places the figure at between 400 and 500. Lawrence, *Storm Over Savannah*, 43.

5. Willcox, ed., *The American Rebellion*, 150.

6. Lilla M. Hawes, ed., "Minutes of the Governor and Council of Georgia, October 4, 1774 . . . through September 20, 1780," Ga. Hist. Soc., *Coll.*, 10 (1952), 50, 70, 92.

7. Commissioners of Claims to James Wright, Apr. 29, 1780, Ga. Hist. Soc., *Coll.*, 3 (1873), 299.

summer of 1780, Governor Wright convened the Assembly and urged it to authorize such a measure. Wright's proposals were quickly enacted: all masters with male slaves from sixteen to sixty were obliged to furnish such as were needed, along with their tools. On the day the impressment bill became law, the Governor collected over four hundred slaves and put them to work on the Savannah fortifications.[8]

The military commander at Savannah, General Prevost, was no stranger to black military laborers, having used them in Florida. "I have besides a number of Negroes employed to repair the Lines," he had written from St. Augustine in June 1778, "making of Redoubts and finishing the Outworks of the Fort." Prevost's successor at St. Augustine, Colonel Lewis von Fuser, reported on October 2, 1779, that he had 130 Negroes currently at work, with more expected every day. Three weeks later Colonel Fuser reported that 300 Negroes were at work and that the covered ways and glacis were almost completed.[9] At St. Augustine, as generally in the South, the British army preferred whenever possible to hire Negroes from loyalist masters rather than resort to impressment.

Nowhere else did the British make greater use of the Negro than at Charleston. During the siege of the city, slaves performed multifarious tasks. They drained ditches. On one occasion when sunken hulks clogged the Cooper River, interfering with offensive operations, the British command ordered a detail of 134 Negroes put to work dragging several large rowboats overland. Following the surrender of the capital on May 12, the British sent out parties of non-commissioned officers and Negroes to dismount and remove the captured guns.[10]

The fall of South Carolina's largest city brought into the British lines a truly embarrassing number of blacks, creating problems of feeding, clothing and controlling them. Confessing his "serious distress" about the excess of Negroes attending

8. Candler, ed., *Col. Rec. of Ga.*, XV, 625-26; Wright to Germain, Dec. 1, 1780, Ga. Hist. Soc., *Coll.*, 3 (1859), 322.

9. Prevost to Sir William Howe, June 5, 1778, L. Von Fuser to Henry Clinton, Oct. 2, 24, 1779, *Amer. MSS in Royal Inst. of G. B.*, I, 261, II, 39. Late the following month, however, Fuser ruefully informed Clinton that with the raising of the siege at Savannah, the planters, including high civilian officials, had taken back their slaves. Fuser to Howe, Nov. 21, 1779, *ibid.*, 64.

10. Edward J. Lowell, *The Hessians in the American Revolution* (New York, 1884), 248; Orderly Book, 1780-1781, of Major Traille, May 25, 1780, George Wray Papers, Clements Lib.

his corps, Lord Cornwallis on May 17 sought the advice of his commander-in-chief, Clinton. Three days later Clinton sent word that headquarters was considering the matter and would announce a policy soon, but that in the meantime officers should discourage any more colored refugees from attaching themselves to the army.[11]

On June 3 Clinton announced his policy, which extended favorable terms to Negroes. Slaves belonging to loyalist masters would be restored only on condition that they would not be punished for running away. Loyalist masters might hire their slaves to the army, receiving full compensation if the slave were killed. "Rebel" masters, of course, had no such choices; Negroes formerly belonging to unfriendly persons, said Clinton, now belonged "to the public." If the escaped slaves of rebel masters served their new master faithfully for the war's duration, they would receive their freedom. For the present they were to be put to work in the various departments of the army and given provisions, clothing, and adequate pay.[12]

To administer the new program, Clinton recommended the appointment of "some humane person with a proper salary." The man chosen was John Cruden, appointed in September 1780 as commissioner for the seizure, care and management of all estates and property sequestered by the British in South Carolina; he was also authorized to employ all slaves who came into his hands.[13] Since he was paid a commission rather than a flat salary, Cruden tried to maximize his operations. To gain civilian goodwill he appointed as deputies such South Carolinians of standing as were available. He signed warrants with 100 overseers who were engaged to manage the more than 5,000 Negroes he had seized.[14]

But everything seemed to conspire against Cruden. The plantations he took over were in a run-down condition typical

11. Cornwallis to Clinton, May 17, 1780, Clinton Papers, Clements Lib.; Clinton to Cornwallis, May 20, 1780, Cornwallis Papers (transcripts), Lib. Cong. Hereafter cited as Cornwallis transcripts.

12. Memorandum for the Commandant at Charlestown and General Earl Cornwallis, June 3, 1780, Carleton photostats.

13. For a copy of Cruden's commission see Cornwallis transcripts, VII. In Aug. 1781 North Carolina was placed under Cruden's jurisdiction, the Negroes there to be used in sawing timber or making naval stores. Nisbet Balfour to Cruden, Aug. 22, 1781, *ibid.*

14. Cruden's report to a Committee to inspect his account appointed by the Commandant at Charleston and the Board of Police, *ibid.*

of abandoned lands which had witnessed guerilla warfare. Equally distressing to Cruden was the large number of needy and ailing Negroes, many of whom were naked or ridden with smallpox. But the greatest obstacle to the successful cultivation of the estates was a series of thrusts by the American armies in the spring of 1781, which reversed the tide of war. "In the short space of five weeks," observed General Clinton, the British commander, "we lost or evacuated every post we possessed in the Carolinas and Georgia with provisions and stores to an immense amount."[15]

As if American military advances were not enough, Cruden had difficulties with his own army officers, many of whom, like the colonel of engineers, James Moncrief, were laggard in furnishing returns of their Negroes. To cap Cruden's problems, the city slaves under his supervision sometimes became drunk or unruly, or they plotted escape, and it became necessary to lock them up in a sugarhouse turned jail.

Nevertheless, Commissioner Cruden's Negroes or those under supervision of other officers furnished substantial aid to various British military departments in Charleston. The quartermaster and the commissary departments procured Negroes from one of Cruden's overseers. Generally the hiring pay rate was 2s. a day for common laborers and a higher rate for mechanics.[16] The royal artillery likewise tapped the pool of blacks. In two returns under date of January 4, 1782, the department listed forty laborers, nineteen servants, ten sawyers, eight carpenters, two smiths, and one teamster.[17] A subsequent return the same year listed sixty-seven laborers, thirty-five teamsters, six carpenters, three sawyers, two turnwheelers, one painter, and one wheeler. Muster rolls of the civil branch of the field train of

15. Willcox, ed., *The American Rebellion*, 296.
16. Account of Negro labourer's employed in the Quarter Master & Commissary General's department . . . from 1st July 1780 to 30th September inclusive, Carleton photostats.
17. Return of Negroes employ'd as Artificers, Labourers and Servants in the Royal Artillery Department, and Return of Negro Servants in the Royal Artillery & Civil Branch of Ordnance, both in Muster Rolls, Journals of Stores, Expense Book, Charleston, 1780-1783, Wray Papers, Clements Lib. The first of these returns appears as a double-page entry which, in tabular form, includes five headings: trades, Negroes' names, remarks, owner's names, and place of residence. The second of these returns, in tabular form, lists the names of the slaves, their owners' names, place of residence, remarks, and whom they served.

artillery in 1782 listed free Negroes as carpenters, wheelers, smiths, sawyers, coopers, painters, armorers, and turnwheelers.[18]

Relations between Negroes and the British forces in occupation of Charleston did not always turn upon labor service. On an evening in January 1782, a group of officers put aside the cares of the day to attend an "Ethiopian Ball," whose managers were three "Negro Wenches assuming their Mistress's names." The female slaves invited to the affair had been "dressed up in taste, with the richest silks, and false rolls in their heads," the expenses borne by their officer escorts. "This Ball was held at a very capital private House in Charlestown," wrote an indignant American prisoner, "and the Supper cost not less than £80 Sterling, and these tyrants danced with these Slaves until four o'clock in the morning."[19]

Despite the indignation of an American patriot, the infrequency of such social notes from Charleston serves but to underscore the Negro's labor contribution to the British armies in the South Carolina theatre. This contribution is cogently illustrated in two lines from an English officer at Camden to General Cornwallis: "Your lordship will not be Surprised that our works are not in greater forwardness. The Negroes took the Small Pox, Deserted, Many Died."[20]

* * *

In the final campaigns of the war the British continued to employ Negroes on a large scale. Blacks accompanied the moving army as Cornwallis departed Charleston in the winter of 1781 and moved northward to meet his destiny at Yorktown.

In his complicated maneuvers across the state of North Carolina his army lived off the country; Negroes were assigned the task of collecting provisions. Going out in parties sometimes numbering into the hundreds, Negro foragers drove off the livestock of enemy farmers and stripped their cellars of food supplies stored for winter use. They brought their "hauls"

18. Return of Negroes employed in the Royal Artillery Department, Charleston, Nov. 5, 1782, Muster Roll of the Civil Branch attending His Majesty's Field Train of Artillery, under dates of Jan. 4, May 14, Aug. 6, Sept. 28, and Oct. 1, 1782, *ibid.*

19. For this affair, including the invitational note from the three managers, see Daniel Stevens to John Wendell, Feb. 20, 1782, "The Boyd-Stevens Letters," Mass. Hist. Soc., *Proc.*, 3rd Ser., 48 (1915), 342-43.

20. George Turnbull to Cornwallis, Nov. 3, 1780, Cornwallis transcripts, IV, Lib. Cong.

back to British regimental quartermasters, each of whom had eight Negroes to assist him in receiving the provisions. Like most operations of this kind, these sallies into the countryside tended to degenerate into mere pillaging expeditions. To prevent Negro foragers from getting out of hand, Cornwallis on February 5, 1781, issued orders that no Negro was to be permitted to carry firearms under any circumstances. Two weeks later Cornwallis ordered that every Negro in the army be given a ticket of identification by the department to which he belonged; an unticketed Negro was to be seized and jailed by the deputy provost.[21]

As Cornwallis moved into Virginia in May 1781 and took up positions, he and other British commanders again pressed Negroes into labor service. General Arnold had already employed them to build dams and "in the several public departments and for the Works." A black corps, numbering nearly five hundred, was soon busy with the trench fortification at Portsmouth,[22] and in constructing the defenses at Yorktown and Gloucester. They also acted as military servants; in mid-July Cornwallis decreed that soldiers could no longer be used as orderlies—such places were to be filled by blacks. Also, it appears, they were of considerable help in impressing horses for the British mounted forces: "Nothing but a treaty of alliance with the Negroes can find us dragoon Horses," wrote Lafayette to Washington, "and it is by this means the enemy have so formidable a Cavalry."[23]

A final service the Negroes performed in the Yorktown campaign was to act as involuntary agents in the contemporary version of germ warfare. Afforded even fewer sanitary precautions than a British private, Negro military laborers were highly susceptible to disease. "An immense number of Negroes have died in the most miserable Manner in York," wrote St. George

21. A. R. Newsome, ed., "A British Orderly Book, 1780-1781," *North Carolina Historical Review*, 9 (1932), 296, 370.

22. Phillips to Clinton, Apr. 3, Alexander Leslie to Cornwallis, June 3, 1781, Cornwallis transcripts, VI, Lib. Cong. The German soldier, Stephan Popp, put the figure of Negro workers as "over a thousand." Joseph G. Rosengarten, "Popp's Journal," *Pa. Mag. of Hist. and Biog.*, 36 (1902), 38.

23. Cornwallis to Clinton, Aug. 22, 1781, "Lord Cornwallis's Movements and Operations in Virginia, in 1781," *Va. Hist. Reg.*, 6 (1853), 189; Bernard A. Uhlendorf, ed., *Revolution in America: Baurmeister Journals* (New Brunswick, 1957), 443; Lafayette to Washington, July 20, 1781, Washington Papers, CLXXX, No. 53, Lib. Cong.

Tucker. At his camp before the town, General Edward Hand observed that almost every thicket held its "Wretched Negroes Carcase"—a scene which also made its impression on another American officer, Ebenezer Denny, who recorded in his journal: "Negroes lie about, sick and dying, in every state of the small pox." British commanders were unhappy about these casualties, but General Leslie thought that the stricken slaves might perform a last service. "About 700 Negroes are come down the River in the Small Pox," he wrote to his superior, "I shall distribute them about the Rebell Plantations."[24]

* * *

Like the Americans the British employed Negroes as spies, guides, and informers. The activities of black spies appear mainly in accounts of their capture by patriotic forces. In December 1776 an American scouting party brought in a Negro spy at Peekskill, the slave of a Tory master. At Red Bank the Americans put to the gallows three spies, one white and two Negroes, who had been with the Hessians. At Charleston in the early months of the war Scipio Handley found ways to bring messages to and from Governor Lord William Campbell, a refugee on board a British vessel off the city; eventually found out, Scipio was imprisoned, only to save his neck by filing his way out of the jail. An even closer brush with eternity was the experience of a free Negro, Benjamin Whitcuff, who for two years operated as a spy in New Jersey. Finally caught by the Americans, Whitcuff was turned over to the hangman and had been dangling in air for three minutes before he was rescued by the sudden arrival of a British detachment.[25]

Ordinarily, Negroes were merely casual informers rather than actual spies. In June 1777 two Negroes from Narragansett, Rhode Island, came to British headquarters bringing information on currency inflation, food supply and army recruiting. The day after the fall of Savannah, Captain Hyde Parker of

24. Coleman, *St. George Tucker*, 74; Edward Hand to Jasper Yeates, Oct. 12, 1781, N. Y. Pub. Lib., *Bulletin*, 6 (1902), 286; W. H. Denny, ed., *Military Journal of Major Ebenezer Denny* (Phila., 1859), 45; Leslie to Cornwallis, July 13, 1781, Cornwallis transcripts, VI, Lib. Cong.

25. *Amer. Arch.*, 5th Ser., III, 1109; Charles J. Bushnell, *The Memoirs of Samuel Smith* (New York, 1860), 10; Robert W. Barnwell, Jr., Loyalism in South Carolina, 1765-1785 (unpubl. Ph.D. diss., Duke University, 1941), 76; John Bakeless, *Turncoats, Traitors and Heroes* (Phila., 1959), 268.

the frigate *Phoenix* received word from Negroes as to the exact location of two American galleys he was anxious to capture. Eight months later when the British were preparing for the American attack on the city, they received information from two Negroes deserted from the enemy.[26] It was in South Carolina, apparently, that Negro informers were most numerous. In the spring of 1780 some Negroes left beleaguered Charleston, bringing information about the defending American forces. One of these was Duncan, slave of a Charleston carpenter. Escaping by foot and canoe, Duncan made his way to British lines where he furnished John André with a full report on the condition of the American warships in the harbor, the food supplies and forage, and the number of troops arriving and those whose time was expiring.[27] The handsome young major, destined himself in six months to be hanged as a spy, took down Duncan's report in some detail.

Another British officer who made use of Negro informers was Lord Francis Rawdon, commander at Camden. Rawdon's dispatches to Cornwallis late in 1780 contain such passages as these:

A Negro asserts that a party of Rebel Cavalry under the command of Major Marshall lay last night at Murphy's beyond Lynches Creek; 25 miles from hence. . . .[28]

A Negro who came in this afternoon says that he was carried Prisoner to Morgan and Washington at Hanging Rock, and escaped from them last night. He reports that in concert with Morgan they were to have attacked this post; & he mentions the point at which the assault was to have been divested, which is indeed the weakest in the line. The dispersion of Morgan's force overturned this plan.[29]

Rawdon's associate, the equally able and youthful Banastre Tarleton, also welcomed intelligence brought by blacks. Told

26. *Diary of Frederick Mackenzie*, I, 145; Parker to Philip Stephens, Jan. 14, 1779, Stevens, ed., *Facsimiles*, XII, No. 1246; "Journal of the Siege of Savannah, September 21, 1779," in Moore, *Materials for History Printed from Original Manuscripts*, 164.

27. "The Siege of Charleston: Journal of Captain Peter Russell, December 25, 1779 to May 2, 1780," *Amer. Hist. Rev.*, 4 (1898-99), 494-95; John André, Report of Intelligence before May 12, 1780, Clinton Papers, Clements Lib.

28. Rawdon to Cornwallis, Dec. 1, 1780, Cornwallis transcripts, IV, Lib. Cong.

29. Rawdon to Cornwallis, Nov. 13, 1780, *ibid.*

by a Negro of a "Party" at Jack's Creek on the Congaree in November 1780, Tarleton realized that General Marion's men had chosen that spot to bivouac. Tarleton soon attacked Jack's Creek, laying waste the houses and plantations of "violent Rebels."[30]

Tarleton's faith in Negro informers was not always shared by Rawdon. On one occasion his lordship informed Cornwallis that it was his opinion that a Negro trusted by Tarleton was deliberately feeding false intelligence to the cavalry officer. Such double dealing was not unprecedented. On Yonge Island a Negro gave misleading information to a party of sixty redcoats in April 1779. Bent on ransacking the Wilkinson estate, the British were deterred when a Negro who knew better told them that the plantation was run-down and abandoned. His mistress, the young and beautiful Eliza Wilkinson, blessed him "for his consideration and pity."[31]

The British were occasionally deceived, but they were not thereby deterred from pumping information from the blacks. In one company of fifty-four Negro laborers in South Carolina, the roster listed not only the slaves' names, where they came from, and who their owners were, but also what they knew. A slave from Lockert's Folly, "knows the roads & Woods a dozen miles round"; a slave from Charleston "knows the back roads as high as Goose Creek." One Negro, Paul, who came from Savannah, "knows nothing," but he was exceptional.[32]

Closely akin to informers were slave guides. Perhaps the best known of these was Quamino Dolly who assisted the British in the capture of Savannah. British commander Archibald Campbell was preparing a frontal attack on the city when Dolly volunteered to conduct the troops through a swamp to the rear of the American position.[33] With alacrity, Campbell sent his light infantry to follow the aged black. The outnumbered and

30. Tarleton to Cornwallis, Nov. 5, Nov. 11, 1780, *ibid.;* Robert D. Bass, *Swamp Fox* (New York, 1959), 80-81.

31. Rawdon to Cornwallis, Nov. 14, 1780, Cornwallis transcripts, IV, Lib. Cong.; Carolina Gilman, ed., *Letters of Eliza Wilkinson* (New York, 1839), 24.

32. "List of the Names of Negroes belonging to Capt. Martin's Company, whom they belonged to, and the respective places they lived at," Clinton Papers, Box 8 of undated and unsigned MSS, Clements Lib.

33. Campbell to Germain, Jan. 16, 1779, Clinton Papers, Clements Lib., also in Stevens, ed., *Facsimiles,* XII, No. 1247.

unsuspecting American regulars and militiamen scarcely knew what hit them. Attacked from the front and from the wooded swamp, they were quickly routed. Eight months later Negro guides were instrumental in the defense of Savannah. On the morning of September 16 the British commander, Prevost, had been summoned to surrender and had asked for a twenty-four hour delay to ponder the matter. Before the time limit expired, he was most providentially re-enforced by a detachment under John Maitland. Colonel Maitland, who had journeyed from Beaufort, owed his good fortune in reaching Savannah to Negro guides. In the final stages of his hurried trip, he had come to the Dawfusie River, where his progress was blocked by French forces. Some Gullah fishermen then volunteered to lead him around the enemy. His party made its way through an obscure and winding waterway, across swamps, bogs, and marshes. Under cover of a dense fog and passing over a terrain never traversed before "but by bears, wolves and runaway Negroes," the British troops reached Savannah undetected by the French.[34] The failure to prevent Maitland from reaching Savannah was "an unpardonable mistake," observed D'Estaing, "which decided the ill success of the operation."[35]

With their intimate knowledge of the countryside, Negroes rendered valuable service not only as guides accompanying British troops, but in directing couriers. Prevost and Maitland employed them in the Georgia theatre to travel with messengers carrying dispatches from one post to another.[36] On February 20, 1780, two Negroes, Bristol and Harry, accompanied a messenger bearing dispatches between British detachments at the siege of Charleston.[37] In Virginia in January 1781 a Negro conducted Colonel John Graves Simcoe to the Charles City courthouse where the Britishers surprised and routed the local militiamen as they were diverting themselves in a tavern. At

34. *Md. Gaz.*, Nov. 5, 1779. For this exploit see Lawrence, *Storm Over Savannah*, 49-50.

35. "Notes from the Observations of Count d'Estaing on M. O'Conner's Journal of the Siege of Savannah," Stevens, ed., *Facsimiles*, XXIII, No. 2018.

36. For such an instance, in which the Americans captured a party of 2 British officers, 4 privates and 10 Negroes, see *Va. Gaz.*, Oct. 9, 1779.

37. "Siege of Charleston: Journal of Captain Peter Russell. . . ." *Amer. Hist. Rev.*, 4 (1899), 486.

Yorktown slave guides were counted as a military asset: a headquarters statement dated September 30, 1781, and entitled "Instructions to Assistant Commissary of Captures," had this advice: "And to get good Guides; You will generally find Negroes at the house where Head Quarters will be; to be very useful and intelligent in these matters."[38]

Early in the war some British officers, like Lord Dunmore, contemplated recruiting masses of black troops. This policy was not adopted. The need for military laborers nearly exhausted the available supply of able-bodied Negroes. Moreover, as the British were not the first to discover, placing a gun in the hands of a former slave created problems of its own. There was, however, a limited use of Negroes in combat. Commanding officers sometimes took the risk of putting small numbers of armed Negroes on the field of battle, and when slaves worked on intrenchments exposed to enemy fire, it was sometimes considered expedient to arm them for their own defense.

One finds occasional mention of Negro soldiers in British forces active in the Northern states. In the spring of 1777 two English deserters in Rhode Island reported that one of the regiments at Newport included a company of about one hundred Negroes. In a skirmish on Long Island late in 1776 Rhode Island troops took twenty-four prisoners, of whom five or six were colored men.[39] At Stony Point in July 1779 three of the prisoners taken by Anthony Wayne were Negroes. A month later at the Battle of Newtown—a decisive action which reduced the power of Britain's Iroquois allies—one of the two prisoners was "an enlisted negro in one of the Tory companies."[40]

38. Henry B. Dawson, *Battles of the United States,* 2 vols. (New York, 1858), I, 645-46; Cornwallis transcripts, VI, Lib. Cong.

39. R. I. Hist. Soc., MSS, III; *Va. Gaz.,* Nov. 29, 1776. In New York in Feb. 1777 a deserter brought information that there were 20 Negroes in the British army on York Island. Paltsits, ed., *Minutes of the Committee for Detecting Conspiracies,* I, 121. But such reports were of a piece with that brought by a Negro captured on Long Island in July 1776 who said that the British were enlisting a company of 800 Negroes on Staten Island. Nathanael Greene to George Washington, July 21, 1776, *Amer. Arch.,* 5th Ser., I, 486.

40. "Journal of Lieut. William McDowell of the First Penn'a Regiment, In the Southern Campaign, 1781-1782," *Pa. Arch.,* 2nd Ser., 15 (1893), 338; John Sullivan to George Washington, Aug. 30, 1779, Hammond, ed., *Letters and Papers of Major-General John Sullivan,* III, 111. See also "Diary of Lieut. Obadiah Gore, Jr., in the Sullivan-Clinton Campaign of 1779," N. Y. Pub. Lib., *Bull.,* 33 (1929), 731.

By 1779, however, it was uncommon to find Negro soldiers in northern British armies, even among loyalist regiments. During the first year of the war loyalist companies had been receptive to Negroes,[41] but by early 1777 this attitude had changed. The officers in these troops were moved by a desire to gain respect for their units in British military circles. Alexander Innes, appointed inspector general of the provincial forces in North America in January 1777, was determined to weed out such recruits as Negroes, mulattoes, Indians, and enemy prisoners. His orders to be more selective in issuing warrants of enlistment were quickly obeyed. General Oliver Delancey required all Negroes and other "improper persons" to be discharged from his brigade at once. A Negro in a loyalist company became a rarity.[42]

The Hessian companies were less particular. Sometimes they filled vacancies in the ranks with runaway slaves; most often they restricted Negroes to non-combatant functions. One battalion of the Brunswick contingent under Baron von Riedesel had a Negro drum corps; Carl von Bose's regiment had a Negro drummer, who on one occasion had to be whipped for stealing.[43]

One Negro, named Tye, became the best known and most hated of the blacks who followed the British standard in the northern states. Tye operated in a somewhat free-lance fashion in and around Monmouth, New Jersey. A former follower of Dunmore, Tye commanded a crew of some twenty-five men, whose racial composition was as varied as the tasks they un-

41. "The Tories at Coram are beating up for volunteers to join our enemies. Negroes as well as whites are taken into pay." Henry B. Livington to Jonathan Trumbull, Sept. 8, 1776, *Amer. Arch.*, 5th Ser., II, 252.

42. Innes to Clinton, Nov. 9, 1779, E. Alfred Jones, "A Letter Regarding the Queen's Rangers," *Va. Mag. of Hist. and Biog.*, 30 (1922), 369; *Orderly Book of the Three Battalions of Loyalists Commanded by Brigadier General Oliver Delancey* (New York, 1917), 6. A check of the Library of Congress photostats of the loyalist muster rolls in the Canada Public Archives will support this statement. A muster roll of Captain Aeneas Shaw's company of the Queen's Rangers in late 1781 lists "Black Prince" as a drummer, but he was perhaps the only Negro in the regiment. Canada Public Archives photostats, Ser. C., No. 1864.

43. Baurmeister to Von Jungkenn, June 2, 1777, Uhlendorf, ed., *Revolution in America: Baurmeister Journals*, 89; "The Brunswick Contingent in America, 1776-1783," *Pa. Mag. of Hist. and Biog.*, 15 (1891), 224; *Journal of Lt. John Charles Philip Von Kraft*, N.-Y. Hist. Soc., *Coll.*, Publication Fund Ser., 15 (1883), 183.

dertook. Tye and his company might be found plundering a neighborhood, spiking a gun, or seizing a militia captain. Eventually Tye was fatally wounded while leading an attack on the home of Captain Joshua Huddy, who put up a spirited one-man defense against the raiders.[44]

In the South the British employed Negroes as soldiers to a greater extent than elsewhere, but the number was still quite limited. The problem of control posed inherent difficulties which restrained the British, as well as their opponents, from giving arms to a large number of Negroes. The British experience at Savannah illustrates this point. Faced by the combined Franco-American forces in the autumn of 1779, the British armed some two hundred Negroes. These black auxiliaries took part in some of the skirmishes on the outskirts of the city. On one occasion they pressed the Americans back before having to retire for lack of ammunition; and on another occasion they captured two dragoons and eight horses. As soon as the siege was lifted, however, a group of Savannah citizens sent a petition to the governor, asking him to disarm the Negroes, who were behaving with "great Insolence." Shortly afterward the governor placed before the Council a grand jury presentment which complained that there were great numbers of Negroes who were suffered to stroll about carrying firearms and other weapons.[45]

British civilian and military authorities in Savannah certainly needed no warnings about the risks involved in giving guns to slaves. Yet sometimes there seemed no alternative. In the autumn of 1780 Governor Wright, facing an American threat to Augusta, asked the legislature's permission to organize a Negro corps as a unit of the militia. The lawmakers grudgingly acquiesced, but stipulated that such a force was to be raised only

44. For Tye see "Documents relating to the Revolutionary History of the State of New Jersey," N. J. Hist. Soc., W. A. Whitehead, et al., eds., Archives of the State of New Jersey, 30 vols., 2nd Ser., 4 (Newark, 1914), 434-35, 457. Hereafter cited as N. J. Arch. The Huddy story, widely copied from the Pennsylvania Packet, Oct. 3, 1870, appears in Moore, Diary of the Amer. Rev., II, 322-23.

45. "Notes from the Observations of Count d'Estaing . . . end of October 1779," Stevens, ed., Facsimiles, XXIII, No. 2018; "Account of the Siege of Savannah from a British Source," Ga. Hist. Soc., Coll., 5, pt. 1 (1901), 138; Moore, Materials for History Printed from Original Manuscripts, 172; The petition was dated Oct. 23, and the presentment was placed before the Council on Dec. 28, 1779, "Proceedings and Minutes of Governor and Council," Ga. Hist. Soc., Coll., 10 (1952), 54, 75.

if the situation became more desperate than it was. Possibly Sir James made some sparing use of this power, for it is to be noted that at the time Augusta surrendered in June 1781 there were "about 200 Negroes" on duty at the fort,[46] and in the following spring Savannah had a corps of some 150 armed and equipped Negro infantrymen under the former commanding officer at Augusta, Colonel Thomas Brown. This latter corps constituted slightly more than one-tenth of Savannah's dwindling garrison.[47]

In South Carolina the British appear to have been as sparing in their use of Negro soldiers as in Georgia. Nathanael Greene reported to George Washington in February 1781 that the British in Charleston were recruiting two regiments of slaves; a month later he sent word that the project had been dropped. However, an American officer reported, from Friday's Ferry about the same time, that in a military action "the enemy oblige the negroes they have to make frequent sallies." This alone, commented General Sumter, was "sufficient to rouse and fix the resentment and detestation of every American who possesses common feelings."[48]

In the spring of 1782 the British formed a small group of Negroes, possibly not more than one hundred, into a cavalry detachment. One of its functions was to patrol outside the lines and pick up deserters, but it also saw combat action. Two of the "Negro horse" were killed in a skirmish at Dorchester in April 1782. Despite their services, these armed blacks created some uneasiness. Loyalist William Bull was alarmed over outrages committed by "our black dragoons," to which "their savage nature prompts them."[49]

46. Wright to Commons House of Assembly, Sept. 27, 1780, Candler, ed., *Col. Rec. of Ga.*, XV, 625-26; Wright to Germain, Dec. 1, 1780, Ga. Hist. Soc., *Coll.*, 3 (1859), 322; William Davis to George Weedon, June 25, 1781, Weedon Correspondence, American Philosophical Society, Philadelphia. Davis also gives the number of British as 160 and Tories as "upwards of 200." See also William B. Stevens, *A History of Georgia*, 2 vols. (New York and Phila., 1847-59), II, 257.

47. *Ibid.*, II, 274.

48. Greene to Washington, Feb. 28, Mar. 30, 1781, Washington Papers, CLXVII, No. 62, CLXIX, 70, Lib. Cong.; Sumter to Marion, Feb. 20, 1781, Gibbes, ed., *Doc. Hist. Amer. Rev.*, III, 28.

49. William Seymour, "A Journal of the Southern Expedition, 1780-1783," Historical Society of Delaware, *Papers*, 2 (1896), 35; Bull to Germain, Mar. 25, 1782, C. O. 5/176, 143.

General Greene notified Washington about this time that the enemy had armed and put into uniform not less than seven hundred Negroes.[50] But Greene's intelligence was wide of the mark. Neither the British command in America nor the king's ministers in London had shown any enthusiasm for general enlistment of Negro troops. As a matter of fact, such proposals advanced by none other than John Murray, Earl of Dunmore, had already been rejected.

Dunmore landed in Charleston on the last day of 1781. Having no assignment and wishing to make his presence felt, he pronounced that the solution to British military problems in the South was Negro soldier recruitment on a large scale. His lordship quickly won the support of commissioner John Cruden, who on January 5 submitted to him an elaborate scheme for raising 10,000 blacks. Inured to fatigue and to the climate, this corps was expected to drive the enemy from the province.[51]

To Cruden's scheme Dunmore added a few touches of his own. In a long letter to Clinton, he advised placing the 10,000 Negro soldiers under the command of provincial officers, many of whom were then inactive. There would be no Negro officers at the outset, but as vacancies occurred in the non-commissioned ranks they might be filled by Negroes. Slaves would be given a guinea and a crown as an enlistment bonus, with a promise of freedom for faithful service; their loyalist masters would be compensated with a receipt bearing 6 per cent interest for their estimated value. Dunmore modestly announced his own availability to execute the whole plan.[52]

Dunmore's scheme made no progress. Sir Henry Clinton, on the point of resigning his command in America, withheld approval. He refused to authorize Negro troops even after both Colonel Moncrief and General Leslie had urged such a

50. Greene to Washington, Apr. 15, 1782, Washington Papers, CXCV, No. 7, Lib. Cong.

51. Copy of a sketch for Embodying Ten Thousand Black Troops in the Province of South Carolina, presented to the Earl of Dunmore by John Cruden, esq., His Majesty's Commissioner for Forfeited Estates, Dated Charles Town, 5th January, 1782, C. O. 5/175, 411-13.

52. Dunmore to Clinton, Feb. 2, 1782, C. O. 5/175, 407-10. Enclosed in Dunmore's letter was Cruden's proposal and also a suggested plan for organizing the proposed corps, including a typical battalion of the specific number of officers of various ranks and privates, *ibid.*, 415-17. The latter may have been a joint product of Dunmore and Cruden.

step, the latter going so far as to say that putting arms in the hands of Negroes would "soon become indispensably necessary shou'd the war continue to be carried on in this part of America."[53] Such advocates of black troops got no more encouragement from London. On February 5 Dunmore had written to Lord Germain on the subject, but Germain, like Clinton, was already on his way out of office. Finally on June 5, 1782, a reply to Dunmore's letter was issued from the office of the colonial secretary, advising him to consult with the new commander in North America, Sir Guy Carleton, who had full instructions on the Negro troops proposal and would transmit them to Dunmore.[54] Even before this letter left London, however, Dunmore was on his way home, doubtless sensing that the king's ministers had written off the war and were no longer concerned with new levies of any hue.

In East Florida the British appear to have armed fewer Negroes than in either South Carolina or Georgia. In June 1781, a month after the Spanish army gained control of West Florida, the legislature of East Florida reacted to the emergency by authorizing the enlistment of black troops. Governor Tonyn was granted power to arm the slaves, who were to be given their freedom if they showed courage in battle. They were also to receive the sum of £2 and in every year of service, a new uniform consisting of a coat and breeches of good red cloth, a pair of shoes and stockings, a hat, and a white linen shirt.[55] It appears, however, that Tonyn never made use of his authority. Perhaps he was as apprehensive about East Florida's swollen Negro population as he was about the Spanish threat. Yet it may be of passing interest to note that some Negroes from St. Augustine played a role in the last military episode of the war— the re-capture of the Spanish-held Bahamas on April 13, 1783. The expedition was led by a young South Carolinian, Andrew Deveaux, who with a force of provincials and Negroes sailed from St. Augustine, landed near Nassau and summoned the fortress to surrender. His audacity bore fruit as the 500 well-

53. Moncrief to Clinton, Mar. 13, 1782, Carleton photostats; Leslie to Clinton, Mar. 1782 (no date of month), *Amer. MSS in Royal Inst. of G. B.*, III, 438.

54. Unsigned letter to Dunmore, June 5, 1782, C. O. 5/175, 419. A penciled notation on this letter bears the surmise that it may have come from Lord Shelburne, colonial secretary.

55. Charles Loch Mowat, *East Florida as a British Province*, University of California Publications in History, 32 (Berkeley, 1943), 129.

equipped Spanish troops laid down their arms, giving up six galleys and seventy pieces of cannon.[56]

* * *

The British were more inclined to use Negroes at sea than on land. Throughout the war, blacks piloted royal vessels in coastal waters, took part in marauding operations, and swelled the ranks of ordinary seamen. Their most valuable function was to act as pilots.

Negro pilots were sometimes pressed into His Majesty's service, others were runaways, and a few were slaves whose service the British hired from loyalist masters. Whatever their origin, they were highly regarded by naval commanders for their intimate knowledge of American waters. In July 1775 Captain Tollemache, of the H.M.S. *Scorpion,* which was operating on the coast of South Carolina, was apprehensive that the patriots would destroy a light house and certain marks that guided ships across a harbor bar. His solution was to take on board a Negro whom Governor Lord William Campbell designated as "by far the best Pilot in this Harbour, and has marks of his own by which he will carry in any vessel in spite of what they [the patriots] can do." A year later, when the British attacked Charleston, three frigates— the *Syren,* the *Sphinx,* and the *Acteon*—which moved up the channel during the assault, were guided by slaves pressed into service. One of these, the pilot Sampson, was considered so valuable that when the action began he was sent below to a safe place.[57]

Negroes were employed as pilots in other areas of the Southern coast. A British captain, William Hotham, operating in Chesapeake waters, detained a black pilot, who although a good one, did not have the irreplaceable quality of a Sampson. Hotham assured the unwilling Edward that he would be released just as soon as the ship found a better pilot. In St. Augustine, the contingent expenses of the garrison listed sums paid "For Pilotage of Negro Caesar," who had put in forty-three days.[58]

56. *Ibid.,* 139 and 208n.

57. Campbell to Dartmouth, July 19, 1775, Clinton Papers, Clements Lib.; John A. Alden, *General Charles Lee* (Baton Rouge, 1951), 126; Christopher Gadsden to William Moultrie, July 1, 1776, Moultrie, *Memoirs,* I, 171.

58. *Va. Gaz.,* Jan. 31, 1777; "Account of Contingent Expenses incurred for the Use of Troops and Garrison of St. Augustine and its Dependencies

Lured by the prospect of plunder, Negroes found ways to join British marauding expeditions, sometimes as irregular volunteers, sometimes as members of the crew. Late in 1775 Captain James Wallace of the *Rose* was conducted around Conanicut Island by Negroes who gave suggestions as to which houses should be despoiled and burned. When Wallace moved to New York he took with him thirty Negroes from Rhode Island, who joined him in his plundering raids around Haverstraw.[59] Negro participation in such forays was most conspicuous, however, in the later campaigns of the war. Early in April 1781 a barge sailed up the Patuxent to Lower Marlboro where its largely Negro crew plundered the town. A similar barge anchored at Courtney's Island in June of the same year carried thirty-five men, of whom, reported a British deserter, not more than eight were white. Along one stretch of the Rappahannock the inhabitants were "daily exposed to the robberies of privateers." Composed mainly of Negroes, this "Banditti" had dispossessed one man of "his Wearing-Apparel, his Household Linen, Furniture, and four Negroes." Not content, they had also "robbed an innocent, worthy, ancient Widow Lady."[60]

Virginia militia colonels frequently called the attention of state officials to the depredations of these raiding parties. In September 1781 Levin Joynes of Accomac County informed the commissioner of war about the "alarming times this summer, all along the shore, from a set of Barges, manned mostly by our own negroes who have run off." Anybody whom they had a grudge against, added Levin, had better watch out for his property.[61] In July 1782 Colonel Hull of Northumberland County asked the governor for arms and ammunition, since the district was exposed to the will of a "wretched infamous crew of plundering barge-men." Two of these vessels were then

---

from 15 January to 30 June, 1780—By Order of Major Beamsly Glasier, 60th Regt.," Cornwallis transcripts, Lib. Cong.

59. Nathanael Greene to Samuel Ward, Dec. 18, 1775, C. P. Monahan, comp., *The Correspondence of Samuel Ward, May 1775-March 1776* (Providence, 1952), 147; *Amer. Arch.,* 5th Ser., I, 453. For the small gain made by the plunderers in one of these raids see George Clinton to Washington, July 23, 1776, *ibid.,* 545.

60. Stephen West to Governor Lee, Apr. 10, 1781, *Arch. of Md.,* XLVII, 177; "Information of John Anderson, a Deserter, July 2, 1781," *ibid.,* 334; *Maryland Journal* (Annapolis), Sept. 17, 1782.

61. Joynes to William Davies, Sept. 10, 1781, *Cal. of Va. State Papers,* II, 411.

cruising about, each with some twenty white men and a like number of Negroes, who frequently went ashore and took almost everything they could lay their hands on.[62]

The attraction of such occupations to escaped slaves or free Negroes is understandable; however, many colored men found themselves engaged in more regular duties as enlisted seamen in the British navy. Always short of hands, His Majesty's officers were not adverse to signing on blacks. A Negro sailor had one special qualification: unlike many whites, he was not likely to find conditions intolerable and jump ship.

A typical instance in which manpower shortage led to the enlistment of Negroes occurred in April 1779, when the British navy added two row galleys to its Savannah River force. The galleys were needed to assist in the defense of Georgia, but it was a problem where to get the sailors to man them. The solution was explained by Captain Hyde Parker: "I thought it expedient to Order Twelve Negroes (out of a number that had taken refuge on board the Kings Ships, and were Rebel Property) for each; to be Borne upon these Ships Books as Ordinary Seamen being part of the Galley's Crews."[63]

As many as twelve Negroes on a British naval vessel was unusual; the number was more likely to be two or three, as may be noted from the listings or descriptions of prisoners taken by Americans. On a "Lord's Day morning" in August 1775, for example, a schooner which had been seized by British Captain Wallace was forced by bad weather to put in at New London. On board was a crew of four, among them three slaves, two of whom belonged to Governor Cooke. The Negroes were returned to their masters and the white man was sent to "Windham goal."[64]

The attitude of American patriots to captured Negro seamen was more lenient than toward the Negro soldiers who fell into their hands. The authorities in Massachusetts had many opportunities to display their position in the matter since, as a result of privateer captures, more cases of Negro naval prisoners came up for judgment in that state, perhaps than in any other.

62. John Hull to Governor Harrison, July 31, 1782, *ibid.*, III, 242.

63. Parker to Philip Stevens, Apr. 17, 1779, Stevens, ed., *Facsimiles*, XII, No. 1283.

64. Jonathan Trumbull to Washington, Sept. 5, 1775, Sparks, ed., *Letters to Washington,* I, 31-32.

In early January 1776, the Council ordered James Middleton, lately taken on the seas but at the moment in custody of the Plymouth jailkeeper, to be restored to his master. In August 1777 the Council was asked to arrange for an exchange of fifteen naval prisoners at Nantucket for a like number of Americans held by the British in New York. Among the American-held prisoners of Nantucket were two Negroes, Joseph Waters and Thomas Brown. The Council gave its consent to the proposal.[65]

A later case was somewhat similar. A British vessel, the *Ranger,* had been captured en route from Nova Scotia to Bermuda. The *Ranger's* crew numbered twenty, of whom six were Negroes. The captain of the captured vessel asked the Council for permission to proceed with his crew to Bermuda prior to making arrangements for a formal exchange of prisoners. The Council gave consent.[66] Sometimes, too, the Council hired out Negro naval prisoners to private citizens; in July 1779 Colonel Paul Revere was ordered to deliver to Henry Gardner three prisoners "from amongst the Negroes taken by the state vessels and committeed to his care on Castle Island."[67]

Possibly the largest number of Negroes taken prisoner at sea at one time was captured off Sandy Hook in April 1782. An American privateer seized a British sloop of war, the *Alert,* which was just starting out on a cruise of four months. On board the *Alert* were forty-six men, of whom eleven were Negroes.[68] Nine of the latter were condemned in a court of admiralty and auctioned off at a Trenton tavern.[69]

There was no uniform policy with respect to captured Negro seamen. Privateers naturally desired to sell them to increase each man's share of the booty. State naval officers and courts of admiralty also tended to sell Negroes taken at sea, but, as

65. Council to Keeper of Plymouth Gaol, Jan. 6, 1776, Revolutionary Rolls Coll., CLXIV, 234, Mass. Arch.; Paul Hussey to Council, Aug. (no day of month) 1777. The Council minutes show that petition was granted on Aug. 12, *ibid.,* CLXVII, 153.

66. John Lightbourne to Council, Oct. 31, 1780, *ibid.,* CLXXVII, 231-33.

67. Order dated July 5, 1779, *ibid.,* CLXXV, 389.

68. John Bray to William Livingston, Apr. 24, 1782, Richard J. Koke, "War, Profit and Privateers along the New Jersey Coast," N.-Y. Hist. Soc., *Quarterly,* 41 (1957), 323. For the names of these 11 Negroes see "Newspaper Extracts Relating to New Jersey, October, 1780-July, 1782," *N. J. Arch.,* 2nd Ser., 5 (1917), 435.

69. *Ibid.,* 446.

the Massachusetts cases illustrate, a state might dispose of black naval prisoners in a number of ways. Neither states nor privateers had any guidance from the central government. In May 1776 Esek Hopkins, head of the Continental navy, asked a friend who was traveling to Philadelphia to obtain instructions from Congress as to what should be done with slaves taken in the bomb brig, *Bolton*. Four months later Congress appointed a committee of three to consider the question, but the committee appears never to have delivered a report.[70]

In the absence of a policy established by Congress, a commander in the Continental navy was free to treat a Negro prisoner like any other prisoner. Such was the case in January 1780 when Abraham Whipple captured the *Lady Crosby*, a frigate which had been separated by a storm from the rest of a Clinton expedition and was making its way from Sandy Hook to Savannah. Whipple sent seventeen of the *Lady Crosby's* crew to General Lincoln, including one who was listed as "Peter Bush, Negro."[71]

* * *

Finally, the British like the Americans used the Negro not to work or to fight but as a piece of property. British commanders gave slaves to loyalists to make up for their losses, and Britishers themselves appropriated slaves as part of the spoils of the campaign. Possibly the largest grant to a loyalist master was made to William Henry Mills of Cheraw, South Carolina. Mills had lost 57 slaves in the summer of 1780 when his plantation was raided by the patriot militia. Later that year he received 100 slaves from Major James Weymss of the British Sixty-third Regiment. Originally taken from Americans, these slaves were turned over to Mills to indemnify him for his losses.[72]

The British officer, General Leslie, explained this policy to the American commander, General Greene. His object, wrote Leslie, was not to plunder American property in slaves; rather it was one of temporary sequestration, and its sole aim was to

70. Hopkins to John Collins, May 21, 1776, Letter Book of Esek Hopkins, Jan. 1776 to Apr. 1777, National Archives; Ford, ed., *Journ. of Cont. Cong.*, VI, 874.

71. Whipple to Benjamin Lincoln, Jan. 22, 1780, *Original Papers Relating to the Siege of Charleston, 1780* (Charleston, 1898), 7.

72. Weymss to Cornwallis, Sept. 26, 1780, and Mills to Cornwallis, Nov. 28, 1780, Cornwallis transcripts, IV, Lib. Cong.

use such slaves to make restitution to loyalists who had been despoiled of their black bondmen.[73]

Leslie's assertion that slaves were being taken in order to right a wrong was not the basis upon which most officers operated. Like their counterparts on the American side British commanders looked upon the slaves of the enemy as booty. They were disposed to turn a profit by taking and selling them. Not only did individual officers hold slaves; sometimes army units owned them in common. Late in 1782 the artillery department at Charleston owned forty-four Negro women and their children, and the "Horse Department" owned six women and their children.[74] After the British occupation of Charleston, every regiment departing for New York took with it a bonus of ten slaves, and hundreds were carried away when the city was evacuated. The number would have been much greater save for a stern warning from Clinton himself, dated June 1, 1780, declaring that ship officers would be held personally responsible for ensuring that no Negro was placed aboard any transport without authorization from the commander-in-chief.[75]

* * *

At the end of the war, British officers and soldiers who had acquired slaves naturally wished to take their human property with them; American masters were desperately anxious to recover their runaways. The situation posed a conflict of interest that cast its shadow over the peace.

73. Leslie to Greene, Apr. 4, 1782, Leslie Letterbooks, N. Y. Pub. Lib. "General Leslie has announced his determination to seize Negroes as a compensation to those adherents of his party whose estates are confiscated by our Legislature," wrote John Laurens from his camp at Bacon Ridge, South Carolina. Laurens to William Bee, Apr. 14, 1782, Laurens MSS, Pennsylvania Historical Society, Philadelphia.

74. "Return of Negro Wenches and Their Children belonging to the Artillery Department, November 5, 1782," Wray Papers, Clements Lib.

75. Lowell, *The Hessians in the American Revolution*, 251; "Orderly Book, 1780-81," Wray Papers, Clements Lib.

CHAPTER IX

EVACUATION WITH THE BRITISH

"If they have a sufficient number of Transports, they will carry with them about Twelve Thousand Negroes, which they have now in Charles Town, and which they have stolen in their various expeditions into the Country."

Ralph Izard to Mrs. Izard, October 7, 1782

The chief concern of Americans about Negroes in the thirty months after Yorktown was their disappearance. Whenever the defeated British made their final withdrawals, whether by land or sea, thousands of slaves went with them. Take what precautions they would, the Americans could not prevent mass exodus of their black bondmen, which began immediately after Cornwallis's defeat.

The articles of capitulation at Yorktown stated that any American property held by the British garrison was subject to recovery.[1] The surrender terms were silent, however, about slaves who would try to escape by going aboard the departing warships of the royal navy. Americans did not need to be told that prompt action was necessary to forestall the flight of slaves. On the very day of the Yorktown surrender, General George Weedon placed sentinels "all along the Beach" to prevent them from reaching the vessels of the royal navy. Prompt as was his action, he feared that many runaways had already "secreted" themselves on board the ships. On the next day Weedon sent a letter to Governor Nelson apprising him of the situation.[2]

Virginia's chief executive had not been idle. Within twenty-four hours after the surrender he had written to Cornwallis

1. Tarleton, *History of the Campaigns in the Southern Provinces*, 439.
2. Weedon to Nelson, Oct. 20, 1781, *Cal. of Va. State Papers*, II, 561.

asking him to prevent Negroes from making their escape by boarding the sloop of war, *Bonetta,* which was allowed to sail to New York with news of the capitulation. These Negroes, cautioned the Governor, would "endeavor to lie concealed from your Lordship's Notice till the Vessel sails."[3]

General Washington lent his support to the effort to keep Negroes from leaving the state. He was disturbed about the number of slaves who attached themselves to the British or posed as freemen in order to deceive American commanders. To put a stop to such irregularities, Washington on October 25 ordered officers of the allied armies to deliver all Negroes who came into their hands to a guard to be established at Yorktown and Gloucester under the superintendency of David Ross, Virginia's commercial agent. Negroes who could prove they were not escaped slaves would be released. Slaves whose masters lived in the vicinity would be issued a pass enabling them to make their way home unmolested. Slaves whose owners were not Virginians would be advertised in newspapers of their home states. While waiting for their masters to claim them, they would be "sent into the Country to work for their Victuals and Cloathes."[4]

Washington's order seems to have placed a check on slave-seizing by American and French officers as well as those of the enemy. Doubtless this was what he intended, for he was fully aware that some American commanders had a weakness for acquiring property in blacks. Ten days before Cornwallis's capitulation Washington requested American army officers to report any Negroes they had "who have come out of York." Henceforth if any officer kept such a person in his service he would be called to the strictest account. Washington's order also applied to officers of the state militia.[5]

Civilians did not come under military regulations, and to prevent them from retaining other people's slaves, the Virginia legislature in May 1782 ordered all holders of runaways to deliver them to their masters, if known. If the master was not known, an advertisement seeking him was to be placed in the *Virginia Gazette.* Any person who could prove his right to a

3. Nelson to Cornwallis, Oct. 20, 1781, *Off. Letters of Govs. of Va.,* III, 88.
4. General Orders, Oct. 25, 1781, Fitzpatrick, ed., *Writings of Washington,* XXIII, 264-65; Washington to Ross, Oct. 24, 1781, *ibid.,* 262.
5. General Orders, Oct. 9, 1781, *ibid.,* 128-29.

slave lost during the Cornwallis invasion might apply to a justice of the peace for a warrant of recovery.[6]

To compel Americans to give slaves back to their owners was a trying task, but it was nothing compared to getting the French to give up their Negroes. In dealing with an ally whose assistance at Yorktown had been almost invaluable, a delicate touch was essential. Washington used a personal approach in writing to the Count de Grasse on behalf of a Maryland master who had lost upwards of forty slaves, five of whom had been taken in the bay by a French ship and carried to the West Indies. "I will take it as a very great favor if your Excellency will direct them to be sent back by any Vessel coming either to Virginia or Maryland." The expenses of their return trip would be paid by Colonel William Fitzhugh, their master.[7]

The difficulties of negotiating with the French were typified by an incident which occurred when the French troops were stationed in Charlotte County in southeastern Virginia. An American militia officer, Colonel Thomas Read, sent a sergeant and a guard to the French camp to apprehend runaways and return them to their owners. The French commander, the Marquis de Choisy, informed Read that he considered his application unnecessary, insisting that he had already come to an agreement with the governor respecting slaves. The rebuked Read dismissed the guard but he informed Governor Harrison that unless the Negroes who had deserted to the French were quickly reclaimed, "those who have Property of that kind in the vicinity of the Camps will suffer by their going off."[8]

With such complaints mounting, Governor Harrison took the matter up with General Count Rochambeau. Expressing his reluctance to trouble the French commander, Harrison nevertheless found it necessary to mention that reports were coming in every day about Negroes harbored by the French troops, and that there was no way in which masters could recover their property except through "your Justice." He asked Rochambeau to issue orders to hold all Negroes within his lines. Simultaneously the Governor ordered the Virginia commissioner

6. Hening, ed., *Statutes of Va.*, XI, 23-24.

7. Washington to de Grasse, Feb. 6, 1782, Fitzpatrick, ed., *Writings of Washington*, XXIII, 488-89.

8. Read to Harrison, Mar. 22, 1782, *Cal. of Va. State Papers*, III, 107.

of war to order a detail "to receive the slaves supposed to be with the French army."[9]

Two days later Rochambeau explained his position. He and many other French officers owned Negroes, but these had come from Rhode Island, having either been captured there by the French fleet or purchased from Rhode Islanders. Moreover, some of the Negroes with the French were hired, others were free. He was ready, said Rochambeau, to help the Virginians recover slaves, but not at the sacrifice of the rights of his fellow Frenchmen.[10]

Rochambeau's response was hardly satisfactory to the state authorities. The Governor notified Virginia's delegates to Congress a week later that the French troops were moving northward with "many Negroes." Since some of these belonged to North and South Carolina masters, he thought that the Congressional delegates from those states should be notified in order to recover the Negroes when the French reached Philadelphia. The exasperated Governor then unburdened himself to George Washington, declaring that he had written so many protests to the French authorities about loss of slaves that "I am wearied out without being able to procure them." Some, indeed, had been returned but most of them had been kept by the French "either for want of their owners having any proof at hand or the negroes declaring themselves free."[11]

Little could be done about runaways who passed themselves off to the French as free men, except to put notices in the press. A Baltimore master advertised for Ned who was "skulking in the neighborhood of this town in order to join the French." They would likely welcome him as a refugee, according to the advertisement, because he was "very capable of being a waiter or hostler to any officer, having been a waiter and coachman to Colonel White, of the State of Georgia, ever since the war commenced."[12] A Virginia mistress advertising for her "artful

9. Harrison to Rochambeau, June 26, 1782, *Off. Letters of Govs. of Va.,* III, 257-58; McIlwaine, ed., *Journal of the Council of State of Va.,* III, 114.

10. Acomb, ed., *Revolutionary Journal of Baron von Closen,* 187-88n.

11. Harrison to Virginia Delegates, July 6, to Washington, July 11, 1782, *Off. Letters of Govs. of Va.,* III, 262-63, 266. The Congressmen replied July 16, "We have informed the Delegates of South Carolina, of what your Excellency mentions. Those of North Carolina are not here." Burnett, ed., *Letters of Members of the Cont. Cong.,* VI, 383.

12. *Maryland Journal* (Baltimore), Sept. 17, 1782.

black Guinea Negro Man, named George, a good waggoner," supposed that he would "attempt to join the French troops, now on the march to the Northward, under the command of Rochambeau."[13]

Particularly vexatious to American masters was the reluctance of the French to release a Negro even after proof was offered that he was a slave. When Edmund Pendleton, Jr., heard that his slave Bob was with the French army at Baltimore he sent his overseer to recover him. Twice before Bob had escaped to the French. This time Pendleton's overseer found that he had taken the job of servant to a French lieutenant. When the overseer appeared, the lieutenant's initial impulse was to throw him into the guard house; however, the officer finally released Bob after charging $20.00 for his maintenance. But the overseer's woes were not over; Bob again escaped, this time with the assistance of the lieutenant; and the overseer returned out of pocket and without Bob. "There are a number of other people who have lost their slaves in the same manner," wrote the influential Edmund Pendleton, "and are in a very ill humor on the occasion."[14]

After the battle of Yorktown, escaped slaves could sometimes be recovered from the British by a search conducted under a flag of truce; however, the procedure was difficult. A Norfolk County planter who had lost ninety slaves asked Governor Harrison to get him a permit to go into the enemy lines. Harrison thereupon wrote to Virginia's representatives at Philadelphia, asking them to find out how Congress felt about an application to the British for a flag. Replying promptly, the delegation informed Harrison that they could not give him a definite answer, "the propriety of applications to the British Commander for a restitution of slaves having never been agitated in Congress." But they added that Congress generally disapproved of negotiations between an individual state and the British as contrary to "the spirit of confederacy." Moreover, such a solicitation to the enemy "might not be very politic," and in any event would probably be denied.[15]

13. *Ibid.,* Aug. 6, 1782.
14. Pendleton to James Madison, Sept. 2, 1782, "Unpublished Letters of Edmund Pendleton," Mass. Hist. Soc., *Proc.,* 2nd Ser., 19 (1905), 162. For the Bob episode see also Pendleton to Madison, July 29, and Aug. 19, 1782, *ibid.,* 158, 159.
15. Harrison to Virginia Delegates, Aug. 30, 1782, *Off. Letters of Govs. of*

This reply spurred Governor Harrison and the Virginia slave-owners to urge both Congress and the commander-in-chief to take positive action in assisting the recovery of slaves in British hands. Indeed, the problem had become one for the federal government to handle, for it existed in all the areas affected by the British evacuation.

* * *

For some months after the surrender at Yorktown, the British appeared "unable to carry on the war, and too proud to make peace."[16] But by April 1782 His Majesty's ministers had decided to evacuate their troops, using three of the major seaports. The first of these departures took place at Savannah in the summer of 1782.

A week before the date set for the evacuation, the Georgia assembly urged Governor John Martin to request of the British commandant of Savannah that no Negroes or other property belonging to Americans be carried off. The legislators also asked Governor Martin to grant permission to citizens having property in British hands to lodge a formal claim. Realizing that Georgia needed all its manpower resources to rebuild the state's economy, the lower house also tried to persuade departing Tories to leave their slaves behind. The commissioners for the sales of forfeited estates were empowered to purchase Negroes from evacuees and sell them to residents, on condition that the purchasers would not carry them out of the state for at least eighteen months.[17]

British military forces formally withdrew from Savannah in July 1782, evacuating loyalists with their slaves as well as troops. On July 6, General Leslie ordered the royal navy to provide shipping accommodations for 50 whites and 1,900 Negoes. An embarkation return of August 10, 1782, lists six ships as having carried 1,568 Negroes to Jamaica. By December 23, 1782, an additional 1,786 Negroes had been taken to St. Augustine; seven months later this figure had reached 1,956, of whom 799 were men, 705 women, and 452 children.[18]

Va., III, 311; Virginia Delegates to Harrison, Sept. 10, 1782, Burnett, ed., *Letters of Members of the Cont. Cong.*, VI, 467-68.

16. Phrase attributed to Benjamin Franklin. Washington to Nathanael Greene, Sept. 23, 1782, Fitzpatrick, ed., *Writings of Washington*, XXV, 195.

17. Candler, ed., *Rev. Rec. of Ga.*, III, 119-20, 122, 127.

18. Leslie to Captain William Swiney, July 6, 1782, Leslie Letter Book,

Five months after the British left Savannah, Charleston was evacuated. Here, too, the Negro problem loomed large. Confronting Leslie were the conflicting hopes and expectations of three groups: his fellow British officers, the Negroes themselves and the victorious Americans.

General Leslie's difficulties in preventing officers from taking possession of Negroes became more acute as the British made ready to leave. In early May 1782 he sent a sharply worded letter to General Charles O'Hara, informing him that a number of Negroes who had been servants of officers, but who belonged to South Carolinians, were then on board the transports about to sail. "I must request," he wrote, "that you will give the most positive orders to have them sent on shore immediately and delivered over to Colonel Ballingal, Commissioner for Claims for Negroes."[19]

Leslie summed up his troubles in a letter to his superiors. Officers who had been in America a long time, he said, looked upon Negroes as their personal property. Now that a general evacuation was near, "every department, and every officer, wishes to include his slave in the number to be brought off. They pretend them spys, or guides, and of course obnoxious [to the Americans], or under promises of freedom from Genl. Prevost. Ld. Cornwallis, Ld. Rawdon, or some other officer of rank, or free by proclamation."[20]

Leslie's problem was compounded by the failure of naval commanders to issue orders against taking Negroes aboard the transports. Once the ship left Charleston it was extremely difficult for American owners to recover their slaves. Rawlins Lowndes was almost alone in managing to reclaim a slave who had been carried to New York by a captain of the engineers.

N.Y. Pub. Lib.; Lists of transports from Savannah to Jamaica, Aug. 10, 1782, C. O. 5/560, 477; Lists of refugees to East Florida, Dec. 23, 1782, authenticated by John Winniett, Inspector of Refugees, C. O. 5/160, 507; Lists of refugees to East Florida, July 18, 1783, C. O. 5/560, 810. For an analytical statement on the number of white and Negro civilian evacuees from Georgia see Kenneth Coleman, *The American Revolution in Georgia, 1763-1789* (Athens, 1958), 145-46.

19. Leslie to O'Hara, May 3, 1782, Leslie Letter Book, N. Y. Pub. Lib.
20. Leslie to Carleton, Oct. 18, 1782, *Amer. MSS in Royal Inst. of G. B.*, III, 175-76. The Carleton photostats have same letter with an unimportant change in one phrase.

He was successful only because he was able to reach the highest echelons—Leslie and Carleton.[21]

Another problem which Leslie laid before his superiors was the British obligation to the Negro. When Leslie learned that Charleston was to be evacuated, he asked the commander-in-chief for instructions as to the disposition of the Negroes under Commissioner Cruden and those employed in the different departments. "There are many negroes who have been very useful, both at the Siege of Savannah and here," he wrote, "Some of them have been guides, and for their loyalty have been promised their freedom." He pointed out that no matter how the sequestered Negroes were disposed of, there was an obligation to those who had voluntarily joined the British. Something was owed them because of the promises made to them and because of their past services. They could not "in justice be abandoned to the merciless resentment of their former masters."[22]

Carleton supported Leslie in refusing to give up Negroes who had borne arms for the king or had otherwise incurred the resentment of American patriots. Leslie therefore appointed a commission, composed largely of military officers, to hear the appeals of Negroes who had served with the British army or who claimed to have fled to the British in response to proclamations offering them their freedom.[23] The responsibility which he felt to the Negroes aggravated his major problem in the evacuation—that of trying to assure the South Carolinians that their property would not be carried off. Masters were already sufficiently alarmed by the difficulty of recovering slaves by legal process; they had to prove ownership, and in establishing such proof they could not employ the testimony of the slaves themselves or of other Negroes—a law which the South Carolinians themselves had enacted.

In August 1782 Governor Mathews warned Leslie that if slaves belonging to patriotic Americans were carried away, he would retaliate by making it impossible for British creditors to collect debts. A believer in the soft answer, Leslie suggested

21. Leslie to Carleton, Aug. 8, Frederick Mackenzie to Lowndes, Sept. 12, 1782, Carleton photostats.

22. Leslie to Carleton, June 27, 1782, *Amer. MSS in Royal Inst. of G. B.*, III, 544; Leslie to Carleton, Aug. 10, 1782, Leslie Letter Book, N. Y. Pub. Lib.

23. Leslie to Carleton, Oct. 18, 1782, *ibid.* For the personnel of this commission see *ibid.*, No. 15675.

that a board of commissioners be appointed to safeguard the interests of both sides—a proposal Mathews found acceptable. On the day before the first meeting of the commissioners, Leslie instructed the two British representatives to pledge the restoration of all British-held slaves except those who had been promised their freedom and those whose services to the British had rendered them *persona non grata* in American circles.[24]

The four commissioners had no trouble getting together, and they agreed to restore all slaves except those who were "obnoxious" and those who had been promised freedom. Restored slaves were not to be punished for having attached themselves to the British. Two Americans were to be permitted to reside in Charleston to assist in returning slaves to their rightful owners.[25] These arrangements were soon completed. Upon presenting themselves at Charleston, the American commissioners were received and accredited without delay, and two additional commissioners were stationed at Accabee near the British lines to receive the recovered Negroes forwarded from Charleston. The outlook for a peaceful settlement appeared most hopeful. Within a week, however, the whole plan had fallen through.

The American commissioners at Charleston found obstacles placed in their way. They were not given full liberty to examine the outbound British transports, and after they had identified 136 Negroes for reclaiming, the British cleared only 73 for delivery. Even before these could be sent to Accabee the Charleston commissioners received a letter from Leslie's headquarters notifying them that the whole plan was at an end unless General Nathanael Greene returned three British soldiers he had just seized.

The surprised commissioners immediately forwarded the note to Governor Mathews. Within a few minutes after the letter reached his hands, the impulsive and outspoken chief executive sent a lengthy reply to Leslie, accusing the British of bad faith. Announcing that he looked upon the agreement as dissolved, he ordered the American commissioners to return from within the British lines.[26] Leslie, on his part, attributed

24. Leslie to Alexander Wright and James Johnson, Oct. 9, 1782, Carleton photostats.

25. Articles of agreement between the commissioners for Governor Mathews and the commissioners for General Leslie, dated Oct. 10, 1782, *ibid.*

26. For this story, with copies of the letters exchanged, see Lee, *Memoirs of the War in the Southern Department,* 566-70.

the failure of the plan to "the behaviour of Mr. Mathews the Rebel Governor and General Greene in insulting the outposts at the very time I was acting with the utmost moderation and forbearance."[27]

As a result of the breakdown of this agreement, the British evacuated Charleston without any supervision of their shipments. When, on December 14, 1782, they finally left the city, they took 5,327 Negroes, of whom one-half were destined for Jamaica. Of the remainder, all but 500 went to East Florida, with a few finding their way to St. Lucia, Halifax, England, and New York.[28]

* * *

The last American port to be evacuated was New York. By November 25, 1783, when the last of His Majesty's troops boarded their transports, the final peace treaty had been signed. Since this treaty included a statement relating to Negroes, the New York evacuations had a broad interest, one involving policy and its observance by the signatories.

The preliminary articles had contained an agreement that His Majesty's forces should withdraw without carrying away any Negroes or other property of Americans. The terms of this agreement, signed at Paris on November 30, 1782, soon became common and official knowledge in America. On April 15, 1783, Commander-in-Chief Sir Guy Carleton issued an order from his New York headquarters warning all masters of British vessels not to commit any breach of the article relative to Negro removals. On the very same day the Congress instructed General Washington to make arrangements to obtain the delivery of the Negroes and other American property then in the hands of the British or their adherents. A week later Washington wrote to Carleton, suggesting a meeting. Sir Guy was willing, if unenthusiastic: "I cannot decline the personal interview proposed by your Excellency."[29]

27. Leslie to Carleton, Nov. 18, 1782, American Dispatches, II, Clinton Papers, Clements Lib.

28. "Return of People Embarked from South Carolina and Georgia. Charleston, 13 December 1782," Mass. Hist. Soc., *Proc.*, 2nd Ser., 3 (1887), 95. For the specific number coming into Florida as of July 15, 1783, see C. O. 5/560, 811-20.

29. "Extract from General Orders, Headquarters, New York, 15 April, 1783," Thomas Jefferson Papers, IX, No. 1455, Lib. Cong.; Carleton to Washington, Apr. 24, 1783, Washington Papers, CCXX, No. 13, Lib. Cong.

This important conference was held at Orangetown on May 6. Washington was accompanied by his military secretary and flanked by three witnesses, one of whom was George Clinton, New York's able war governor. Washington led off by stating that he had asked for a personal conference as the speediest way of reaching agreement over the major problems connected with the British evacuation, namely, taking over the posts occupied by the British troops, and recovering Negroes and other property belonging to Americans.[30] Carleton replied that the British were leaving the country as fast as they could—6,000 civilians had already been sent away, including some Negroes. Expressing surprise, Washington observed that transporting Negroes was contrary to the provisional treaty. Carleton then advanced a point of view which dismayed the American negotiators, despite its familiar ring. It could not have been the intention of his government, said Carleton, to ignore its obligations to Negroes who had come into the British lines under proclamations of freedom issued by his predecessors. To deliver up such persons, some of whom would thereby be executed and others seriously punished, would be a "dishonorable Violation of the public Faith." However, if British evacuation of the Negroes was subsequently declared to be a treaty infraction, the Crown would compensate their owners. With this possibility in mind, Carleton had directed that a register be kept of all Negroes involved.

Washington made no attempt to conceal his dissatisfaction. He told Carleton that he felt that his conduct departed from the letter and the spirit of the treaty. He pointed out that Carleton's proposal to compensate owners could not be executed. It would be impossible to ascertain the value of a slave from a mere register; a slave's worth depended upon his industry and sobriety. Also, a slave might falsify his name or that of his master. Carleton countered by observing that since the Negroes whom the British refused to deliver would have obtained their freedom they would have no reason to conceal facts about their

30. The summary that follows is from "The Substance of the Conference between General Washington and Sir Guy Carleton at an Interview at Orangetown, May 6th 1783," in Washington Papers, CCXX, No. 71, Lib. Cong. See also "Extract from the Substance of the Conference between General Washington and Sir Guy Carleton at an Interview at Orange Town, 6th May 1783," in Thomas Jefferson Papers, IX, Nos. 1471-72, Lib. Cong.

past. By keeping a register, as he was doing, he was actually helping the slave-owners, for if no record was kept and no control exercised over the Negroes, they would do as they pleased, to the inevitable loss of their former proprietors. His plan left open some chance of later compensation. On this note the lengthy conference came to a close.

Washington hoped that he and Carleton could reconcile some of their differences at a dinner meeting scheduled the next day, but Carleton fell ill. Even if the second meeting had been held it would probably have had little result. "I have discovered enough," Washington wrote a few hours after the initial interview, "to convince me that the slaves which have absconded from their masters will never be restored."[31]

When Washington learned that Carleton could not see him, he sent word signifying his readiness to enter into any agreement to prevent further evacuating of American-owned Negroes. Carleton replied that when he came to New York he found the Negroes free, and that he had no right to keep them from going anywhere in the world they pleased. However, he approved the establishment of an American commission to inspect the British embarkation, and was gratified to learn that Washington had already taken this action.[32]

Three weeks before the Orangetown interview, Carleton had proposed that Congress appoint persons to enter New York to assist the British in inspecting and superintending the embarkations. Congress had referred the suggestion to Washington who, two days after the interview, named a three-man commission: Egbert Benson, attorney-general of New York, Colonel William S. Smith, and army contractor Daniel Parker. Washington charged them with the task of reporting both to Carleton and himself any treaty infractions relative to American property.[33]

The American commissioners got to work slowly. They arrived in New York on May 10, but were unable to get an audience with Carleton until five days later. At the end of the month they wrote to the impatient Washington asking specific instructions as to whether they should superintend outbound

31. Washington to Benjamin Harrison, May 6, 1783, Fitzpatrick, ed., *Writings of Washington,* XXVI, 401.

32. Washington to Carleton, May 6, 1783, Carleton to Washington, May 12, 1783, Washington Papers, CCXX, Nos. 71-72, 104-5, Lib. Cong.

33. Washington to Commissioners, May 8, 1783, *ibid.,* CCXX, No. 77.

merchant vessels as well as official transports. Washington replied that they were the best judges of such matters.[34]

In early June the commissioners carefully selected a case that would furnish a test of their powers. They reported to Carleton that an ex-slave, Thomas Francis, was on board the *Fair American,* then about to sail for the West Indies. Escaped from an American master, Francis had come within the British lines on November 2, 1782, and had enlisted in the Jamaica Rangers.[35] To the chagrin of the commissioners, Carleton sent no reply.

The disillusioned commissioners asked Washington whether further protests would serve a useful purpose in view of the Francis case. They informed him that American-owned Negroes numbering at least 130 men were then aboard ships sailing for Nova Scotia. A month later one of the commissioners reported that although seven Negroes had been salvaged from the recently sailed fleet, he considered further remonstrance useless since about one thousand ex-slaves were scheduled to embark within a day or two. Nevertheless, he concluded, he would continue to supervise the examination of the ships and the registering of slaves.[36]

By mid-July, both Washington and Congress were ready to abolish the impotent commission. Acting as an agent of Congress, the Commander-in-Chief had sent to that body a report of his interview with Carleton, and advised that the commission be discontinued. Congress needed no prodding, having already unanimously voted to instruct the American ministers in Europe to protest to Great Britain the carrying off of "a considerable number of negroes belonging to citizens of these States." Sharing Washington's sentiment that the commission was little more than a farce, Congress on July 16 instructed him to abolish it unless some change should have occurred which dictated otherwise.[37]

34. Washington to Commissioners, May 27, Commissioners to Washington, May 30, Washington to Commissioners, June 10, 1783, *ibid.,* CCXXI, No. 45, CCXXI, Nos. 72-74, CCXXII, No. 13.

35. Commissioners to Carleton, June 9, 1783, *ibid.,* CCXXII, No. 10, Lib. Cong.

36. Benson and Parker to Washington, June 14, Smith to Washington, July 15, 1783, *ibid.,* CCXXII, No. 47, CCXXIII, No. 66, Lib. Cong.

37. Washington to Congress, June 23, 1783, *ibid.,* CCXXII, No. 83, Lib. Cong.; Congress to Washington, July 16, 1783, *ibid.,* CCXXIII, No. 73,

Thus the British evacuation of New York, as of Savannah and Charleston, proceeded with little American hindrance. Alexander Hamilton found the British point of view on slaves defensible,[38] but his was an almost solitary voice in non-loyalist circles. Indignation over the carrying away of slaves was both widespread and enduring; it was to affect American diplomatic relations with Great Britain for nearly half a century. Years after the war Americans were still hammering the point that the payment of pre-war debts in London and Glasgow should be withheld until His Majesty's government made restitution for the lost blacks.

It appears that the position Britain finally adopted on the return of slaves was formulated by Guy Carleton,[39] whose view became standard policy: Negroes who were with the British prior to the signing of the provisional treaty on November 30, 1782 were free; those acquired after that date were to be given up.[40] In arriving at this dictum, Carleton was doubtless moved, as he claimed, by a sense of responsibility to the Negroes. A far-seeing man, Carleton may also have felt that if Britain defaulted on promises of freedom made during the war, any similar proclamations in future conflicts would not be trusted.

Nevertheless, he carefully fulfilled his assurances to Washington that he would keep a register of Negroes to facilitate the compensation of their American owners. He assigned a board of three men to keep the register, and every Wednesday morning the board met for two hours at Fraunces Tavern with the three American commissioners.

By the time His Majesty's forces officially withdrew from New York on November 30, 1783, the British commissioners had compiled a detailed list of 3,000 Negroes they had inspected, com-

Lib. Cong.; "The United States in Congress assembled, May 26, 1783," Jefferson Papers, IX, Nos. 1487-88, Lib. Cong.; Hunt, ed., *Writings of Madison*, I, 471. For Robert Livingston's instructions to the American Peace Commissioners, dated May 28, 1783, see Francis Wharton, *The Revolutionary Diplomatic Correspondence of the United States*, 6 vols. (Washington, 1889), VI, 453.

38. Camillus: "Defence of Mr. Jay's Treaty," in J. C. Hamilton, ed., *Works of Hamilton*, VII, 190-94.

39. For a cogent statement on the Negro evacuation policy of the British see an undated draft headed "Negroes" in C. O. 5/8, 113-15.

40. Nothing came of Congress's referral of the matter to the American ministers abroad; moreover, as concerned the slaves, the definitive treaty of Sept. 3, 1783, merely repeated the language of its predecessor.

prising 1,336 men, 914 women, and 750 children.[41] This massive "Inspection Roll of Negroes" bore eight columns listing the names of the Negroes, their former masters, and the names of the vessels on which they were embarking. One heading was entitled, "Description," and bore such arresting comments as "fine boy," "an idiot," "likely rascal," "snug little wench," and "nearly worn out."

To these 3,000 Negroes who left New York must be added the hundreds of unregistered ones carried away in private vessels. The total number of colored persons who left that city, as well as other ports, can only be guessed. Perhaps it would be safe to say that during the evacuations the numbers of Negroes leaving Savannah was 4,000, Charleston 6,000, and New York 4,000. If anything, these figures are a bit low, and they do not, of course, include those who went off with the French, nor the thousands—perhaps around five thousand—whom the British carried away prior to the surrender of Yorktown.

*   *   *

Many Negroes were carried off without regard for their own wishes. This would be particularly true of slaves belonging to departing loyalists. Likewise, many Negroes who had deserted to the British were not consulted about their being taken off in the evacuations. Perhaps most of these former runaways would have left America voluntarily, since the British had assiduously spread the idea that those who went back to their American masters would be severely whipped and then assigned the hardest kind of labor.

The belief that their former masters would treat them harshly for having fled was no doubt a strong factor in shaping the conduct of Negroes who had a free choice. In peacetime a recovered runaway was not likely to get off lightly; in wartime a slave who not only had taken to his heels but had joined the enemy had reason to feel nervous about the welcome he would receive upon his return to the home plantation. To allay this

41. This lengthy document may be seen in the Carleton photostats, Book of Negroes Registered & certified after having been Inspected by the Commissioners appointed by His Excellency Sir Guy Carleton, K. B. General & Commander in Chief, on Board Sundry Vessels in which they were embarked Previous to the time of sailing from the Port of New York between the 23 Apr. and 31st July, 1783, both days included. This is book I. Book II bears the same heading with the exception of the final line which lists the period as extending from July 31 to Nov. 30, 1783.

fear, some masters promised a pardon. Virginia's Theodorick Bland, Jr., sent word to his slaves, Isaac and Kitt, who were in New York, that if they would come back to Framingdell, the family plantation in Prince George County, he would let bygones be bygones. Neither would listen; Isaac informed Bland's emissary that he had heard that once a slave had returned to his master he was "treated with great severity."[42]

Exclusive of the thousand or more youngsters who were born within the British lines and who therefore might be considered born free, a small number of adult free Negroes, perhaps a few hundred, went off in the evacuations. There were 8 free Negroes among the 2,563 colored refugees who came to East Florida from South Carolina as of July 15, 1783. Numbered in the 1,956 black emigrants from Georgia to East Florida as of July 18, 1783, were 3 free Negroes. Accompanying the British from Charleston to New York late in 1782 was free Negro Bacchus, a smith by trade. Thirteen free Negroes, 7 men and 6 women, were included in the 232 adults sailing out of New York in November 1783 on the *Peggy, Concord,* and *Diannah.*[43]

One free Negro who was not near an evacuation point besought Carleton's aid in getting out of America. Originally from England, Towers Bell had been brought to Baltimore and sold into slavery. His four years in bondage were a time in which he had "suffered with the Greatest Barbarity in this Rebellious Country." For the last six years he had been free, but had neither friends nor money, and needed assistance to get home.[44]

Not all the Negroes within British lines were evacuated. Aside from a handful successfully reclaimed by Washington's commissioners, there were some slaves who were deliberately left behind. They were the sick, the helpless, and the aged,

42. Jacob Morris to Bland, July 17, 1783, Campbell, ed., *Bland Papers,* II, III.

43. C. O. 5/560, 810, 811-20; Return of the Civil Branch of Ordnance and Horse Department, arrived at New York from Charleston in South Carolina, Jan. 19, 1783, Wray Papers, Clements Lib.; Inspection Roll of Negroes, taken on board the undernamed vessels, on the 30th day of Nov. 1783 at Anchor near Statten Island, previous to their Sailing for Port-Mattoon in the province of Nova Scotia, The Papers of the Continental Congress, LIII, 276-95, National Archives. These lists carry a descriptive statement on each of the Negroes who embarked on the three transports.

44. Bell to Carleton, June 7, 1783, Carleton photostats.

whom evacuating loyalists simply abandoned.[45] Some departing masters sold their slaves.

One slave thus disposed of was to have a notable career. James Derham had been the property of a surgeon in the British Sixteenth Regiment. While his master was with the army, Derham was allowed to perform medical duties, since he had already acquired some experience in compounding medicines and acting as a male nurse. At the close of the war, the surgeon sold him to a New Orleans physician, who employed him as a paid assistant. While still in his early twenties, Derham was able to buy his freedom, and by 1789 he had built up a thriving medical practice in Philadelphia, with an income of over $3,000 a year. The celebrated Dr. Benjamin Rush was impressed by his fellow practitioner—by his fluency in French and Spanish, and, more importantly, by his knowledge of the healing arts: "I expected to have suggested some new medicines to him," wrote Rush, "but he suggested many more to me."[46]

While most Negroes whom the British left behind had no choice in the matter, a corps of some three hundred ex-slaves in Georgia remained there by preference. This group had been arms-bearers for the British during the occupation of Savannah, and they proposed neither to return to their masters nor leave in the evacuation. Styling themselves the "King of England's soldiers," they settled along the swamps bordering the Savannah River, plundering by night and disappearing by day. It was not until May 1786 that they were dispersed, following the discovery and burning of their fortified encampment at Bear Creek by militia from Georgia and South Carolina.[47]

The Negroes who left the United States at war's end traveled to widely separated points on the globe. Over a thousand, as will be noted, went to the west coast of Africa. An odder destination was reserved for a Negro drum corps which arrived in central Europe, accompanying General Riedesel to Brunswick, where, on a mid-October day in 1783, it formed part of an infantry battalion received with military honors in a public

45. Harry B. Yoshpe, *The Disposition of Loyalist Estates in the Southern District of the State of New York* (New York, 1939), 91-93.

46. For a sketch of Derham by Rush see *The American Museum*, 5 (Phila., 1789), 61-62.

47. Charles C. Jones, *The Life and Services of the Honorable Major General Samuel Elbert* (Cambridge, 1887), 47; Stevens, *A History of Georgia*, II, 376-78.

market place.[48] The overwhelming majority of black evacuees, however, settled in the British Caribbean islands or in Canada, although thousands of these were at first taken into East Florida, where their sojourn proved to be temporary.

Before the British evacuation of Savannah, many Georgia loyalists contemplated a removal to East Florida. Just south of the state border, it offered a climate and conditions to which they were accustomed. Uncertain as to what disposition would be made of the province after the war, they urged British authorities to retain it. Responding to their entreaties, Sir Guy Carleton, successor to Henry Clinton as commander-in-chief, merely informed Governor Leslie that the province would remain as it was. Georgia loyalists construed his remark to mean that the British did not intend to give it up. Accordingly, many of them migrated into the neighboring province, bearing with them a large number of slaves. By the summer of 1783, as we have seen, a total of 1,956 slaves had been taken into East Florida.[49]

Within a few months the newcomers knew that East Florida was destined to go to Spain, and that they would have to move again; Spanish rule had no attraction for Anglo-Americans. The treaty that ceded East Florida to Spain, signed in September 1783, gave the inhabitants of the province eighteen months to get out. The nearly eight thousand Negroes in the province at that time included not more than one thousand who were free and could therefore choose whether to go or stay.[50] The others followed the dictates of their masters.

Of the 6,540 Negroes recorded as leaving the province, over 2,500 were brought back to the United States,[51] many of them to Georgia. As early as October 1782 the Georgia Council

48. "The Brunswick Contingent in America, 1776-1783," *Pa. Mag. of Hist. and Biog.,* 15 (1891), 224.

49. Candler, ed., *Col. Rec. of Ga.,* XV, 664-65; Lists of refugees to East Florida, July 18, 1783, C. O. 5/560, 810; Coleman, *Amer. Rev. in Ga.,* 145-46.

50. Joseph Bryne Lockey, *East Florida, 1783-1785* (Berkeley, 1949), 23, 340.

51. For the specific figures on white and black migrants to the varying destination points see "Return of Persons who emigrated from East Florida to different parts of the British Dominions &c," C. O. 5/561, 817. Dated London, 1786, this return is signed by Colonel William Brown, Commissioner of Embarkation.

voted to permit its citizens to purchase slaves from loyalists who had gone to East Florida, and to export produce and lumber to pay for such purchases. The Council granted individual petitions to those wishing to go to St. Augustine to recover or to purchase slaves, such petitions generally specifying the product or commodity to be used in defraying expenses. In the spring of 1783 the state of South Carolina sent a commissioner to St. Augustine to seek recovery of her expatriated blacks.[52] "There is," wrote the governor of East Florida, "a considerable influx of transient people from Georgia and South Carolina to recover their property in Negroes."[53] Apart from such efforts, slaves amounting to "upwards of 1,000" were brought back from St. Augustine to South Carolina by former loyalists who were legally permitted to return.[54] Some of East Florida's free Negroes returned to America, but they tended to move northwestward toward the Mississippi River rather than northeastward toward the Savannah and the Santee.

By no means was all the black emigration out of East Florida to the United States; over 2,200 Negroes went to the Bahamas, and lesser numbers went to other points, ranging from the 714 transported to Jamaica to the 35 that crossed the Atlantic to an English port. In addition to those whose departure was officially recorded, there were hundreds of refugees, white and black, who left in small groups, sailing away without authorization, leaving not a trace behind. A few hundred Negroes remained in the province; presumably they were of the free class.

As the migration figures illustrate, the Bahamas attracted slave-owning refugees, not only from East Florida, but from the United States. Over a twenty-two month span from June 1783 to April 1785 these British islands received from six to seven thousand refugees, white and colored.[55] A few of the black newcomers were destined to return to the mainland. Late in 1784 General James Grant sold to three South Carolinians twenty-seven of his slaves—ten men, five women, eleven children

52. Candler, ed., *Rev. Rec. of Ga.*, II, 388, 477, 478; James Clitherall to John Cruden, May 31, 1783, *Amer. MSS in Royal Inst. of G. B.*, IV, 115.

53. Tonyn to Thomas Townshend, May 15, 1783, C. O. 5/560, 550.

54. Ralph Izard to Jefferson, with "Reports on the Trade of South Carolina, June 10, 1785, Boyd, ed., *Papers of Jefferson*, VIII.

55. Wilbur H. Siebert, "The Legacy of the American Revolution in the British West Indies, and Bahamas," Ohio State University, *Bulletin*, 17 (1913), 22.

and an infant just christened "Providence."[56] But most of the other Negroes remained in the Bahamas, giving its agriculture, particularly its cotton culture, a new impetus.

Thousands of Negroes were taken to other islands in the British West Indies; from 1775 to 1787 the colored population of Jamaica showed an increase of 60,000. Practically all of the black immigrants were slaves. Many had been brought in as slaves, but many others who came expecting to be free were seized by those holding no legal title, and sold for rum, coffee, sugar, and fruits.[57]

Perhaps the most noteworthy of the Negroes taken to Jamaica was George Liele who as a slave and a free man in Georgia had been a dedicated preacher. Brought to Kingston in 1782 as an indentured servant, Liele worked out his time in two years. Once he obtained his certificate of freedom, Liele resumed his work in religion, preaching in private homes and then organizing a church—the only Baptist church on the island. By 1790 more than 450 persons had received baptism at his hands.[58]

Many of the Negroes evacuated from the United States did not go southward; thousands went to Canada. Perhaps their lot may be suggested by focussing on the story of African-born Thomas Peters. Dark-skinned and of large frame, Peters had in 1776 fled from his master and joined the British.[59] During the war he served as a sergeant in a Negro arms-bearing pioneer company, being twice wounded in battle. With the coming of peace, he and his wife settled at Annapolis in Nova Scotia, a province to which many of the Canada-bound Negroes went.

The British had promised Peters and his comrades not only freedom but a farm. His Majesty's officers were slow in making

56. For this list of Negroes and the contract of sale see James Grant folder in Personal Papers: Miscellaneous, GI to GRA, Manuscript Division, Lib. Cong.

57. Siebert, "Legacy of American Revolution in British West Indies and Bahamas," Ohio State Univ., *Bull.,* 17 (1913), 16, 38.

58. See Carter G. Woodson, *The History of the Negro Church* (Washington, 1921), 43-45; and "Letters showing the Rise and Progress of the early Negro Churches of Georgia and the West Indies," *Journal of Negro History,* 1 (1916), 69-92, *passim.*

59. For sketches of Peters see C. H. Fyfe, *Thomas Peters: History and Legend* (a 10-page pamphlet, no date, no place, but republished from *Sierra Leone Studies* [Freetown], Dec. 1953), and F. W. Butt-Thompson, *Sierra Leone in History and Tradition* (London, 1926), 89-96.

good the promise of a farm, and the civilian authorities were likewise dilatory.[60] The black settlers in Nova Scotia felt cheated: either the surveyor was too busy to mark out their lands, or the plots they received were largely thick pine forest and hard to clear. Finding themselves landless, or holders of land that would produce little, many Negroes apprenticed themselves to farmers or congregated in Burchtown, a nearly all-Negro community.

Peters was a patient man, but after six years of waiting he determined to go to England to seek redress from the king's ministers. By virtue of a small sum raised by his fellows, and by working as a "hand" to pay his passage aboard ship, Peters arrived in London early in 1791. Here he received a welcome that must have made up for much of the disappointment of the preceding years. Granville Sharp and his fellow reformers took Peters in tow, and soon the former slave-soldier became a London celebrity. "His eloquence, his passion, his spirit, made him the rage of the newspaper world, the latest fashionable craze, and the newest object of philanthropy."[61]

To assist Peters, his abolitionist friends drew up a memorial in his name and sent it to William W. Granville, secretary of state for foreign affairs. This document described the plight of 102 colored families at Annapolis Royal and 100 families at New Brunswick. These Negroes would remain in those provinces, it was said, if they could obtain the full grant of land and provisions originally promised them; otherwise many would be willing to migrate to any country which would make them a "competent" offer.[62]

This petition, which Peters signed by making his mark, brought quick action. The Secretary of State ordered the governor of Nova Scotia to investigate the matter. If the charges were true, the governor was informed that the province must

60. There were a number of Negroes at Port Roseway, and some expected at Halifax, "for whom Lands are not yet located, nor other provisions made," wrote Colonel Robert Morse to General H. E. Fox on Aug. 23, 1783, Carleton photostats.

61. Butt-Thompson, *Sierra Leone,* 93-94.

62. John Clarkson, Clarkson's Mission to America (478-page handwritten document in diary form, dated from Aug. 6, 1791 to Mar. 18, 1792, is in the N.-Y. Hist. Soc.), 6. Another copy, handwritten but with a different pagination, may be seen at the Moorland Library, Howard University, Washington, D. C. In these footnotes I use the pagination of the former.

fulfill its obligation or send these families to Sierra Leone. A removal to Sierra Leone would entail some expense, but His Majesty's government had an obligation to these Negroes for their wartime services.[63]

The idea of transporting the Canadian Negroes to Africa originated with the directors of the recently incorporated Sierra Leone Company. Founded to enable destitute Negroes in London to make a new start by settling them on the west coast of Africa, the company had acquired a site and begun operations by the time Peters visited London. On its board of directors in 1791 the company counted such well-known abolitionists as Thomas Clarkson, William Wilberforce and Granville Sharp. It was Sharp who introduced Peters to the other board members, and enlisted their interest in the black Nova Scotians. In turn Peters was favorably impressed by the kindness of the board members—by their assurance that he and his associates would be welcome to Sierra Leone, and by their belief that his group would be better off there than in frigid Canada.

With the tacit support of Parliament, and the approval of Peters, the Sierra Leone Company got busy.[64] On August 12, 1791 the company authorized two agents, Lawrence Hartshorn of Halifax and John Clarkson, to screen out the candidates for resettlement and get written testimonials as to their character, sobriety and industry. The agents were authorized to offer twenty acres of land to each prospective migrant, with ten additional acres for his wife and five for each child.

The choice of Clarkson as an agent was a happy one. A former naval lieutenant and the younger brother of Thomas Clarkson, he brought a spirit of dedication to his task. Reaching Halifax in early October 1791, he took the leadership in recruiting prospective emigrants. First he interviewed the applicant, optimistically assuring him that in Sierra Leone he would have every opportunity to become his own master. The interview was followed by an investigation, and if the applicant came out well, he received a certificate of character.

63. Clarkson's Mission to America, 8, N.-Y. Hist. Soc.

64. For this Nova Scotian project of the Sierra Leone Company see *Report by Court of Directors of the Sierra Leone Company, 1794* (London, 1794), 3-8; Adams G. Archibald, "Story of the Deportation of Negroes from Nova Scotia to Sierra Leone," Nova Scotia Historical Society, *Collections,* 7 (1889-1891), 129-54.

The deeply religious and sensitive Clarkson was often moved by the interviews. He noted that the greatest number of applicants were not thinking of their own future but that of their children "whom they wished to see established (as they expressed it) upon a better foundation."[65] Particularly touching to Clarkson was the incident in which a Negro slave, John Coltress, came to enroll his free wife and children. Putting the Atlantic between himself and his family was heart-rending to Coltress, but he was willing to face it because it would bring "a better life for them."[66]

Many of the candidates were personally enlisted by Peters, who returned to the province prior to Clarkson's arrival. Including his family, Peters recruited a total of eighty-four persons from St. John, New Brunswick and Annapolis, and brought them to Halifax. Some applicants made their way alone; many of these arrived at the headquarters city only after hard journeys of up to 340 miles through wooded and little known country.

Once gathered in Halifax and awaiting the date of departure, the migrants kept Clarkson busy with all kinds of requests and petitions. Typical was the request of the thirty-eight residents of the township of Preston (one of whom bore the incongruous name "British Freedom") that in Sierra Leone they be permitted to settle side by side.[67] Another group which sought to keep together and managed to make arrangements to cross the ocean in the same brig, was the congregation of the Baptist minister, David George. George had been a slave until the British seized Savannah and his master fled. He resided in Charleston during the last years of the war, and in 1782 came to Nova Scotia, where for nearly ten years he had preached at Burchtown and Shelburne. When he learned of the Sierra Leone proposal, George enrolled his own family of six, and persuaded fifty-nine of his congregation to sign up.[68]

Thanks to men like George and Peters, there was no problem in recruiting good prospects; indeed, the directors of the Sierra Leone Company were surprised and gratified by the number of applicants. By the end of the year a large enough

65. Clarkson's Mission to America, 86, N.-Y. Hist. Soc.
66. Ibid., 88.
67. Ibid., 300.
68. For a brief sketch of George see Woodson, History of the Negro Church, 41-42.

group had been recruited and the ships chartered. On January 15, 1782, a bit over three months after his arrival at Halifax, agent John Clarkson could joyfully write: "I am now under sail with a fair wind and fine weather, having on board 1190 souls in fifteen ships, properly equipped and I hope destined to be happy."[69]

For the next few weeks the embarking Nova Scotians were not as happy as Clarkson had hoped. The expedition ran into heavy squalls, temporarily separating one ship from another. Some sixty-five of the voyagers died at sea, and another hundred were too ill to be landed when the fleet pulled into Kru Bay in early March. When the remaining thousand stepped ashore they found that little preparation had been made to receive them. They knew they would have to work long hours if they were to succeed in throwing up enough shelters before the rainy season set in. But if at the moment their new dwelling site lacked adequate housing, it bore a sweet sounding name—Freetown.

69. Clarkson's Mission to America, 399.

CHAPTER X

HEIRS OF THE SAME PROMISE

Tell them that if I am Black I am free born American
& a revolutionary soldier & therefore ought not to be
thrown intirely out of the scale of notice.

John Chavis to Willie P. Mangum
March 10, 1832

Putting aside for the moment the tragedy of her personal life, thirty-one-year-old Phillis Wheatley Peters turned out a lengthy poem in 1784 under the title, "Liberty and Peace." Its closing lines expressed the hope of the many Negroes to whom the war had brought rising expectations:

To every realm shall peace her charms display,
And heavenly freedom spread her golden ray.[1]

Writing three years later, elderly Jupiter Hammon, like Phillis, a poet with a religious turn of mind, but unlike her, never free, summed up the feelings of many Negroes—their high hopes as the war ended and their sense of some disappointment during the years that immediately followed:

That liberty is a great thing we know from our
own feelings, and we may likewise judge so from
the conduct of the white people in the late war.
How much money has been spent and how many lives
have been lost to defend their liberty! I must
say that I have hoped that God would open
their eyes, when they were so much engaged for
liberty, to think of the state of the poor blacks,
and to pity us.[2]

1. Charles F. Heartman, ed., *Phillis Wheatley: Poems and Letters* (New York, 1915), 57.
2. Oscar Wegelin, *Jupiter Hammon* (New York, 1915), 27. Wegelin's frontispiece is a reproduction of the title page of the original "Address."

Hammon could not fail to note that with the removal of the British threat to American liberties, the generous idealism of the Revolution had abated. The Negro was again mired in his old status. Nevertheless, he had made some progress. One indubitable fact was that many slaves became free men from taking part in the struggle for independence. Those who joined the army upon the promise of freedom usually obtained it.

The one notable attempt to repudiate this pledge and return Negro soldiers to slavery occurred in Virginia. Since only free men could enlist in the state forces, some masters had entered slaves as their substitutes, passing them off to the authorities as free men and privately promising them their freedom, but when the term of enlistment expired, they tried to repossess their former chattels. One such incident came to public attention in the last days of the war. In November 1782 the Virginia Council ordered five counties to furnish 3,500 men to level the works at Yorktown. Anyone summoned to duty was permitted to "send an able bodied [free] Negro Man in his stead."[3] Consequently, the force contained a goodly number of Negroes. When the time came for the black substitutes to be discharged, their former masters in numerous instances tried to re-enslave them.

Governor Harrison, like many other Virginians, was indignant at this violation of the "common principles of justice and humanity," and was determined to "Lay the matter before the Assembly, not doubting but they will pass an act giving to those unhappy creatures that liberty which they have been in some measure instrumental in securing to us." Harrison quickly got what he wanted. Declaring that the slaves who enlisted had contributed to American liberty and independence, and that their former masters were acting "contrary to the principles of justice, and to their own solemn promise," the legislature decreed that each slave who had served as a substitute was henceforth fully and completely emancipated. The attorney general was charged with acting on behalf of any former slave who was being detained in servitude.[4]

A few similar incidents occurred elsewhere. In North Carolina the legislature liberated Ned Griffin who, in violation of

3. McIlwaine, ed., *Journal of the Council of the State of Va.,* III, 171.
4. Harrison to Charles Dabney, Oct. 7, 1783, Boyd, ed., *Writings of Jefferson,* VI, 430-31*n.*; Hening, ed., *Statutes of Va.,* XI, 308-9.

the promise made to him, had been re-enslaved following his honorable discharge.[5] In Connecticut the Superior Court liberated a slave, Jack Arabas. Arabas had enlisted in the army with his master's consent, served three years, and upon his discharge was reclaimed by his master. Attempting flight, he was apprehended and brought back to New Haven, where he brought the court action which gave him his freedom.[6]

On occasion a slave became free as a reward for work service. In 1783 the Virginia legislature emancipated the slave, Aberdeen, for his years of public service spent in labor at the lead mines.[7] Sometimes a slave became free in recognition of an act of bravery. Such a case was that of Latchom, a Virginia bondman whose freedom was purchased by General John Cropper. While retreating at Henry's Point in 1781, Cropper fell into a boggy marsh and was soon stuck fast in soft mud up to his waist. He was about to be bayoneted when Latchom shot the British squad leader, dragged Cropper through the mud, and then carried him to safety, even though he "weighed in the neighborhood of two hundred pounds."[8] Another Virginia Negro who similarly merited his freedom was Jupiter, who, according to Colonel George Muter, "saved two guns during the time the enemy were at Richmond, which he afterwards delivered to me."[9] In January 1782 the Rhode Island legislature freed the slave, Quaco, for having rendered the state "and the public in general" an important service in furnishing information about activities of the British in Newport when they occupied that city. Quaco had escaped from the British lines after his master sold him to an officer in the king's army.[10]

At war's end some Negroes in the North achieved freedom as an incidental result of the confiscation of loyalist estates. Local governments in New York often liberated the slaves of departed loyalists during the war and in 1784 the legislature declared that loyalist masters had forfeited their property in

5. Clark, ed., *State Rec. of N. C.*, XXIV, 639.

6. For this case, Arabas *vs.* Ivers, see Bernard C. Steiner, *History of Slavery in Connecticut*, Johns Hopkins Univ. Studies in Hist. and Poli. Science, 11th Ser., Nos. IX, X (1893), 37.

7. Hening, ed., *Statutes of Va.*, XI, 309.

8. "Memoir of General John Cropper," Virginia Historical Society, *Proceedings*, 2 (Richmond, 1891-92), 296-97.

9. *Cal. of Va. State Papers*, I, 604.

10. Bartlett, ed., *Records of the Colony of Rhode Island*, IX, 494-510.

slaves. Two years later all slaves whose masters had been banished were made free.[11] In New Jersey, the legislature on three separate occasions passed laws setting free slaves who had become state property through the confiscation of loyalist holdings. Two such liberated slaves, Peter Williams and Cato, served in both the state and Continental armies.[12]

The states below the Mason-Dixon line did not free the slaves of loyalists. In Maryland the office for confiscated estates, with headquarters at Annapolis, took possession of the slaves of loyalists and sold them at public auction for the benefit of the state.[13] Virginia not only sold the slaves of loyalists but also the "public" slaves which the state had purchased for service in wartime industry. One or two might be freed, as in the case of Aberdeen, mentioned above, but as a rule, such Negroes were placed on auction and sold for hard money, tobacco, or state warrants.[14] South Carolina and Georgia were likewise not disposed to free the slaves of loyalists, having found other uses for them long before the British surrendered.

*   *   *

In its total influence toward freedom the Revolutionary War extended beyond the manumission of Negroes who had served as soldiers. Since the war had been fought in the name of liberty, many Americans were led to reflect seriously upon the impropriety of holding men in bondage. The feeling that slavery was inconsistent with the ideals of the war cropped out in many quarters, becoming manifest in the attitude of prominent national figures, in the formation of abolitionist societies, in the concern for Negroes displayed by religious sects, and in the anti-slavery activities of state and federal governments.

One of those who came out of the war with convictions about slavery was Lafayette, whose influence is worth noting because it extended to the Old World. Prior to 1782 the young Marquis apparently had no strong opinion, but early in 1783

11. *Cal. of Hist. MSS Relating to Rev. War in the Office of Sec. of State*, I, 650. Yoshpe, *Disposition of Loyalist Estates*, 91.
12. Cooley, *A Study of Slavery in New Jersey*, 53.
13. *Md. Gaz.*, Oct. 18, 1781.
14. For orders issued by the state council directing the sale of public Negroes as of June 10, 1783, Oct. 29, 1783, Apr. 5, 1784 and Mar. 14, 1785, see McIlwaine, ed., *Journals of the Council of State of Va.*, III, 267, 302, 335, 424.

while at Cadiz, he wrote to George Washington proposing a plan "which might greatly benefit the black part of mankind." He and the General would jointly purchase a small estate on which slaves might be settled as free tenants. He desired Washington's participation because his name would influence others. Washington discreetly replied that the idea was a good one, but that before going into details he preferred to wait until they could discuss the matter in person. Despite Washington's gentle rejection, Lafayette persisted in his plan, eventually purchasing a plantation in the French Colony of Cayenne for his own Negroes.[15]

Lafayette's convictions led him to give vigorous support to the movement in France to abolish slavery in the French colonies and prohibit the slave trade. When the Society of the Friends of the Blacks was organized in 1788, Lafayette insisted on becoming a charter member although the founders had not wished to enroll men of the titled nobility. Thomas Clarkson, who met him in Paris on four occasions, said he was "as uncompromising an enemy of the slave-trade and slavery, as any man I ever knew."[16] Respected on two continents, Lafayette personified the international scope of the anti-slavery crusade, the cross fertilization of the reform and revolutionary spirit in America and Western Europe.[17]

Although Lafayette did not succeed in persuading Washington to sponsor a settlement for free Negroes, he may have contributed to his friend's growing uneasiness about the rightness of slavery. In an interview following dinner at Mount Vernon on a May evening in 1785, Washington told his guests, the Methodist clergymen Herbert Asbury and Thomas Coke, that "he was of our sentiments" about freeing those in bondage.

15. Melvin D. Kennedy, *Lafayette and Slavery* (Easton, Pa., 1950), 3; Lafayette to Washington, Feb. 5, 1783, Sparks, ed., *Letters to Washington,* III, 547; Washington to Lafayette, Apr. 5, 1783, Fitzpatrick, ed., *Writings of Washington,* XXVI, 300; Lafayette to Washington, July 14, 1785 and Feb. 6, 1786, Louis Gottschalk, ed., *The Letters of Lafayette to Washington, 1777-1799* (New York, 1944), 301, 309. For the fate of this experiment see Walter H. Mazyck, *George Washington and the Negro* (Washington, 1932), 96-97.

16. Clarkson to Maria W. Chapman, Oct. 3, 1845, *The Liberator* (Boston), May 2, 1846.

17. On this point see Michael Kraus, "Slavery Reform in the Eighteenth Century: an Aspect of Transatlantic Intellectual Cooperation," *Pa. Mag. of Hist. and Biog.,* 60 (1936), 53-66.

Washington "did not see it proper to sign" a petition for slave emancipation which Coke and Asbury presented,[18] but the following year he pointedly expressed his antagonism to slavery. "There is not a man living," he wrote to Robert Morris, "who wishes more sincerely than I do, to see a plan adopted for the gradual abolition of it." To another correspondent he revealed his determination never "to possess another slave by purchase, it being among my first wishes to see some plan adopted by which slavery may be abolished by law."[19]

Disturbed by scruples regarding slavery, Washington was a considerate master. When Billy Lee wanted him to bring a free Negro, Margaret Thomas, to Mount Vernon, Washington wrote Clement Biddle in Philadelphia asking him to locate her and arrange passage for her by boat or stage. Washington said that he had hoped never to lay eyes on Margaret again but that he could not refuse the request, especially since Billy "has been with me all the War," following his fortunes with fidelity.[20]

More apprehensive about slavery than Washington was his fellow-Virginian, Thomas Jefferson, who trembled for his country when he reflected that God was just.[21] He regarded slavery as harmful to both master and bondman, breeding boisterous passions in one and degrading submission in the other. Jefferson's conviction that slavery was an evil was but little stronger, however, than his belief that the Negro was inferior to the white man in mental endowment.[22] He had a poor opinion of even the most celebrated Negroes. Religion had produced a Phillis Wheatley, he wrote, but it could not produce a poet—the proof being the inferior quality of her compositions.[23] Hardly more

18. For this meeting see Albert Matthews, "Notes on the Proposed Abolition of Slavery in Virginia in 1785," Colonial Society of Massachusetts, *Publications*, 6 (1900), 377; also *Journal of Rev. Francis Asbury*, 3 vols. (New York, 1852), I, 496.

19. Washington to Morris, Apr. 12, to John F. Mercer, Sept. 9, 1786, Fitzpatrick, ed., *Writings of Washington*, XXVIII, 408, XXIX, 5.

20. Washington to Biddle, July 28, 1784, *ibid.*, XXVII, 451.

21. Thomas Jefferson, *Notes on the State of Virginia* (Baltimore, 1800), 241.

22. In a letter to Chastellux in 1785 Jefferson qualified his opinion of the limited capacity of the Negro, stating that it would be hazardous to say that if the black men were "equally cultivated for a few generations" they would reach the level of anybody else. Jefferson to Chastellux, June 7, 1785, Boyd, ed., *Papers of Jefferson*, VIII, 186. On Jefferson's attitude toward slavery vis-à-vis the Negro slave as a mental equal to whites see Dumas Malone, *Jefferson and the Rights of Man* (Boston, 1951), 95-97.

23. Jefferson, *Notes on Virginia*, 208.

flattering was his estimate of Benjamin Banneker, who had sent him an almanac, and which he in turn sent to Condorcet, a founder of the Society of the Friends of the Blacks: "We know he had spherical geometry enough to make almanacs, but not without the suspicion of aid from Ellicot, who was his neighbor and friend, and never missed an opportunity of puffing him. I have a long letter from Banneker, which shows him to have had a mind of very common stature indeed."[24]

The inferiority of the Negro did not signify, in Jefferson's thinking, that he was to be deprived of his rights. A man's rights were not contingent upon his abilities; hence, the Negro should be free. But since Jefferson did not believe whites and blacks could live together in peace, his conclusion was that Negroes should be sent away.[25] To Jefferson, as to Lincoln after him, the emancipation of the slave was inseparable from his deportation; his place to be taken by free white laborers. It needs scarcely be added, however, that a man of Jefferson's broad humanity was kind to his own slaves. Monticello-born Isaac expressed the feeling of his fellows in calling Jefferson "a mighty good master," always encouraging them and giving the best workers "a suit of red or blue."[26]

Knowing Jefferson's interest in seeing all men become free, his Polish friend, Thaddeus Kosciuszko, named him as executor of his will, in which he authorized the use of his American funds for the purchase and education of slaves so that they might become good citizens of their country and defenders of its liberties.[27] The Polish patriot was a believer in liberty for all men as a matter of principle, but he had had some wartime contacts with Negroes. Perhaps as he drew up this will he recalled his once asking General Greene for permission to give two nearly naked Negro orderlies of John Laurens a part of

24. Jefferson to Joel Barlow, Oct. 1, 1809, Paul Leicester Ford, ed., *The Writings of Thomas Jefferson*, 10 vols. (New York, 1892-99), IX, 261. Compare Richard B. Davis, ed., *Jeffersonian America: Notes on the United States of America . . . by Sir Augustus John Foster* (San Marino, Calif., 1954), 149-50.

25. Jefferson, *Notes on Virginia*, 204.

26. Rayford W. Logan, ed., *Memoirs of a Monticello Slave* (Charlottesville, 1951), 35-36.

27. For the story of this will and its aftermath see Miecislaus Haiman, *Kosciuszko: Leader and Exile* (New York, 1946), 76-79, 125-26, and Marion M. Thompson Wright, *The Education of Negroes in New Jersey* (New York, 1941), 92-97.

the slain young colonel's clothing. Perhaps, too, he remembered Prince, who often served him as a messenger when he was in charge of the intelligence service between the patriots in Charleston and the American army command. Perhaps running through Kosciuzko's mind as he composed this will, was the recollection of a skirmish at Port Johnston in South Carolina in November 1782, in which he led the American forces in the last skirmish of the war—one of the casualties was a mulatto who died of shoulder wounds.[28]

As the views of Washington and Jefferson display attitudes toward slavery of notable public figures in the South, so the thought of Benjamin Franklin reveals an even more liberal trend above the Potomac. A slaveowner in his early days, Franklin had abandoned the practice before the Revolution, moved by his reading of Quaker pamphlets brought to his print shop for publication, and by his correspondence with Anthony Benezet and Granville Sharp. While in London in the early summer of 1773, Franklin paid a visit to Phillis Wheatley: "I went to see the black poetess," he wrote, "and offered her any services I could do for her."[29] Two years after his return from France in 1785, he was elected President of the "Pennsylvania Society for Promoting the Abolition of Slavery and the Relief of Free Negroes unlawfully held in Bondage." In November 1789 the aged Franklin signed the Society's public appeal for funds to extend relief to freed men, secure them employment, and provide schooling for their children.[30] Three months later, performing his last public act, he put his signature to the society's memorial, presented to the first Congress on February 12, 1790, which entreated the legislators "to countenance the restoration of liberty to those unhappy men, who alone, in this land of freedom are degraded into perpetual bondage."[31]

28. Miecislaus Haiman, *Kosciuszko in the American Revolution* (New York, 1943), 133, 135; Alexander Garden, *Anecdotes of the Revolutionary War* (Charleston, 1822), 92; W. Dancey to unknown, Nov. 25, 1782, Joseph W. Barnell, ed., "Letters to General Greene and Others," *S. C. Hist. and Gen. Mag.*, 17 (1916), 54.

29. Franklin to Jonathan Williams, July 7, 1773, Albert Henry Smyth, *The Writings of Benjamin Franklin*, 10 vols. (New York, 1905-07), VI, 96.

30. For this petition see Livermore, *An Historical Research Respecting Negroes*, 46-48.

31. Joseph Gales, Sr., *The Debates and Proceedings in the Congress of the United States, 1789-1824*, 42 vols. (1834-56), I, 1239-40.

Congress, however, took the stand that it had no power to interfere in the internal activities of the states. In the course of the debates, James Jackson of Georgia supported this point of view, thereby drawing from Franklin's pen one of the cleverest satires in American political letters. Franklin took Jackson's arguments and put them into the mouth of one "Sidi Mehemet Ibrahim, a member of the Divan of Algiers." A few sentences will suggest the flavor and content of this famous parody: "If we cease our cruises against the Christians, how shall we be furnished with the commodities their countries produce, and which are so necessary for us? If we forbear to make slaves of their people, who, in this hot climate, are to cultivate our lands. . . . And is there not more compassion and favor due to us as Mussulmen than to these Christian dogs?"[32]

Franklin's public activities in the anti-slavery cause were undertaken mainly in connection with his presidency of an abolitionist society. Within a decade after the war, these societies experienced a rapid growth. The Pennsylvania Society, first formed in 1775 at Philadelphia, was revived in April 1784. Less than a year later, New York organized a society, with John Jay as president. New Jersey came next, and by the end of 1790, Delaware, Maryland, Connecticut, and Rhode Island had followed suit. Supplementing these state-wide organizations were numerous local societies. The abolitionist groups held their first national convention at Philadelphia in 1794, with representatives from ten state organizations, including Maryland and Virginia.[33]

Unlike the key figures in the abolitionist movement of half a century later, the leaders in these early societies could never be charged with being hot-headed zealots; on the contrary, they were men of property and standing—orderly, law abiding, quiet-mannered. Franklin and John Jay were not odd figures in a company which included leading justices in the state courts, public figures like Luther Martin of Maryland, and Alexander Hamilton, well-known physicians such as George Buchanan of Maryland and Benjamin Rush, and such pioneer notables in the world of learning as the historian Jeremy Belknap, the geographer Jedidiah Morse, and the lexicographer Noah Webster.

32. For this satire see Smyth, *Writings of Franklin*, X, 87-91.
33. William F. Poole, *Anti-Slavery Opinions Before the Year 1800* (Cincinnati, 1873), 59-62.

Meeting quarterly and working through standing and special committees, these societies engaged in a variety of activities. Although they sent petitions to the state and national legislatures, their essential technique was persuasion rather than political agitation, soft impeachment rather than declamation. They urged the abolition of the slave trade, foreign and domestic, and the gradual abolition of slavery itself. In some instances they paid masters to free slaves; in other instances they guaranteed to a master that if he freed his slave, they would be legally responsible if the slave failed to support himself. They tried to strike at slavery by refusing to buy the products of slave labor.[34]

These societies protected the free Negro from being seized and sold back into slavery. They assisted him in finding a job, furnished recommendations, and saw to it that the employer did not take advantage of him. Believing that the former slave should be educated for a life of freedom, they conducted night classes for adults and opened schools for children. In 1787 the New York Manumission Society founded the African Free School, which opened its doors to some forty pupils.[35]

To shape public opinion, the societies published broadsides and pamphlets for gratuitous distribution to public officials, as well as to private citizens. The essays of Anthony Benezet, Samuel Hopkins and Thomas Clarkson, and the "Address" of Jupiter Hammon were reproduced by the thousands. One society offered a gold medal for the best anti-slavery oration delivered at the commencement exercises of Columbia College.[36]

* * *

The early abolitionist movement owed much of its strength to the influence of church groups, which almost without exception showed a quickening interest in the welfare of Negroes. Some fundamentalists attributed the war itself to divine displeasure at things in general and slavery in particular. A contemporary minister of the gospel wrote that there were many who did not rightly estimate the true source of all freedom, "in

34. Edward R. Turner, "The First Abolition Society in the United States," *Pa. Mag. of Hist. and Biog.*, 36 (1912), 102-3.

35. For this enterprise see Charles C. Andrews, *The History of the New-York African Free-Schools* (New York, 1830).

36. Wegelin, *Jupiter Hammon*, 51; Poole, *Anti-Slavery Opinions Before the Year 1800*, 48.

consequence of which God sent them liberty, and with it leanness of soul."[37] The religiously minded were concerned about America's spiritual outlook; the war had been won, but had her iniquities been pardoned?

No Protestant group was more forthright in opposing slavery than the Quakers. The first anti-slavery society in America in 1775 had been comprised largely of Quakers, and they were foremost in the movement which led Pennsylvania to ·become the first state to abolish slavery. Concerned about the emancipated Negro, they had become pioneers in establishing schools, like that of Benezet, for colored girls and boys. Interested too in his spiritual welfare, some of the "meetings" held regular worship services for the Negro, and they permitted Negroes to marry by Friends' ceremony.[38]

Other religious denominations became concerned about the Negro in the years just after the war. The Baptists licensed Negro preachers, both slave and free. In addition to George Liele and David George, both of whom left America with the British, the Baptists also licensed Jesse Peter who in 1783 took over the church at Silver Bluff, South Carolina—the first Negro Baptist church in the United States. At Savannah five years later Andrew Bryan was certified as minister of the Ethiopian Church of Jesus Christ; he built its membership up to 700 within ten years. Another noteworthy early Negro Baptist was Joseph Willis, who was born in South Carolina, became a licensed preacher, and some time prior to 1798 moved into the Mississippi Territory. Willis had the distinction of delivering the first Protestant sermon west of the Mississippi River; he also became first moderator of the first Baptist state-wide organization in that distant territory—the Louisiana Association.[39]

Among Methodists anti-slavery sentiment was deepened by John Wesley's castigation of human bondage. In 1780, six years after Wesley had penned his *Thoughts Upon Slavery*, the Methodist conference, meeting at Baltimore, left no doubt as to its attitude: it expressed disapproval of members who held

37. Robert B. Semple, *A History of the Rise and Progress of the Baptists of Virginia*, ed. G. W. Beale (Richmond, 1894), 55.

38. Henry J. Cadbury, "Negro Membership in the Society of Friends," *Journal of Negro History*, 21 (1936), 157, 159.

39. For a sketch of Willis see Benjamin Quarles, "Joseph Willis: Pioneer Churchman," *Negro Hist. Bull.* (1949), 110-11.

slaves, and required traveling preachers to free their slaves. This forthright stand was re-affirmed in 1784, but in the following year the conference suspended the rule against slaveholding. A feature of the early Methodist churches, however, was their racially mixed congregations. Of the fifty-one churches at the 1789 conference, thirty-six reported having colored members. "Black Harry" Hosier, a free Negro, was a traveling companion of Francis Asbury, and sometimes preached as his substitute.[40]

Like other Protestant groups, the Methodists continued to have their difficulties over slavery and the Negro. The forthright anti-slavery statements of the early conferences and the coolness with which these sentiments were received in the slaveholding sections foreshadowed the sectional divisions among Methodists that wracked the church in the eighteen-forties. The problems incident to white and black worship under the same roof were dramatized at Philadelphia's St. George's Methodist Episcopal Church on a winter Sunday in 1787, when, in the hush of the morning service, a white trustee advanced upon the kneeling Absalom Jones and ordered him and the other Negro communicants to get themselves to the gallery.[41]

* * *

Through such agencies as abolitionist societies and religious denominations, the anti-slavery impulse spread. The movement was strongest in the North where slaves were least numerous. Pennsylvania and Massachusetts, as has been noted, did not wait until the war was over to take action. Less than a year after the peace treaty was signed, Connecticut and Rhode Island passed gradual abolition measures. The Connecticut act stated that no child thereafter should be held to service after reaching twenty-five years of age, and Rhode Island declared that all children born of slave mothers after March 1, 1784, would be free.[42] In 1788 the New York legislature permitted masters to set free without incurring bonded responsibility any able-bodied slave under fifty years of age. In Delaware the movement for gradual emancipation was a failure despite the work of such

40. W. D. Weatherford, *American Churches and the Negro* (Boston, 1957), 87. This whole topic is treated in L. C. Matlack, *The History of American Slavery and Methodism from 1780 to 1849* (New York, 1849), 11-37.

41. Charles H. Wesley, *Richard Allen* (Washington, 1935), 52-53.

42. On this whole topic of emancipation in the states see Locke, *Anti-Slavery in America*, 112-33.

men as John Dickinson who, while president of the state legislature, freed six of his slaves.[43]

The South, too, had its voices crying out, however futilely, against slavery. St. George Tucker, professor of law at William and Mary, his reflections on abolition having been deepened by his correspondence with Jeremy Belknap, sent to the Virginia legislature a copy of *A Dissertation on Slavery*. A gradualist even among gradualists, Judge Tucker proposed to free only the females who had reached twenty-eight. Their children, however, would be free after they had worked out the cost of rearing them in infancy and childhood. Free Negroes were not to be permitted to hold any public office, own land, or bear arms. Tucker's hope was that such restrictions would cause them to leave the state.[44] He wished to protect the whites; nevertheless he had his sympathies for the Negro: "Whilst America hath been the land of promise to Europeans, and their descendants," he wrote, "it hath been a vale of tears to millions of the wretched sons of Africa."[45] Tucker's proposals were not acted upon by the legislature, other than by a routine acknowledgment in one house and a tabling in the other.

Although not willing to adopt a general emancipation bill, the Virginia legislature encouraged private manumission and took steps to protect the status of free Negroes. In 1782 it authorized a master to free his bondman without first obtaining legislative consent. Five years later, the assembly decreed death without benefit of clergy to anyone who knowingly sold a free person as a slave.[46] But although Virginia made it easier to free slaves, and the Maryland legislature in 1785 actually mustered twenty-two votes against slavery, as against thirty-two for it,[47] this degree of abolitionism was not possible in the lower South where Negroes were more numerous and slavery was more profitable.

The movement to abolish slavery itself was less widespread and less successful than the drive to abolish the slave trade. At one time or another during the war, every state except Georgia

43. J. H. Powell, "John Dickinson, President of the Delaware State, 1781-1782," *Delaware History*, I (1916), 11.
44. St. George Tucker, *A Dissertation on Slavery* (Phila., 1796), 91-94.
45. *Ibid.*, 9.
46. Hening, ed., *Statutes of Va.*, XI, 39, XII, 53, 182.
47. Locke, *Anti-Slavery in America*, 120.

and South Carolina prohibited or limited the traffic in men. In Massachusetts the liberal spirit triumphed in 1788 as a direct result of public indignation at the abduction of three free Negroes employed as day laborers on a boat in Boston harbor. Sent into the hold to work, they were carried off when the vessel suddenly raised sail and set out to sea. Governor Hancock sent letters to governors in the West Indies advising them to be on the lookout for the abducted blacks, and they were finally rescued by the authorities at the Danish port of St. Bartholomew. Back in Massachusetts, groups of clergymen and Quakers urged the General Court to prevent a recurrence of such kidnappings, and Prince Hall, grand master of the Negro Masons, brought forward a strongly worded statement calling for the total abolition of the traffic in human beings. The legislature quickly responded by passing an act prohibiting the slave trade and establishing a procedure by which persons who were kidnapped or decoyed out of the commonwealth could obtain redress. Boston's colored population held a day of celebration July 29, when the three shanghaied Negroes were returned to the city.[48]

But just as the lower South resisted any abolition of slavery, so it refused to countenance restriction of the slave trade. The importation of slaves increased heavily in the two southernmost states after the war, whereas by 1790 it had declined to a standstill above the Potomac.[49] The decline in the North registered the force of humanitarian protest, but it was facilitated by economic changes. With the China trade opening up, the New England states could afford a reduction of the traffic in Negroes and rum. South Carolina and Georgia, on the other hand, had need of additional slaves to make up for those carried off by the British.

* * *

With limited powers and little ability to enforce its enactments, the Confederation Congress was reluctant to approach such explosive issues as slavery and the slave trade. The Negro

48. Jeremy Belknap to Ebenezer Hazard, Mar. 2, 1788, "The Belknap Papers," Mass. Hist. Soc., *Coll.*, 5th Ser., 3 (1877), 22; "Judge Tucker's Queries Respecting Slavery," Mass. Hist. Soc., *Coll.*, 1st Ser., 4 (1795), 204-5; also Robert S. Rantoul, Sr., "Negro Slavery in Massachusetts," Essex Institute Historical Society, *Collections*, 14 (1887), 94-95.
49. Dubois, *Suppression of the African Slave-Trade*, 50-51.

figured incidentally, however, in several matters of a federal
nature. One question was whether Negroes should be counted
as part of a state's population in determining the number of
soldiers it should furnish to the Continental army. The slave
states gained an advantage from the stipulation in the Articles
of Confederation, ratified in March 1781, that quotas should
be based solely on the number of white inhabitants. A more
controversial issue arose in determining Congressional assess-
ments of money upon the different states. Under the Articles
of Confederation, a state's quota of money was to be based on
the relative value of its land. This mode of determining a state's
proportion of federal expenses proved impractical, and at the
end of the war Congress asked the states to ratify an amendment
to the Articles which would substitute population as the basis
of assessment. In drawing up its proposal, Congress debated
whether slaves should be counted as population; the resulting
compromise, by which three-fifths of the slaves were to be
counted, anticipated the famous compromise at the Constitutional
Convention. It was never ratified by the states during the Confederation.

The cession of state claims to western lands compelled
Congress to define its position with respect to slavery in the
new federal domain beyond the Alleghanies. In the debate over
the Ordinance of 1784, Jefferson moved that Congress prohibit slavery after 1800 in the region from the Great Lakes
to the Gulf of Mexico. The proposal lost by a vote of seven
states to six, but three years later Congress wrote a clause
into the Northwest Ordinance prohibiting slavery in the territory above the Ohio. While practical considerations may have
dictated this policy, it was nevertheless an indication of growing antipathy to slavery.

With the Northwest Ordinance this study may properly be
brought to a close. To go into the work of the Founding Fathers
and the new federal union would be outside its scope. Suffice
it to say that in President Washington's America, the Negro
would meet with discriminations contrary to the ideals proclaimed in the America of General Washington. Nevertheless,
that America was the land of promise remained to Negroes the
abiding significance of the Revolutionary War. This sentiment
was expressed in an address given at Rutland, Vermont, on the

twenty-fifth anniversary of the Declaration of Independence by Lemuel Haynes, Negro Congregationalist pastor, who had been a minuteman and a Ticonderoga volunteer: "Explore every corner of the globe for an equal asylum, tired in the fruitless chase, you would most eagerly seek the refreshing shades of happy Columbia. Still it is a land of improvement; we are not to conclude that the fair tree of liberty hath reached its highest zenith; may we not add to its lustre."[50]

* * *

The American Revolution touched all classes in society, even Negroes. On the eve of the conflict, the same religious and political idealism that stirred the resistance to Britain deepened the sentiment against slavery. The memorable phrases of the Declaration of Independence which asserted the equality of man set forth a principle which could never be wholly reconciled with the existence of slavery. During the war itself, the abolition movement bore its first fruits, and within two decades after the war's end, all the Northern states were emancipating their slaves.

The actual fighting presented more immediate opportunities for obtaining freedom. Britain and America both needed black manpower, and both were prepared to give the Negro the freedom he sought. Since liberating the slaves of American rebels cost her nothing and at the same time hampered the patriot war effort, Britain was first to make the offer. Lord Dunmore, at bay in Virginia during the opening months of the yet undeclared war, initiated the practice of inviting slaves to desert their American masters. Although Dunmore was soon driven from the Old Dominion, the number of Negroes who tried to join his forces disclosed the readiness of slaves to seek freedom within the British lines. Henceforth, solicitation of Negroes became a key factor in British policy.

On the American side, free Negroes served in the military and naval forces from the beginning of the war, but the enlistment of slaves raised so many difficulties and aroused such opposition, particularly in the South, that it was at first avoided. The need to counteract British appeals and the shortage of manpower soon caused a change of heart. Congress and most

50. For Haynes see Timothy Mather Cooley, *Sketches of the Life and Character of the Rev. Lemuel Haynes, A. M.* (New York, 1837).

of the states north of the Potomac endorsed a policy of recruiting slaves for military duty, granting freedom as the reward for faithful service.

As an American soldier, the Negro proved to be much like his fellows. His morale was likely to be above average—military service was a step up in life for him, and active campaigning was often no more arduous and certainly more exciting than the routine of the plantation. With little investment in a civilian existence or occupation, Negroes were suitable recruits for the Continental army, which Congress desired to enlist on the basis of three years or the duration of the war. Serving in racially mixed units, the Negro did not stand out distinctly; his military personality blended into the composite portrait of the undistinguished but indispensable foot soldier.

Negroes also served in state forces, particularly in the North. In the plantation areas of the South, the heavy slave population made it seem a risky venture to employ slaves as soldiers, moreover inducting them into the army took them away from the tobacco or rice fields, where their labor was of paramount importance. The plantation states all took a few free Negroes into their armed forces, and Maryland provided for the enlistment of slaves. Georgia and the Carolinas were never willing to take this last step, and resisted it to the end.

Service at sea offered a better field of opportunity for Negroes; even in the South there was less reluctance to employ them aboard ship than as soldiers. The Continental navy welcomed black recruits, especially free Negro sailors from New England coastal towns. Generally, however, the Continental service was outbid by the state navies: Massachusetts and Connecticut took all the Negroes they could get for maritime service. Among Southern states, Virginia was most inclined to use black seamen, enlisting nearly 150 during the war. The highest function open to Southern Negro sailors was to act as pilots in local waters, and several attained considerable reputation for their diligence and success. Apart from duty in regular maritime forces, Negroes went to sea on privateers. As the captains of these private ships of war seldom bothered to inquire into the status of the black members of their crews, many runaway slaves thus found sanctuary.

Individuals who bore arms or served on ships or who took

advantage of opportunities to act as spies, guides, or informers stand out from the general mass of the Negro population whose contribution to the American cause was anonymous labor. Negroes erected fortifications, manufactured cannon and gun carriages, worked in the salt and lead mines, repaired roads, and drove wagons. To procure Negro labor, state governments and Continental military officers resorted to a variety of techniques: impressing, hiring, or purchasing slaves. Whatever the method, it never yielded a sufficient supply to meet the need.

The military potential represented by America's large Negro population was available to the British in the regions they occupied or controlled. In the South, some hundreds of runaway slaves were converted into shock troops, but the British needed blacks less as soldiers than as military laborers. Thousands of Negro carpenters, hostlers, axemen, miners, and blacksmiths increased the striking power of the British forces. Unable to get enough slaves for their purposes, many British commanders induced free Negroes to take employment, paying them 2s. or 3s. a day as smiths, sawyers, armorers, and turnwheelers. Unskilled Negroes were often sent out on foraging parties to run off the livestock of American patriots and strip their fields, barns, and cellars.

Since slaves were property, they constituted a source of wealth which both the British and the Americans exploited for a variety of purposes. Southern state governments used them to pay official salaries, enlistment bounties, and back-pay due to the troops. To Americans as well as the British, the slaves of the enemy were legitimate spoils of war, which not only provided booty but deprived the enemy of vital resources. In the South, especially in the later stages of the conflict, slave-raiding was one of the primary objects of war.

When the British evacuated American ports, they took with them most of the Negroes who had come into their lines. Alert to this possibility, which entailed immense loss of property to Americans, General Washington personally presented the American case to Sir Guy Carleton, the British commander-in-chief. Joint commissions were set up to supervise the evacuation, but they were of little help to Americans in recovering slaves. The British never yielded in their contention that the terms of the peace treaty did not cover Negroes who accepted British protection before the preliminary articles of peace were signed. Irate Americans could only fume as their former slaves were evacuated. Their losses gave rise to a diplomatic issue that plagued Anglo-American relations for a quarter of a century.

Negroes who went with the British were shipped to the West Indies, Canada, England, and Continental Europe. Those owned by loyalists or British subjects remained slaves, of course, and merely followed their masters. Others who had achieved freedom by embracing the British side in the Revolution often failed to improve their lot significantly. Some, in fact, were forced back to slavery; in other instances, they had difficulty in obtaining the land grants which had been promised them. In Nova Scotia, a group of disillusioned Negroes numbering nearly twelve hundred, obtained permission from the Sierra Leone Company in 1792 to settle on its territory in West Africa.

Negroes who remained in America likewise found the post-war period a disappointment to their hopes. The condition of slaves on the plantations was unchanged. Nevertheless, the Negro had made some gains. Many slaves had become free, and some free Negroes had improved their status. The emancipation movement was gaining strength in the North. Ultimately, the colored people of America benefited from the irreversible commitment of the new nation to the principles of liberty and equality.

BIBLIOGRAPHY

PRIMARY SOURCES

I. *Manuscripts*

Adams, John. Papers, 1775. Massachusetts Historical Society. Boston.

Canada. Public Archives of Canada, Series C. Photostats. Library of Congress.

Carleton, Sir Guy. Papers. Photostats, Colonial Williamsburg and New York Public Library.

Carrollton Manuscripts. Maryland Historical Society. Baltimore.

Clarkson, John. Mission to America. New-York Historical Society.

Clinton, Sir Henry. Papers. William L. Clements Library. Ann Arbor.

Colonial Office Papers. Class 5: American and West Indies. British Public Record Office. Transcripts. Library of Congress.

Cornwallis, Charles, Lord. Papers. British Public Record Office. Transcripts. Library of Congress.

Emmet, Thomas Addis. Collection. Miscellaneous Manuscripts, EM-F. New York Public Library.

Force-Bancroft. Peter Force—George Bancroft Transcripts. Virginia: Official Correspondence. Library of Congress.

Gage, Thomas. Papers: British and American Series. William L. Clements Library. Ann Arbor.

Glover, John. Letters and Orderly Books, 1776-1781. Transcripts. New York Public Library.

Greene, Nathanael. Papers. William L. Clements Library. Ann Arbor.

Hamond, Andrew Snape. Diaries, 1775-1777. University of Virginia Library.

Hopkins, Esek. Letterbook and Papers. Navy Department Records Division. National Archives.

Jefferson, Thomas. Papers. Vols. 8, 9. Library of Congress.

Laurens, John. Manuscripts. Historical Society of Pennsylvania. Philadelphia.

Laurens, John. Papers. Library of Congress.
Lee, Arthur. Papers. Houghton Library. Harvard University.
Lee, Richard Henry. Family Papers. University of Virginia Library.
Leslie, Alexander. Letterbooks. New York Public Library.
Marine Committee, Continental Congress. Letterbook, 1776-1780. Papers of the Continental Congress, Foreign Affairs Section, National Archives.
Maryland. Revolutionary Papers, boxes 2 and 6. Hall of Records. Annapolis.
Massachusetts Archives. Commonwealth of Massachusetts, Archives Division. Boston.
Miscellaneous Manuscripts. William L. Clements Library. Ann Arbor.
New York. Revolutionary Papers, vol. 1. New York Public Library.
Poems of the American Revolution, 1779-1782. New-York Historical Society. New York.
Ranger (U. S. Ship of War). Navy Department Records Division. National Archives.
Rhode Island. Manuscripts, vol. 3. Rhode Island Historical Society. Providence.
Rhode Island. Military Papers, vols. 2-4. Rhode Island Historical Society. Providence.
Schuyler, Philip. Papers. New York Public Library.
Virginia. List of Virginia soldiers and seamen receiving certificates for balance of pay. Virginia State Library.
Virginia. Officers, Seamen, and Vessels, Virginia Navy, 1776-1779. Virginia State Library.
Virginia. Papers Concerning the State Navy. Virginia State Library.
Washington, George. Papers. Vols. 1-223. Library of Congress.
Weedon, George. Correspondence. American Philosophical Society. Philadelphia.
Wild, Ebenezer. A Journal of a March from Cambridge on an Expedition against Quebeck in Colo. Arnold's Regiment, September 13, 1775. Houghton Library, Harvard University.
Williams, Otho Holland. Papers. Maryland Historical Society. Baltimore.
Woodson, Carter G. Papers. Library of Congress.
Wray, George. Papers. William L. Clements Library. Ann Arbor.

II. *Unpublished Dissertations*

Barnwell, Robert W., Jr. Loyalism in South Carolina, 1765-1785. Ph.D. Dissertation, Duke University, 1941.
Caley, Percy Burdelle. Dunmore: Colonial Governor of New York and Virginia. Ph.D. Dissertation, University of Pittsburg, 1939.

Morse, Sidney G. New England Privateering in the American Revolution. Ph.D. Dissertation, Harvard University, 1941.

Roe, Clara Goldsmith. Major General Nathanael Greene and the Southern Campaign of the American Revolution, 1780-1783. Ph.D. Dissertation, University of Michigan, 1943.

III. *Printed Official Records*

Connecticut

Public Records of the State of Connecticut, ed. by C. J. Hoadly and L. W. Labaree. Hartford, 1894-1951. 8 vols.

"Rolls and Lists of Connecticut Men in the Revolution," Connecticut Historical Society, *Collections,* 8 (1901), 1-280.

"Rolls of Connecticut Men in the French and Indian War," Connecticut Historical Society, *Collections,* 9 (1903-05), 1-378.

Delaware

"Council of Safety Minutes," ed. by Leon de Valinger, Jr., *Delaware History,* 1 (1946), 55-78.

Laws of the Government of New-Castle, Kent, and Sussex, upon Delaware. Wilmington, 1783.

Georgia

Colonial Records of the State of Georgia, 1732-1782, ed. by Allen D. Candler. Atlanta, 1904-16. 26 vols.

"Proceedings of the First Provincial Congress of Georgia, 1775," Georgia Historical Society, *Collections,* 5, pt. 1 (1901), 1-13.

The Revolutionary Records of the State of Georgia, ed. by Allen D. Candler. Atlanta, 1908. 3 vols.

Maryland

Archives of Maryland, ed. by William H. Browne, *et al.* Baltimore, 1883-1952. 65 vols.

Laws of Maryland Passed at a Session of the Assembly in the Year One Thousand and Seven Hundred and Eighty. Annapolis, 1781.

Unpublished Revolutionary War Records of Maryland, comp. by Margaret R. Hodges. Baltimore, 1939. 6 vols.

Massachusetts

Acts and Resolves, Public and Private of the Province of the Massachusetts Bay. Boston, 1869-1922. 21 vols.

Boston Town Records, 1770 through 1777. Boston, 1887.

Boston Town Records, 1758 to 1769. Boston, 1886.

"Extract from Orderly Book of the Massachusetts Regiment Under the Command of Colonel John Jacobs," *Rhode Island Historical Tracts,* 6 (1878), 113-14.

Massachusetts Soldiers and Sailors of the Revolutionary War. Boston, 1896-1908. 17 vols.

New Hampshire

An Act for forming and regulating the Militia within the State of New Hampshire. Exeter, 1776.

Miscellaneous Revolutionary Documents of New Hampshire, ed. by Albert S. Batchellor. Manchester, 1910.

Revolutionary War Rolls and Documents of New Hampshire, ed. by Isaac W. Hammond. Manchester, 1889.

Revolutionary War Rolls of the State of New Hampshire, ed. by Isaac W. Hammond. Manchester, 1887-89. 4 vols.

New Jersey

Archives of the State of New Jersey, 1631-1800, ed. by W. A. Whitehead, *et al.* Newark, etc., 1880-1906. 30 vols.

Laws of the State of New-Jersey. Newark, 1800.

Minutes of the Provincial Congress and Council of Safety of the State of New Jersey. Trenton, 1879.

"Proceedings of the Committees of Freehold and Shrewsbury," New Jersey Historical Society, *Proceedings,* 1 (1845-46), 184-97.

New York

The Colonial Laws of New York. Albany, 1894-96. 5 vols.

Laws of the State of New-York. Poughkeepsie, 1782.

Minutes of the Commissioner for Detecting Conspiracies in the State of New York: Albany County Sessions, 1778-1781, ed. by V. H. Paltsits. Albany, 1909. 2 vols.

"Minutes of the Committee and of the First Commission for Detecting and Defeating Conspiracies in the State of New York, December 11, 1776—September 23, 1778," New York Historical Society, *Collections,* 57-58 (1924-25). 2 vols.

"Muster Rolls of New York Provincial Troops, 1755-1764," New-York Historical Society, *Collections,* 24 (1892), 1-498.

North Carolina

Colonial Records of North Carolina (1662-1776), ed. by William L. Saunders. Raleigh, 1886-90. 10 vols.

The Public Acts of the General Assembly of North-Carolina. Newbern, 1804.

State Records of North Carolina, 1777-1790, ed. by Walter Clark. Winston and Goldsboro, 1895-1905. 16 vols.

Pennsylvania

Pennsylvania Archives [1664-   ], ed. by Samuel Hazard, *et al.* Harrisburg and Philadelphia, 1852-1949. 138 vols.

Statutes at Large of Pennsylvania from 1682 to 1801, ed. by J. T. Mitchell and Henry Flanders. Harrisburg, 1896-1908.

South Carolina

Documents relating to the History of South Carolina during the War, ed. by A. S. Salley, Jr. Columbia, 1908.

Journal of the Commissioners of the Navy of South Carolina, October 9, 1776—March 1, 1779, ed. by A. S. Salley, Jr. Columbia, 1916.

"Journal of the Council of Safety for South Carolina," South Carolina Historical Society, *Collections,* 2 (1858), 22-64.

Journal of the House of Representatives of South Carolina, January 8, 1782—February 26, 1782, ed. by A. S. Salley, Jr. Columbia, 1916.

"Journal of the Second Council of Safety," South Carolina Historical Society, *Collections,* 3 (1859), 35-271.

"Papers of the First Council of Safety of the Revolutionary Party in South Carolina, June—November, 1775," *South Carolina Historical and Genealogical Magazine,* 2 (1901), 3-26.

The Public Laws of South Carolina down to 1790, ed. by John F. Grimké. Philadelphia, 1790.

Statutes at Large of South Carolina. Charleston, 1838.

Stub Entries to Indents, Books C-F, ed. by Wylma A. Wates. Columbia, 1960.

Stub Entries to Indents, Books G-H, ed. by Wylma A. Wates. Columbia, 1955.

Stub Entries to Indents, Book K, ed. by Wylma A. Wates. Columbia, 1956.

Stub Entries to Indents, Books L-N, ed. by A. S. Salley. Columbia, 1910.

Stub Entries to Indents, Books U-W, ed. by A. S. Salley. Columbia, 1918.

United States

The Debates and Proceedings in the Congress of the United States, 1789-1824 [Annals of Congress]. Washington, 1834-56. 42 vols.

Journals of the Continental Congress, 1774-1789, ed. by Worthington C. Ford and Gaillard Hunt. Washington, 1904-37.

Outletters of the Continental Marine Committee and Board of Admiralty, ed. by Charles Oscar Paullin. New York, 1914. 2 vols.

The Records of the Federal Convention of 1787, ed. by Max Farrand. New Haven, 1911-37. 4 vols.

The Revolutionary Diplomatic Correspondence of the United States, ed. by Francis Wharton. Washington, 1889. 6 vols.

Virginia

Calendar of Virginia State Papers and Other Manuscripts . . . Preserved . . . at Richmond [1652-1869], ed. by W. P. Palmer, *et al.* Richmond, 1875-93. 11 vols.

Journals of the Council of the State of Virginia, 1776-1781, ed. by H. R. McIlwaine and Wilmer L. Hall. Richmond, 1931-32, 1952. 3 vols.

Journals of the House of Burgesses of Virginia, 1773-1776, ed. by John P. Kennedy. Richmond, 1905.

Official Letters of the Governors of the State of Virginia, ed. by H. R. McIlwaine. Richmond, 1926-29. 3 vols.

Revolutionary War Records, Vol. I: Virginia, ed. by Gaius Marcus Brumbaugh. Washington, 1936.

The Statutes at Large: Being a Collection of All the Laws of Virginia [1619-1792], ed. by William W. Hening. Richmond, 1809-23. 13 vols.

IV. *Other Printed Sources*

Adams, John. *The Works of John Adams,* ed. by Charles Francis Adams. Boston, 1850-56. 10 vols.

Adams, Samuel. *The Writings of Samuel Adams,* ed. by Henry Alonzo Cushing. New York, 1904-08. 4 vols.

African Society. *Laws of the Sons of the African Society, Instituted at Boston, Anno Domini, 1798.* Boston, 1802.

Andrews, E. W. and C. M. (eds.). *Journal of a Lady of Quality.* New Haven, 1923.

Aptheker, Herbert (ed.). *A Documentary History of the Negro People in the United States.* New York, 1951.

Asbury, Rev. Francis. *The Heart of Asbury's Journal.* New York, 1904.

———. Journal of Rev. Francis Asbury. New York, 1852. 3 vols.

Balch, Thomas. *Papers Relating Chiefly to the Maryland Line.* Philadelphia, 1857.

Belknap, Jeremy. "The Belknap Papers," Massachusetts Historical Society, *Collections,* 5th Ser., 3 (1877), 1-371.

———. "Extracts from Dr. Belknap's Note-books," Massachusetts Historical Society, *Proceedings,* 1st Ser., 14 (1876), 92-98.

———. "Queries Respecting the Slavery and Emancipation of Negroes in Massachusetts, Proposed by the Honorable Judge Tucker of Virginia, and Answered by Reverend Dr. Belknap," Massachusetts Historical Society, *Collections,* 1st Ser., 4 (1795), 191-211.

Bentham, Capt. James. "Regimental Book of Captain James Bentham, 1778-1800," *South Carolina Historical and Genealogical Magazine,* 7 (1906), 26.

The Bland Papers, ed. by Charles Campbell. Petersburg, 1840-43. 2 vols.

"Boyle's Journal of Occurrences in Boston, 1759-1788," *New England Historical and Genealogical Register,* 74 (1930), 142-71.

"The Boyd-Stevens Letters," Massachusetts Historical Society, *Proceedings,* 3rd Ser., 48 (1915), 335-43.

Boston. "Historical Manuscripts from the Public Library of the City of Boston," Public Library of Boston, *Monthly Bulletin,* 2nd Ser., 7 (1902), 460-66.

Boston Massacre. *Orations Delivered at the Request of the Inhabitants of The Town to Commemorate the Evening of the Fifth of March 1770.* Boston, 1785.

————. *A Short Narrative of the Horrid Massacre in Boston.* Boston, 1770, repub. in New York, 1849.

British army. "Proceedings of a Board of General Officers of the British Army at New York, 1781," New-York Historical Society, *Collections,* 49 (1916), 1-258.

"A British Orderly Book, 1780-1781," ed. by A. R. Newsome, *North Carolina Historical Review,* 9 (1932), 366-92.

Burnett, Edmund C. (ed.). *Letters of Members of the Continental Congress.* Washington, 1921-36. 8 vols.

Calendar of 'Historical Manuscripts Relating to the War of the Revolution. Albany, 1868. 2 vols.

Carter, Col. Landon. "Diary of Col. Landon Carter," *William and Mary Quarterly.* 1st Ser., 20 (1912), 173-86.

Charleston, S. C. "Return of People Embarked from South Carolina and Georgia, Charlestown, 13 December 1782," Massachusetts Historical Society, *Proceedings,* 2nd Ser., 3 (1888), 95-96.

————. *The Siege of Charleston,* ed. by Bernard A. Uhlendorf. Ann Arbor, 1938.

————. "The Siege of Charleston: Journal of Captain Peter Russell, December 25, 1779 to May 2, 1780," *American Historical Review,* 4 (1898-99), 478-501.

Clark, George Rogers. *George Rogers Clark Papers. 1781-1784,* ed. by James Alton James. Springfield, Illinois, 1926.

Clinton, Sir Henry. *The American Rebellion: Sir Henry Clinton's Narrative of his Campaigns, 1775-1782,* ed. by William B. Willcox. New Haven, 1954.

Dartmouth, Earl of. *Manuscripts of the Earl of Dartmouth,* publ. by the Historical Manuscripts Commission. London, 1887-96. 3 vols.

Denny, Maj. Ebenezer. *Military Journal of Major Ebenezer Denny.* Philadelphia, 1859.

Deane, Charles. "Remarks of Charles Deane, Esq.," Massachusetts Historical Society, *Proceedings,* 1st Ser., 10 (1869), 332-34.

Drayton, John. *Memoirs of the American Revolution.* Charleston, 1821. 2 vols.

Dunmore, Lord. *Dunmore's Proclamation of Emancipation,* ed. by Francis L. Berkeley, Jr. Charlottesville, 1941.

Force, Peter (ed.). *American Archives . . . A Documentary History of . . . the American Colonies,* 4th Ser., 6 vols.; 5th Ser., 3 vols. Washington, 1837-53.

Foster, Sir Augustus John. *Jeffersonian America: Notes on the United States of America . . . by Sir Augustus John Foster,* ed. by Richard B. Davis. San Marino, 1954.

Fortescue, Jonn W. (ed.). *The Correspondence of King George the Third from 1760 to December 1783.* London, 1927-28. 6 vols.

Frazer, Gen. Persifor. "Some Extracts from the Papers of General Persifor Frazer," *Pennsylvania Magazine of History and Biography,* 31 (1907), 129-44.

Freneau, Philip. *The Poems of Philip Freneau,* ed. by Fred Lewis Pattee, Princeton, 1902-07. 3 vols.

Franklin, Benjamin. *The Writings of Benjamin Franklin,* ed. by Albert Henry Smyth. New York, 1905-07. 10 vols.

Gage, Gen. Thomas. *The Correspondence of General Thomas Gage,* ed. by Clarence E. Carter. New Haven, 1931-33. 2 vols.

————. "Queries of George Chambers with the Answers of General Gage," Massachusetts Historical Society, *Collections,* 4th Ser., 6 (1858), 367-72.

Gibbes, R. W. (ed.). *Documentary History of the American Revolution.* New York, 1853-57. 3 vols.

Gore, Lieut. Obadiah, Jr. "Diary of Lieut. Obadiah Gore, Jr., in the Sullivan-Clinton Campaign of 1779, ed. by R. W. G. Vail, New York Public Library, *Bulletin,* 33 (1929), 711-42.

Graydon, Alexander. *Memoirs of a Life.* Harrisburgh, 1811.

Greene, Gen. Nathanael. "Letters to General Greene and Others." ed. by Joseph W. Barnwell, *South Carolina Historical and Genealogical Magazine,* 16 (1915), 139-50.

Hamilton. Alexander. *The Works of Alexander Hamilton,* ed. by John C. Hamilton, New York, 1850-51, 7 vols.

————. *The Works of Alexander Hamilton,* ed. by Henry Cabot Lodge. New York, 1904. 12 vols.

Hand, General Edward. *The Unpublished Letters of Major-General Edward Hand of Pennsylvania.* New York, 1907.

"The Heath Papers, 1775-1779," Massachusetts Historical Society, *Collections,* 7th Ser., 4 (1904), 1-341.

Henshaw, Col. William. *The Orderly Book of Colonel William Henshaw,* ed. by Harriet E. Henshaw. Boston, 1881.

Hopkins, Esek. *Correspondence of Esek Hopkins, Commander-in-Chief of the United States Navy,* ed. by Alverda S. Beck. Providence, 1933.

———. *Letter Book of Esek Hopkins, Commander-in-Chief of The United States Navy, 1775-1777,* ed. by Alverda S. Beck. Providence, 1932.

"Huntington Papers," Connecticut Historical Society, *Collections,* 20 (1923), 1-474.

Huntington, Ebenezer. *Letters Written by Ebenezer Huntington During the American Revolution.* New York, 1914.

Hutchinson, Thomas. "Letters of Thomas Hutchinson to Lord Hillsborough, March, 1770." Massachusetts Historical Society, *Proceedings,* 1st Ser., 6 (1863), 484-87.

Izard, Ralph. *Correspondence of Mr. Ralph Izard.* New York, 1844. 2 vols.

Jefferson, Thomas. *Notes on the State of Virginia.* New York, 1801.

———. *The Papers of Thomas Jefferson,* ed. by Julian P. Boyd. Princeton, 1950—in progress.

———. *The Writings of Thomas Jefferson,* ed. by Paul Leicester Ford. New York, 1892-99. 10 vols.

Jensen, Merrill (ed.). *American Colonial Documents to 1776. English Historical Documents,* vol. 9, ed. by David C. Douglass. London, 1955.

Jones, Joseph. *Letters of Joseph Jones, 1777-1787,* ed. by Worthington C. Ford. Washington.

The Keith Papers, ed. by W. G. Perrin and Christopher Lloyd. London, 1926-55. 3 vols.

Lafayette, Marquis de. *The Letters of Lafayette to Washington, 1777-1799,* ed. by Louis Gottshalk. New York, 1944.

———. "Letters to Lafayette in Virginia State Library," *Virginia Magazine of History and Biography,* 5 (1898), 374-83.

Laurens, Col. John. *The Army Correspondence of Colonel John Laurens, with a Memoir,* ed. by William Gilmore Simms. New York, 1907.

Lee, Richard Henry. *The Letters of Richard Henry Lee,* ed. by James C. Ballagh. New York, 1912-14. 2 vols.

"Letters Colonial and Revolutionary Selected from the Dreer Collection of the Historical Society of Pennsylvania," *Pennsylvania Magazine of History and Biography,* 47 (1918), 75-85.

"Letters showing the Rise and Progress of the early Negro Churches of Georgia and the West Indies," *Journal of Negro History,* 1 (1916), 69-92.

"The Leven Powell Correspondence," Randolph-Macon College, *John P. Branch Historical Papers,* 1 (1902), 111-38.

Lincoln, Levi. "Brief of Levi Lincoln in the Slave Case Tried in 1781." Massachusetts Historical Society, *Collections,* 5th Ser., 3 (1877), 438-42.

Lincoln, Capt. Rufus. *The Papers of Captain Rufus Lincoln,* ed. by James M. Lincoln. Cambridge, 1903.

Logan, Rayford W. (ed.). *Memoirs of a Monticello Slave.* Charlottesville, 1951.

Loyalists. *Orderly Book of the Three Battalions of Loyalists Commanded by Brigadier General Oliver Delancey.* New York, 1917.

———. "United Empire Loyalists," in "Proceedings of Commissioners on Loyalist Claims," Ontario Bureau of Archives, *Second Report* (Ontario, 1905). 2 vols.

McDowell, Lt. William. "Journals of Lieut. William McDowell of the First Penn'a Regiment, in the Southern Campaign, 1781-1782," *Pennsylvania Archives* [1664——], ed. by Samuel Hazard, *et al.* [138 vols., Harrisburg and Phila., 1852-1949] 2nd Ser., 15 (1893), 297-340.

McIntosh, Lachlan. "Letter Book of Lachlan McIntosh, 1776-1777," ed. by Lilla M. Hawes, *Georgia Historical Quarterly,* 38 (1954), 251-67.

Mackenzie, Lieut. "Description of the Battle of Lexington by Lieutenant Mackenzie of the Royal Welsh Fusileers," Massachusetts Historical Society, *Proceedings,* 2nd Ser., 5 (1890), 391-96.

Mackenzie, Frederick. *Diary of Frederick Mackenzie.* Cambridge, 1930. 2 vols.

Madison, James. *The Papers of James Madison,* ed. by Henry D. Gilpin. Washington, 1840. 3 vols.

———. *The Writings of James Madison,* ed. by Gaillard Hunt. New York, 1900-10. 9 vols.

Mathews, Albert. "Notes on the Proposed Abolition of Slavery in Virginia in 1785," Colonial Society of Massachusetts, *Publications,* 6 (1899-1900), 370-80.

Meade, Richard Kidder. "Two Letters of Richard Kidder Meade," *Southern Literary Messenger,* 25 (1857), 22-25.

Middleton, Arthur. "The Correspondence of Arthur Middleton," *South Carolina Historical and Genealogical Magazine,* 26 (1925), 183-213.

"Miscellaneous Colonial Documents," *Virginia Magazine of History and Biography,* 19 (1911), 263-75.

Moore, Frank. *Diary of the American Revolution*. New York, 1865. 2 vols.

Morris, Gen. Lewis. "Letters to General Lewis Morris," New-York Historical Society, *Collections*, 7 (1876), 433-512.

Muhlenberg, Henry Melchior. *The Journals of Henry Melchior Muhlenberg*, trans. by Theodore G. Tappert and John W. Doverstein. Philadelphia, 1942-58. 3 vols.

Navy Board. "Excerpts from the Letter Book of the Navy Board," *The Researcher*, 1 (1927), 17-28.

"Newspaper Extracts Relating to New Jersey, October 1780—July 1782," *New Jersey Archives* [ed. by W. A. Whitehead, et al. Newark, etc., 1880-1906. 30 vols.] 2nd Ser., 5 (1917), 1-490.

Niles, Hezekiah. *Principles and Acts of the Revolution*. Baltimore, 1822.

Paine, Thomas. *The Writings of Thomas Paine*, ed. by Moncure D. Conway. New York, 1894-96. 3 vols.

Pargellis, Stanley (ed.). *Military Affairs in North America, 1748-1765*. New York, 1936.

Parker, Col. Josiah. "Revolutionary Correspondence of Col. Josiah Parker, of Isle of Wight County, Va.," *Virginia Magazine of History and Biography*, 22 (1914), 257-66.

Pendleton, Edmund. "Unpublished Letters of Edmund Pendleton," Massachusetts Historical Society, *Proceedings*, 2nd Ser., 19 (1905), 107-67.

Pennsylvania. "Journals and Diaries of the War of the Revolution with Lists of Officers and Soldiers, 1775-1783," *Pennsylvania Archives* [1664——], ed. by Samuel Hazard, et al. [138 vols., Harrisburg and Phila., 1852-1949] 2nd Ser., 15 (1893), 7-775.

———. "Officers and Men of the Pennsylvania Navy, 1775-1781," *Pennsylvania Archives* [1664——], ed. by Samuel Hazard, et al. [138 vols., Harrisburg and Phila., 1852-1949] 2nd Ser., 1 (1874), 229-405.

"Popp's Journal," ed. by Joseph G. Rosengarten. *Pennsylvania Magazine of History and Biography*, 26 (1880), 1-86.

Pynchon, William. *The Diary of William Pynchon of Salem*, ed. by Fitch Oliver Edward. Boston, 1890.

Ramsay, David. *A History of the American Revolution*. London, 1793. 2 vols.

Randolph, John. "Deposition of John Randolph in Regard to the Removal of the Powder," *Virginia Magazine of History and Biography*, 15 (1907), 149-50.

Report of American Manuscripts in the Royal Instituiions of Great

Britain, publ. by the Historical Manuscripts Commission. London, Dublin, Hereford, 1904-09. 4 vols.

"Report of the Committee of Claims: Wm. Hazzard Wigg—Claim for Slaves Taken By the British in the Revolutionary War," 36th Cong., 1st sess. (1860), *House Report,* no. 471, 1-16.

Rowe, John. "Extracts from the Diary of John Rowe," Massachusetts Historical Society, *Proceedings,* 2nd Ser., 10 (1896), 60-108.

Rush, Benjamin. *The Autobiography of Benjamin Rush,* ed. by George W. Corner. Princeton, 1948.

———. "Certificate Communicated by Dr. Rush," *The American Museum,* 5 (1789), 61-62.

———. *Letters of Benjamin Rush,* ed. by L. H. Butterfield. Princeton, 1951. 2 vols.

Savannah, Ga. "Account of the Siege of Savannah from a British Source," Georgia Historical Society, *Collections,* 5, pt. 1 (1901), 129-39.

Saffell, W. T. R. (ed.). *Records of the Revolution.* New York, 1858.

St. Clair, Gen. Arthur. "The Trial of Major General St. Clair, August, 1778," New-York Historical Society, *Collections,* 13 (1881), 1-171.

Saint-Marc, Meyronnet de. "Meyronnet de Saint-Marc's Journal," ed. by Roberta Leighton, *New-York Historical Society Quarterly,* 36 (1952), 225-87.

Seymour, William. "A Journal of the Southern Expedition, 1780-1783," Historical Society of Delaware, *Papers,* 2 (1896), 3-42.

Sierra Leone Company. *Report by Court of Directors of the Sierra Leone Company, 1794.* London, 1794.

Smith, Richard. "Diary of Richard Smith in the Continental Congress, 1775-1776," *American Historical Review,* 1 (1895-96), 288-310.

Stevens, Benjamin F. (ed.). *Facsimiles of Manuscripts in European Archives Relating to America, 1773-1783.* London, 1889-95. 26 vols.

Stiles, Ezra. *The Literary Diary of Ezra Stiles.* New York, 1901. 3 vols.

Stopford-Sackville, Mrs. *Report on the Manuscripts of Mrs. Stopford-Sackville.* London, 1904-1910. 2 vols.

Sullivan, Gen. John. *Letters and Papers of Major-General John Sullivan,* ed. by Otis G. Hammond. Concord, N. H., 1930-39. 3 vols.

Summers, William. "Obituary Notices of Pennsylvania Soldiers of the Revolution," *Pennsylvania Magazine of History and Biography,* 38 (1914), 443-60.

Tarleton, Banastre. *A History of the Campaign in the Southern Provinces.* Dublin, 1787.

Thayer, Capt. Simeon. "Journal of Captain Simeon Thayer," Rhode Island Historical Society, *Collections,* 6 (1867), 1-56.

Tucker, St. George. *A Dissertation on Slavery.* Phila., 1796.

Tudor, William (ed.). *Deacon Tudor's Diary.* Boston, 1896.

Uhlendorf, Bernard A. (ed.). *Revolution in America: Baurmeister Journals.* New Brunswick, 1957.

Von Closen, Baron Ludwig. *The Revolutionary Journal of Baron Ludwig von Closen, 1780-1783,* ed. by Evelyn M. Acomb. Chapel Hill, 1958.

Von Krafft, John Charles Philip. "Journal of Lt. John Charles Philip von Krafft, 1776-1784," New-York Historical Society, *Collections,* 15 (1883), 1-200.

Ward, Gov. Samuel. *The Correspondence of Governor Samuel Ward, May 1775—March 1776,* comp. by C. P. Monahan. Providence, 1952.

Warren, James and Mercy [Otis]. "Warren-Adams Letters," ed. by W. C. Ford. Massachusetts Historical Society, *Collections,* 72-73 (1917-25). 2 vols.

Warren, Mercy. *History of the American Revolution.* Boston, 1805. 3 vols.

Washington, George. *Correspondence of the American Revolution: Being Letters of Eminent Men to George Washington,* ed. by Jared Sparks. Boston, 1853. 4 vols.

———. *Washington-Irvine Correspondence,* ed. by C. W. Butterfield. Madison, Wisc., 1882.

———. *The Writings of George Washington,* ed. by John C. Fitzpatrick. Washington, 1931-44. 39 vols.

Wells, Bayze. "Journal of Bayze Wells of Farmington, in the Canadian Expedition, 1775-1777," Connecticut Historical Society, *Collections,* 7 (1899), 239-96.

Wheatley, Phillis. *Phillis Wheatley: Poems and Letters,* ed. by Charles F. Heartman. New York, 1915.

———. *Poems on Various Subjects, Religious and Moral.* London, 1773.

Wilkinson, Eliza. *Letters of Eliza Wilkinson,* ed. by Carolina Gillman. New York, 1839.

Willard, Margaret W. (ed.). *Letters on the American Revolution.* Boston, 1925.

"The Woodford Howe, and Lee Letters," Richmond College, *Historical Papers,* 1 (1915), 96-163.

Wright, Sir James. "Letters from Governor Sir James Wright to the Earl of Dartmouth and Lord George Germain," Georgia Historical Society, *Collections*, 3 (1873), 180-375.

V. *Newspapers*

Boston Gazette, 1770.
Boston Evening Post, 1779.
Connecticut Courant (Hartford), 1778.
Dunlap's Maryland Gazette (Baltimore), 1777.
Maryland Gazette (Annapolis), 1775, 1776, 1779, 1780, 1781.
Maryland Journal (Baltimore), 1782.
New-Jersey Gazette (Trenton), 1781.
Pennsylvania Evening Post (Phila.), 1777.
Pennsylvania Gazette (Phila.), 1775, 1777.
Pennsylvania Packet (Phila.), 1778.
Royal Gazette (New York: Rivington's), 1779.
Virginia Gazette (Purdie and Dixon), 1772.
Virginia Gazette (Purdie), 1775, 1776.
Virginia Gazette (Dixon and Hunter), 1776, 1777.
Virginia Gazette (Dixon and Nicolson), 1779.

SECONDARY SOURCES

I. *Books*

Allyn, Charles. *The Battle of Groton Heights*. New London, 1882.
Andrew, Charles C. *The History of the New-York African Free-Schools*. New York, 1830.
Andrews, Charles M. *The Colonial Period of American History*. New Haven, 1934-38. 4 vols.
Aptheker, Herbert. *The Negro in the American Revolution*. New York, 1940.
Arnold, Samuel G. *History of the State of Rhode Island and Providence Plantations*. Providence, 1878. 2 vols.
Barney, Samuel E. *Songs of the Revolution*. New Haven, 1893.
Barry, William. *A History of Framingham, Massachusetts*. Boston, 1847.
Bass, Robert D. *Swamp Fox*. New York, 1949.
Belcher, Henry. *The First American Civil War, 1775-1778*. New York, 1911. 2 vols.
Bowman, Allen. *The Morale of the American Revolutionary Army*. Washington, 1943.
Bragg, George F. *History of the Afro-American Group of the Episcopal Church*. Baltimore, 1922.

A Brief Sketch of the Schools for Black People and Their Descendants Established by the Religious Society of Friends in 1770. Philadelphia, 1867.

Brock, Robert K. *Archibald Cary of Ampthill.* Richmond, 1937.

Brookes, George S. *Friend Anthony Benezet.* Philadelphia, 1937.

Buell, August C. *Paul Jones, Founder of the American Navy.* New York, 1900. 2 vols.

Bunker Hill. *Proceedings of the Bunker Hill Memorial Association.* Boston, 1911.

Burk, John. *The History of Virginia.* Petersburg, 1805-16. 4 vols.

Butt-Thompson, F. W. *Sierra Leone in History and Tradition.* London, 1926.

Callahan, North. *Henry Knox.* New York, 1958.

Caulkins, Frances M. *The Stone Records of Groton.* Norwich, 1903.

Chapin, Howard M. *Privateering in King George's War, 1739-1748.* Providence, 1927.

Charleston, S. C. *Year Book of the City of Charleston.* Charleston, 1899.

Coburn, Frank W. *The Battle of April 19, 1775.* Lexington, Mass., 1912.

Coleman, Kenneth. *The American Revolution in Georgia, 1763-1789.* Athens, 1958.

Coleman, Mary H. *St. George Tucker: Citizen of No Mean City.* Richmond, 1938.

Connecticut Military Record, 1775-1848. Hartford, 1889.

Cooley, Henry S. *A Study of Slavery in New Jersey.* Baltimore, 1896.

Cooley, Timothy Mather. *Sketches of the Life and Character of the Rev. Lemuel Haynes, A. M.* New York, 1837.

Cowell, Benjamin. *Spirit of '76 in Rhode Island.* Boston, 1850.

Curtis, Edward E. *The Organization of the British Army in the American Revolution.* New Haven, 1926.

David, Harry E. *A History of Free Masonry Among Negroes in America.* (No place) 1946.

Davis, William T. *History of the Town of Plymouth.* Philadelphia, 1885.

Dawson, Henry B. *The Assault on Stony Point.* Morrisania, N. Y., 1863.

Drake, Thomas E. *Quakers and Slavery in America.* New Haven, 1950.

DuBois, W. E. B. *The Suppression of the African Slave-Trade.* New York, 1896.

Fiske, John. *The American Revolution.* Boston, 1891. 2 vols.

Forbes, Esther. *Paul Revere and the World He Lived In.* Boston, 1942.

Franklin, John Hope. *From Slavery to Freedom.* New York, 1956.

Freeman, Douglas S. *George Washington: A Biography.* New York, 1948-54. 6 vols.

Garden, Alexander. *Anecdotes of the Revolutionary War.* Charleston, 1822.

Gilmer, George W. *Sketches of Some of the First Settlers of Upper Georgia.* New York, 1855.

Goold, Nathan. *History of Colonel James Scamman's Thirtieth Regiment Foot.* Portland, Me., 1899.

Gordon, William. *The History of the United States.* London, 1788. 4 vols.

Gottschalk, Louis. *Lafayette and the Close of the American Revolution.* Chicago, 1942.

Greene, Lorenzo J. *The Negro in Colonial New England.* New York, 1942.

Haiman, Miecislaus. *Kosciuszko in the American Revolution.* New York, 1943.

———. *Kosciuszko: Leader in Exile.* New York, 1946.

Harrell, Isaac S. *Loyalism in Virginia.* Philadelphia, 1926.

Hibbard, Benjamin H. *A History of the Public Land Policies.* New York, 1924.

History of the Town of Hingham, Massachusetts. Hingham, 1893. 3 vols.

Hinman, Royal R. *Historical Collection of the Part Sustained by Connecticut During the War of the Revolution.* Hartford, 1842.

Hopkins, Samuel. *Timely Articles on Slavery.* Boston, 1854.

Howard, James L. *Seth Harding, Mariner.* New Haven, 1930.

Humphreys, Frank Landon. *The Life and Times of David Humphreys.* New York, 1916. 2 vols.

Jackson, Luther P. *Virginia Negro Soldiers and Sailors in the Revolutionary War.* Norfolk, 1944.

James, William D. *A Sketch of the Life of Brigadier General Francis Marion,* ed. by A. S. Salley. Marietta, 1948.

Jameson, J. Franklin (ed.). *Essays in the Constitutional History of the United States.* Boston, 1889.

———. *Privateering and Piracy in the Colonial Period.* New York, 1923.

———. *The American Revolution Considered as a Social Movement.* Princeton, 1940.

Jones, Charles C. *The Life and Services of the Honorable Major General Samuel Elbert.* Cambridge, 1887.

———. *The History of Georgia.* Boston, 1883. 2 vols.

Jones, Thomas. *History of New York During the Revolutionary War*. New York, 1879. 2 vols.

Kennedy, Melvin D. *Lafayette and Slavery*. Easton, Pennsylvania, 1950.

Kidder, Frederic. *History of the Boston Massacre*. Albany, 1870.

Knight, Lucian Lamar. *Georgia's Roster of the Revolution*. Atlanta, 1920.

Kull, Irving (ed.). *New Jersey: A History*. New York, 1930-36. 6 vols.

Lawrence, Alexander A. *Storm Over Savannah*. Athens, 1951.

Lecky, William E. *The American Revolution, 1763-1783*. New York, 1929.

Lee, Richard Henry. *Memoir of the Life of Richard Henry Lee*. Philadelphia, 1825.

Livermore, George. *An Historical Research Respecting the Opinions of the Founders of the Republic on Negroes as Slaves, as Citizens, and as Soldiers*. Boston, 1862.

Locke, Mary S. *Anti-Slavery in America*. Boston, 1901.

Lockey, Joseph Bryne. *East Florida, 1783-1785*. Berkeley, 1949.

Loggins, Vernon. *The Negro Author*. New York, 1931.

Lossing, Benson. *Pictorial Field Book of the Revolution*. New York, 1860. 2 vols.

Lovell, Louise L. *Israel Angell*. New York, 1921.

Lowell, Edward J. *The Hessians in the American Revolution*. New York, 1884.

McCrady, Edward. *The History of South Carolina in the Revolution, 1780-1783*. New York, 1902.

Mandelbaum, David G. *Soldier Groups and Negro Soldiers*. Berkeley, 1952.

Matlack, L. C. *The History of American Slavery and Methodism from 1780 to 1849*. New York, 1849.

Mazyck, Walter H. *George Washington and the Negro*. Washington, 1932.

A Memorial of Crispus Attucks, Samuel Maverick, James Caldwell, Samuel Gray and Patrick Garr, from the City of Boston. Boston, 1889.

Merriam, John M. *Five Framingham Heroes of the American Revolution*. Framingham, 1925.

Middlebrook, Louis F. *History of Maritime Connecticut during the American Revolution*. Salem, Mass., 1925. 2 vols.

Miller, John C. *Sam Adams: Pioneer in Propaganda*. Boston, 1936.

Moore, George H. *Notes on the History of Slavery in Massachusetts*. New York, 1866.

Muhlenberg, Henry A. *The Life of Major-General Peter Muhlenberg.* Philadelphia, 1849.

Nell, William C. *The Colored Patriots of the American Revolution.* Boston, 1855.

Newcomer, Lee N. *The Embattled Farmers: A Massachusetts Countryside in the American Revolution.* New York, 1953.

Nourse, Henry S. *The Military Annals of Lancaster, Massachusetts, 1740-1865.* Lancaster, 1889.

Paullin, Charles O. *The Navy of the American Revolution.* Cleveland, 1906.

Poole, William F. *Anti-Slavery Opinions Before the Year 1800.* Cincinnati, 1873.

Powell, J. H. *Bring Out Your Dead.* Philadelphia, 1949.

Rogers, Ernest E. *Connecticut's Naval Office at New London During the War of the American Revolution.* New London, 1933.

Russell, Phillips. *John Paul Jones, Man of Action.* New York, 1927.

Scharf, John T. *History of Maryland.* Baltimore, 1879. 3 vols.

Schlesinger, Arthur M. *Prelude to Independence: The Newspaper War on Britain, 1764-1776.* New York, 1958.

Seeber, Edward D. *Anti-Slavery Opinions in France During the Second Half of the Eighteenth Century.* Baltimore, 1937.

Semple, Robert B. *A History of the Rise and Progress of the Baptists of Virginia,* ed. by G. W. Beale. Richmond, 1894.

Sheppard, John H. *The Life of Samuel Tucker.* Boston, 1868.

Sparks, Jared. *The Life of Gouverneur Morris.* Boston, 1832.

Steiner, Bernard C. *History of Slavery in Connecticut.* Baltimore, 1893.

Stevens, William B. *A History of Georgia.* New York and Phila., 1847-59. 2 vols.

Stewart, Robert A. *The History of Virginia's Navy of the Revolution.* Richmond, 1934.

Swett, Samuel. *Historical and Topical Sketch of Bunker Hill Battle.* Boston, 1818.

———. *Notes to His Sketch of Bunker-Hill Battle.* Boston, 1825.

Townsend, Sara Bertha. *An American Soldier: The Life of John Laurens.* Raleigh, N. C., 1958.

Turner, Edward R. *The Negro in Pennsylvania, 1639-1861.* Washington, 1911.

Tyler, Moses Coit. *The Literary History of the American Revolution.* New York, 1897. 2 vols.

Wallace, David D. *The Life of Henry Laurens.* New York, 1915.

Ward, John. *A Memoir of Lieut.-Colonel Samuel Ward.* New York, 1875.

Weatherford, W. D. *American Churches and the Negro.* Boston, 1957.

Weeden, William B. *The Economic and Social History of New England.* Boston, 1890. 2 vols.

Wegelin, Oscar. *Jupiter Hammon.* New York, 1915.

Wesley, Charles H. *Richard Allen.* Washington, 1935.

Wild, Helen Tilden. *Medford in the Revolution.* Medford, 1903.

Wilkes, Laura E. *Missing Pages in American History.* Washington, 1919.

Williams, George Washington. *History of the Negro Race in America.*

Woodson, Carter G. *The History of the Negro Church.* Washington, 1921.

————. *The Negro in Our History.* Washington, 1945.

Wright, Marion T. *The Education of Negroes in New Jersey.* New York, 1941.

Yoshpe, Harry B. *The Disposition of Loyalist Estates in the Southern District of the State of New York.* New York, 1939.

II. *Articles*

Adams, Randolph G. "New Light on the Boston Massacre," American Antiquarian Society, *Proceedings,* 47 (1937), 259-354.

Alexander, Arthur J. "How Maryland Tried to Raise Her Continental Quotas," *Maryland Historical Magazine,* 62 (1947), 184-96.

Allen, Gardner W. "Captain Hector McNeill, Continental Navy," Massachusetts Historical Society, *Proceedings,* 3rd Ser., 55 (1923), 46-152.

Andrews, Charles M. "Slavery in Connecticut," *Magazine of American History,* 21 (1889), 422-23.

Aptheker, Herbert. "Eighteenth Century Petitions of South Carolina Negroes," *Journal of Negro History,* 31 (1946), 98-99.

Archibald, Adams G. "Story of the Deportation of Negroes from Nova Scotia to Sierra Leone," Nova Scotia Historical Society, *Collections,* 7 (1891), 129-54.

"The Battle of Great Bridge," *Virginia Historical Register,* 6 (1853), 1-6.

Bettle, Edward. "Negro Slavery as Connected with Pennsylvania," Historical Society of Pennsylvania, *Memoirs,* 1 (1826), 367-416.

Billington, Ray Allen. "James Forten: Forgotten Abolitionist." *Negro History Bulletin,* 13 (1949), 31-36.

"A British Officer in Boston in 1775," *Atlantic Monthly*, 39 (1877), 389-401, 544-54.

Bruce, Kathleen. "Manufacture of Ordnance in Virginia During the American Revolution," *Army Ordnance*, 7, nos. 39, 41 (1926-27), 187-93, 385-91.

"The Brunswick Contingent in America, 1776-1783," *Pennsylvania Magazine of History and Biography*, 15 (1891), 218-24.

"Bunker's Hill," *Historical Magazine*, 2nd Ser., 3 (1868), 321-40.

Cadbury, Henry J. "Negro Membership in the Society of Friends," *Journal of Negro History*, 21 (1936), 151-213.

Channing, Edward. "The American Board of Commissioners of the Customs," Massachusetts Historical Society, *Proceedings*, 3rd Ser., 43 (1910), 477-90.

Coleman, Charles W. "The Southern Campaign, 1781," *Magazine of American History*, 7 (1881), 201-16.

Collier, Thomas S. "The Revolutionary Privateers of Connecticut," New London Historical Society, *Records and Papers*, 1, pt. 4 (1892), 3-45.

"Collier's and Mathew's Invasion of Virginia in 1779," *Virginia Historical Register*, 4 (1851), 185-91.

Cornwallis. "Lord Cornwallis's Movements and Operations in Virginia, in 1781," *Virginia Historical Register*, 6 (1853), 121-31.

Crocker, James F. "The Parkers of Macclesfield, Isle of Wight, Va.," *Virginia Magazine of History and Biography*, 6 (1889), 420-24.

Cropper, Gen. John. "Memoir of General John Cropper," by Burton H. Wise. Virginia Historical Society, *Proceedings*, 2 (1892), 275-315.

Davis, Andrew M. "The Employment of Indian Auxiliaries in the American War," *English Historical Review*, 2 (1887), 709-28.

Davis, Arthur P. "Personal Elements in the Poetry of Phillis Wheatley," *Phylon*, 13 (1953), 191-98.

Dickerson, Oliver M. "The Commissioners of Customs and the 'Boston Massacre'," *New England Quarterly*, 27 (1954), 307-25.

Diman, J. Lewis. "The Capture of Prescott," *Rhode Island Historical Tracts*, 1 (1877), 11-44.

"Eighteenth Century Slaves as Advertised by Their Masters," *Journal of Negro History*, 1 (1916), 163-216.

Fisher, J. B. "Who was Crispus Attucks?" *American Historical Record*, 1 (1872), 531-33.

Fisher, Ruth Anna. "Manuscript Materials Bearing on the Negro in the British Museum," *Journal of Negro History*, 27 (1942), 83-93.

Fogg, John S. H. "Inquest on Michael Johnson Alias Crispus Attucks," *New-England Historical and Genealogical Register,* 44 (1890), 382-83.

Gasperetti, Elio, trans. "An Italo-American Newspaper's Obituary of a Negro Revolutionary War Veteran," *Negro History Bulletin,* 15 (1954), 58.

Gobbel, Luther L. "The Militia in North Carolina in Colonial and Revolutionary Times," Trinity College Historical Society, *Historical Papers,* 13 (1919), 35-61.

Green, Samuel A. "Slavery at Groton in Provincial Times," Massachusetts Historical Society, *Proceedings,* 3rd Ser., 42 (1909), 196-202.

Greene, Lorenzo J. "Some Observations on the Black Regiment of Rhode Island in the American Revolution," *Journal of Negro History,* 27 (1952), 142-72.

Hadaway, William S. "Negroes in the Revolutionary War," Westchester County Historical Society, *Quarterly Bulletin,* 6 (1930), 8-12.

Hammond, Isaac W. "Slavery in New Hampshire," *Magazine of American History,* 21 (1889), 62-65.

"Historical Notes," *South Carolina Historical and Genealogical Magazine,* 8 (1907), 222-23.

"Historical Notes on Slavery in the Northern Colonies and States," *Historical Magazine,* 10 (1866), 237-38.

"J. B.," "The Schooner Liberty," *Virginia Historical Register,* 1 (1848), 127-31.

Jackson, Luther P. "Negro Soldiers and Seamen in the American Revolution," *Journal of Negro History,* 27 (1942), 247-87.

Johnson, Cecil. "Expansion in West Florida, 1770-1779," *Mississippi Valley Historical Review,* 20 (1934), 481-96.

Kellogg, Louise Phelps. "The Paul Revere Print of the Boston Massacre," *Wisconsin Magazine of History,* 1 (1918), 377-87.

Koke, Richard J. "War, Profit and Privateers along the New Jersey Coast," *New-York Historical Society Quarterly,* 41 (1957), 279-337.

Kraus, Michael. "Slavery Reform in the Eighteenth Century: an Aspect of Trans-Atlantic Intellectual Cooperation," *Pennsylvania Magazine of History and Biography,* 60 (1936), 53-66.

Morse, C. H. "Crispus Attucks," *New England Historical and Genealogical Register,* 13 (1859), 300.

Morse, Sidney G. "The Yankee Privateersman," *New England Quarterly,* 17 (1944), 71-86.

Moss, Simeon F. "The Persistence of Slavery and Involuntary

Servitude in a Free State," *Journal of Negro History,* 35 (1950), 289-314.

Payne, A. H. "The Negro in New York Prior to 1860," *Howard Review,* 1 (1923), 23-35.

Pennington, Edgar L. "East Florida in the American Revolution, 1775-1778," *Florida Historical Quarterly,* 9 (1930), 24-46.

Phillips, David E. "Negroes in the American Revolution," *Journal of American History,* 5 (1911), 143-46.

Powell, J. H. "John Dickinson, President of the Delaware State, 1781-1782," *Delaware History,* 1 (1946), 1-54.

Pugh, Robert C. "The Revolutionary Militia in the Southern Campaign, 1780-1781," *William and Mary Quarterly,* 3rd Ser., 14 (1957), 154-75.

Quarles, Benjamin. "The Colonial Militia and Negro Manpower," *Mississippi Valley Historical Review,* 45 (1959), 643-52.

———. "Lord Dunmore as Liberator," *William and Mary Quarterly,* 15 (1958), 494-507.

Rantoul, Robert S., Sr. "Negro Slavery in Massachusetts," Essex Institute, *Historical Collections,* 14 (1887), 81-108.

Reynolds, Helen W. "The Negro in Dutchess County in the Eighteenth Century," Dutchess County Historical Society, *Yearbook* (1941), 89-99.

Rider, Sidney S. "The Rhode Island Black 'Regiment' of 1778," *Rhode Island Historical Tracts,* 10 (1880), 1-86.

"The Schooner Patriot," *Virginia Historical Register,* 1 (1848), 76-80.

Shaffer, E. T. H. "The Rejected Laurens—A Carolina Tragedy," South Carolina Historical Association, *Proceedings for 1934* (Columbia, 1934), 14-24.

Siebert, Wilbur H. "The Legacy of the American Revolution in the British West Indies and Bahamas," Ohio State University, *Bulletin,* 17 (1913), 6-50.

Silverman, E. H. "Painter of the Revolution," *American Heritage,* 9 (1958), 40-51.

"Slaves in the Revolutionary Army," *Historical Magazine,* 2nd Ser., 2 (1867), 44.

Smith, Anna Bustill. "The Bustill Family," *Journal of Negro History,* 10 (1925), 638-44.

Smith, Jonathan. "How Massachusetts Raised Her Troops in the Revolution," Massachusetts Historical Society, *Proceedings,* 3rd Ser., 55 (1923), 345-70.

Stravisky, Leonard P. "Negro Craftsmanship in Early America," *American Historical Review,* 54 (1948-49), 315-25.

Sweat, Edward P. "Social Status of the Free Negro in Antebellum Georgia," *Negro History Bulletin*, 21 (1958), 129-31.

Thwaites, Reuben Gold. "The British Regime in Wisconsin," State Historical Society of Wisconsin, *Collections*, 18 (1908), 223-468.

Turner, Edward R. "The First Abolition Society in the United States," *Pennsylvania Magazine of History and Biography*, 36 (1912), 92-109.

Virginia. *The Lower Norfolk County, Virginia Antiquary* [periodical], vols. 1-5, publ. at Norfolk, Va., 1897-1906. Reprinted, New York, 1951.

Von Eelking, Max. "Military Operations in Rhode Island," *Rhode Island Historical Tracts*, 6 (1878), 37-65.

Washburn, Emory. "Somerset's Case, and the Extinction of Villenage and Slavery in England," Massachusetts Historical Society, *Proceedings*, 1st Ser., 7 (1864), 307-26.

Weeks, Stephen B. "Anti-Slavery Sentiment in the South, Southern Historical Association, *Publications*, 2 (1898), 87-130.

INDEX